STOIC CLASSICS COLLECTION

Marcus Aurelius's Meditations, Epictetus's Enchiridion, Seneca's On a Happy Life, On the Shortness of Life, On Peace of Mind & On Providence

by

Marcus Aurelius
Epictetus
Lucius Annaeus Seneca

Translated by

George Long
Aubrey Stewart

C L A S S Y
PUBLISHING

STOIC CLASSICS COLLECTION
by Marcus Aurelius, Epictetus & Lucius Annaeus Seneca
Published by Classy Publishing, 2023

www.classypublishing.com
info@classypublishing.com

ISBN: 978-93-5522-373-9

No part of this publication may be reproduced, stored in a retrieval system, or transmitted, in any form or by any means, electronic, mechanical, photocopying, recording or otherwise, without the prior permission of the publisher.

Cover Design by Classy Publishing

CONTENTS

Meditations 1

Enchiridion 103

On a Happy Life 128

On the Shortness of Life 154

On Peace of Mind 176

On Providence 202

MEDITATIONS

Marcus Aurelius

Translated by
George Long

BOOK I

From my grandfather Verus[1] [I learned] good morals and the government of my temper.

2. From the reputation and remembrance of my father, modesty and a manly character.[2]

3. From my mother,[3] piety and beneficence, and abstinence, not only from evil deeds, but even from evil thoughts; and further, simplicity in my way of living, far removed from the habits of the rich.

4. From my great-grandfather,[4] not to have frequented public schools, and to have had good teachers at home, and to know that on such things a man should spend liberally.

5. From my governor, to be neither of the green nor of the blue party at the games in the Circus, nor a partisan either of the Parmularius or the Scutarius at the gladiators' fights; from him too I learned endurance of labor, and to want little, and to work with my own hands, and not to meddle with other people's affairs, and not to be ready to listen to slander.

6. From Diognetus,[5] not to busy myself about trifling things, and not to give credit to what was said by miracle-workers and jugglers about incantations

---

[1] Annius Verus was his grandfather's name. There is no verb in this section connected with the word "from," nor in the following sections of this book; and it is not quite certain what verb should be supplied. What I have added may express the meaning here, though there are sections which it will not fit. If he does not mean to say that he learned all these good things from the several persons whom he mentions, he means that he observed certain good qualities in them, or received certain benefits from them, and it is implied that he was the better for it, or at least might have been: for it would be a mistake to understand Marcus as saying that he possessed all the virtues which he observed in his kinsmen and teachers.

[2] His father's name was Annius Verus.

[3] His mother was Domitia Calvilla, named also Lucilla.

[4] Perhaps his mother's grandfather, Catilius Severus.

[5] In the works of Justinus there is printed a letter to one Diognetus, whom the writer names "most excellent." He was a Gentile, but he wished very much to know what the religion of the Christians was, what God they worshipped, and how this worship made them despise the world and death,

and the driving away of daemons and such things; and not to breed quails [for fighting], nor to give myself up passionately to such things; and to endure freedom of speech; and to have become intimate with philosophy; and to have been a hearer, first of Bacchius, then of Tandasis and Marcianus; and to have written dialogues in my youth; and to have desired a plank bed and skin, and whatever else of the kind belongs to the Grecian discipline.

7. From Rusticus[6] I received the impression that my character required improvement and discipline; and from him I learned not to be led astray to sophistic emulation, nor to writing on speculative matters, nor to delivering little hortatory orations, nor to showing myself off as a man who practices much discipline, or does benevolent acts in order to make a display; and to abstain from rhetoric, and poetry, and fine writing; and not to walk about in the house in my outdoor dress, nor to do other things of the kind; and to write my letters with simplicity, like the letter which Rusticus wrote from Sinuessa to my mother; and with respect to those who have offended me by words, or done me wrong, to be easily disposed to be pacified and reconciled, as soon as they have shown a readiness to be reconciled; and to read carefully, and not to be satisfied with a superficial understanding of a book; nor hastily to give my assent to those who talk overmuch; and I am indebted to him for being acquainted with the discourses of Epictetus,[7] which he communicated to me out of his own collection.

8. From Apollonius[8] I learned freedom of will and undeviating steadiness of purpose; and to look to nothing else, not even for a moment, except to reason; and to be always the same, in sharp pains, on the occasion of the loss of a child, and in long illness; and to see clearly in a living example that the same man can be both most resolute and yielding, and not peevish in giving his instruction; and to have had before my eyes a man who clearly considered his experience and his skill in expounding philosophical principles as the smallest of his merits;

---

and neither believe in the gods of the Greeks nor observe the superstition of the Jews; and what was this love to one another which they had, and why this new kind of religion was introduced now and not before. My friend Mr. Jenkins, rector of Lyminge in Kent, has suggested to me that this Diognetus may have been the tutor of M. Antoninus.

[6] Q. Junius Rusticus was a Stoic philosopher, whom Antoninus valued highly, and often took his advice (Capitol. *M. Antonin.* iii).

[7] Antoninus says, τοῖς Ἐπικτείοις ὑπομνήμασιν, which must not be translated, "the writings of Epictetus," for Epictetus wrote nothing. His pupil Arrian, who has preserved for us all that we know of Epictetus, says, ταῦτα ἐπειράθην ὑπομνήματα ἐμαυτῷ διαψυλάξαι τῆς ἐκείνου διανοίας (*Ep. ad. Gell.*).

[8] Apollonius of Chalcis came to Rome in the time of Pius to be Marcus' preceptor. He was a rigid Stoic.

and from him I learned how to receive from friends what are esteemed favors, without being either humbled by them or letting them pass unnoticed.

9. From Sextus,[9] a benevolent disposition, and the example of a family governed in a fatherly manner, and the idea of living conformably to nature; and gravity without affectation, and to look carefully after the interests of friends, and to tolerate ignorant persons, and those who form opinions without consideration: he had the power of readily accommodating himself to all, so that intercourse with him was more agreeable than any flattery; and at the same time he was most highly venerated by those who associated with him: and he had the faculty both of discovering and ordering, in an intelligent and methodical way, the principles necessary for life; and he never showed anger or any other passion, but was entirely free from passion, and also most affectionate; and he could express approbation without noisy display, and he possessed much knowledge without ostentation.

10. From Alexander[10] the grammarian, to refrain from fault-finding, and not in a reproachful way to chide those who uttered any barbarous or solecistic or strange-sounding expression; but dexterously to introduce the very expression which ought to have been used, and in the way of answer or giving confirmation, or joining in an inquiry about the thing itself, not about the word, or by some other fit suggestion.

11. From Fronto[11] I learned to observe what envy and duplicity and hypocrisy are in a tyrant, and that generally those among us who are called Patricians are rather deficient in paternal affection.

12. From Alexander the Platonic, not frequently nor without necessity to say to any one, or to write in a letter, that I have no leisure; nor continually to excuse the neglect of duties required by our relation to those with whom we live, by alleging urgent occupations.

13. From Catulus,[12] not to be indifferent when a friend finds fault, even if he should find fault without reason, but to try to restore him to his usual disposition; and to be ready to speak well of teachers, as it is reported of Domitius and Athenodotus; and to love my children truly.

---

[9] Sextus of Chaeronea, a grandson of Plutarch, or nephew, as some say; but more probably a grandson.

[10] Alexander was a Grammaticus, a native of Phrygia. He wrote a commentary on Homer; and the rhetorician Aristides wrote a panegyric on Alexander in a funeral oration.

[11] M. Cornelius Fronto was a rhetorician, and in great favor with Marcus. There are extant various letters between Marcus and Fronto.

[12] Cinna Catulus, a Stoic philosopher.

14. From my brother[13] Severus, to love my kin, and to love truth, and to love justice; and through him I learned to know Thrasea, Helvidius, Cato, Dion, Brutus;[14] and from him I received the idea of a polity in which there is the same law for all, a polity administered with regard to equal rights and equal freedom of speech, and the idea of a kingly government which respects most of all the freedom of the governed; I learned from him also consistency and undeviating steadiness in my regard for philosophy; and a disposition to do good, and to give to others readily, and to cherish good hopes, and to believe that I am loved by my friends; and in him I observed no concealment of his opinions with respect to those whom he condemned, and that his friends had no need to conjecture what he wished or did not wish, but it was quite plain.

15. From Maximus[15] I learned self-government, and not to be led aside by anything; and cheerfulness in all circumstances, as well as in illness; and a just admixture in the moral character of sweetness and dignity, and to do what was set before me without complaining. I observed that everybody believed that he thought as he spoke, and that in all that he did he never had any bad intention; and he never showed amazement and surprise, and was never in a hurry, and never put off doing a thing, nor was perplexed nor dejected, nor did he ever laugh to disguise his vexation, nor, on the other hand, was he ever passionate or suspicious. He was accustomed to do acts of beneficence, and was ready to forgive, and was free from all falsehood; and he presented the appearance of a man who could not be diverted from right, rather than of a man who had been improved. I observed, too, that no man could ever think that he was despised by Maximus, or ever venture to think himself a better man. He had also the art of being humorous in an agreeable way.

16. In my father[16] I observed mildness of temper, and unchangeable resolution in the things which he had determined after due deliberation; and no vain-glory in those things which men call honors; and a love of labor and perseverance; and a readiness to listen to those who had anything to propose for the common weal; and undeviating firmness in giving to every man according to his deserts; and a knowledge derived from experience of the occasions for vigorous action

---

[13] The word brother may not be genuine. Antoninus had no brother. It has been supposed that he may mean some cousin. Schultz in his translation omits "brother," and says that this Severus is probably Claudius Severus, a peripatetic.

[14] We know, from Tacitus (*Annal.* xiii., xvi. 21; and other passages), who Thrasea and Helvidius were. Plutarch has written the lives of the two Catos, and of Dion and Brutus. Antoninus probably alludes to Cato of Utica, who was a Stoic.

[15] Claudius Maximus was a Stoic philosopher, who was highly esteemed also by Antoninus Pius, Marcus' predecessor. The character of Maximus is that of a perfect man. (See viii. 25.)

[16] He means his adoptive father, his predecessor, the Emperor Antoninus Pius. Compare vi. 30.

and for remission. And I observed that he had overcome all passion for boys; and he considered himself no more than any other citizen;[17] and he released his friends from all obligation to sup with him or to attend him of necessity when he went abroad, and those who had failed to accompany him, by reason of any urgent circumstances, always found him the same. I observed, too, his habit of careful inquiry in all matters of deliberation, and his persistency, and that he never stopped his investigation through being satisfied with appearances which first present themselves; and that his disposition was to keep his friends, and not to be soon tired of them, nor yet to be extravagant in his affection; and to be satisfied on all occasions, and cheerful; and to foresee things a long way off, and to provide for the smallest without display; and to check immediately popular applause and all flattery; and to be ever watchful over the things which were necessary for the administration of the empire, and to be a good manager of the expenditure, and patiently to endure the blame which he got for such conduct; and he was neither superstitious with respect to the gods, nor did he court men by gifts or by trying to please them, or by flattering the populace; but he showed sobriety in all things and firmness, and never any mean thoughts or action, nor love of novelty. And the things which conduce in any way to the commodity of life, and of which fortune gives an abundant supply, he used without arrogance and without excusing himself; so that when he had them, he enjoyed them without affectation, and when he had them not, he did not want them. No one could ever say of him that he was either a sophist or a [home-bred] flippant slave or a pedant; but every one acknowledged him to be a man ripe, perfect, above flattery, able to manage his own and other men's affairs. Besides this, he honored those who were true philosophers, and he did not reproach those who pretended to be philosophers, nor yet was he easily led by them. He was also easy in conversation, and he made himself agreeable without any offensive affectation. He took a reasonable care of his body's health, not as one who was greatly attached to life, nor out of regard to personal appearance, nor yet in a careless way, but so that through his own attention he very seldom stood in need of the physician's art or of medicine or external applications. He was most ready to give without envy to those who possessed any particular faculty, such as that of eloquence or knowledge of the law or of morals, or of anything else; and he gave them his help, that each might enjoy reputation according to his deserts; and he always acted conformably to the institutions of his country, without showing any affectation of doing so. Further, he was not fond of change nor unsteady, but he loved to stay in the same places, and to employ himself about the same things; and after his paroxysms of headache he came immediately fresh and vigorous

---

[17] He uses the word κοίνονοημοσύνη. See Gataker's note.

to his usual occupations. His secrets were not many, but very few and very rare, and these only about public matters; and he showed prudence and economy in the exhibition of the public spectacles and the construction of public buildings, his donations to the people, and in such things, for he was a man who looked to what ought to be done, not to the reputation which is got by a man's acts. He did not take the bath at unseasonable hours; he was not fond of building houses, nor curious about what he ate, nor about the texture and color of his clothes, nor about the beauty of his slaves.[18] His dress came from Lorium, his villa on the coast, and from Lanuvium generally.[19] We know how he behaved to the toll-collector at Tusculum who asked his pardon; and such was all his behavior. There was in him nothing harsh, nor implacable, nor violent, nor, as one may say, anything carried to the sweating point; but he examined all things severally, as if he had abundance of time, and without confusion, in an orderly way, vigorously and consistently. And that might be applied to him which is recorded of Socrates,[20] that he was able both to abstain from, and to enjoy, those things which many are too weak to abstain from, and cannot enjoy without excess. But to be strong enough both to bear the one and to be sober in the other is the mark of a man who has a perfect and invincible soul, such as he showed in the illness of Maximus.

17. To the gods I am indebted for having good grandfathers, good parents, a good sister, good teachers, good associates, good kinsmen and friends, nearly everything good. Further, I owe it to the gods that I was not hurried into any offence against any of them, though I had a disposition which, if opportunity had offered, might have led me to do something of this kind; but, through their favor, there never was such a concurrence of circumstances as put me to the trial. Further, I am thankful to the gods that I was not longer brought up with my grandfather's concubine, and that I preserved the flower of my youth, and that I did not make proof of my virility before the proper season, but even deferred the time; that I was subjected to a ruler and a father who was able to take away all pride from me, and to bring me to the knowledge that it is possible for a man to live in a palace without wanting either guards or embroidered dresses, or torches and statues, and such-like show; but that it is in such a man's power to bring himself very near to the fashion of a private person, without being for this reason either meaner in thought, or more remiss in action, with respect to the things which must be done for the public interest in a manner that befits a ruler. I thank the gods for giving

---

[18] This passage is corrupt, and the exact meaning is uncertain.
[19] Lorium was a villa on the coast north of Rome, and there Antoninus was brought up, and he died there. This also is corrupt.
[20] Xenophon, Memorab. i. 3, 15.

me such a brother,[21] who was able by his moral character to rouse me to vigilance over myself, and who at the same time pleased me by his respect and affection; that my children have not been stupid nor deformed in body; that I did not make more proficiency in rhetoric, poetry, and the other studies, in which I should perhaps have been completely engaged, if I had seen that I was making progress in them; that I made haste to place those who brought me up in the station of honor, which they seemed to desire, without putting them off with hope of my doing it some other time after, because they were then still young; that I knew Apollonius, Rusticus, Maximus; that I received clear and frequent impressions about living according to nature, and what kind of a life that is, so that, so far as depended on the gods, and their gifts, and help, and inspirations, nothing hindered me from forthwith living according to nature, though I still fall short of it through my own fault, and through not observing the admonitions of the gods, and, I may almost say, their direct instructions; that my body has held out so long in such a kind of life; that I never touched either Benedicta or Theodotus, and that, after having fallen into amatory passions, I was cured, and though I was often out of humor with Rusticus, I never did anything of which I had occasion to repent; that, though it was my mother's fate to die young, she spent the last years of her life with me; that, whenever I wished to help any man in his need, or on any other occasion, I was never told that I had not the means of doing it; and that to myself the same necessity never happened, to receive anything from another; that I have such a wife,[22] so obedient, and so affectionate, and so simple; that I had abundance of good masters for my children; and that remedies have been shown to me by dreams, both others, and against bloodspitting and giddiness[23]. . .; and that, when I had an inclination to philosophy, I did not fall into the hands of any sophist, and that I did not waste my time on writers [of histories], or in the resolution of syllogisms, or occupy myself about the investigation of appearances in the heavens; for all these things require the help of the gods and fortune.

Among the Quadi at the Granua.[24]

---

[21] The emperor had no brother except L. Verus, his brother by adoption.
[22] *See the* Life of Antoninus.
[23] This is corrupt.
[24] The Quadi lived in the southern part of Bohemia and Moravia; and Antoninus made a campaign against them. (See the *Life*.) Granua is probably the river Graan, which flows into the Danube.

If these words are genuine, Antoninus may have written this first book during the war with the Quadi. In the first edition of Antoninus, and in the older editions, the first three sections of the second book make the conclusion of the first book. Gataker placed them at the beginning of the second book.

BOOK II

Begin the morning by saying to thyself, I shall meet with the busybody, the ungrateful, arrogant, deceitful, envious, unsocial. All these things happen to them by reason of their ignorance of what is good and evil. But I who have seen the nature of the good that it is beautiful, and of the bad that it is ugly, and the nature of him who does wrong, that it is akin to me; not [only] of the same blood or seed, but that it participates in [the same] intelligence and [the same] portion of the divinity, I can neither be injured by any of them, for no one can fix on me what is ugly, nor can I be angry with my kinsman, nor hate him. For we are made for co-operation, like feet, like hands, like eyelids, like the rows of the upper and lower teeth.[25] To act against one another, then, is contrary to nature; and it is acting against one another to be vexed and to turn away.

2. Whatever this is that I am, it is a little flesh and breath, and the ruling part. Throw away thy books; no longer distract thyself: it is not allowed; but as if thou wast now dying, despise the flesh; it is blood and bones and network, a contexture of nerves, veins, and arteries. See the breath also, what kind of a thing it is; air, and not always the same, but every moment sent out and again sucked in. The third, then, is the ruling part; consider thus: Thou art an old man; no longer let this be a slave, no longer be pulled by the strings like a puppet to unsocial movements, no longer be either dissatisfied with thy present lot, or shrink from the future.

3. All that is from the gods is full of providence. That which is from fortune is not separated from nature or without an interweaving and involution with the things which are ordered by providence. From thence all things flow; and there is besides necessity, and that which is for the advantage of the whole universe, of which thou art a part. But that is good for every part of nature which the nature of the whole brings, and what serves to maintain this nature. Now the universe is preserved, as by the changes of the elements so by the changes of things compounded of the elements. Let these principles be enough for thee; let

---

[25] Xenophon, Mem. ii. 3. 18.

them always be fixed opinions. But cast away the thirst after books, that thou mayest not die murmuring, but cheerfully, truly, and from thy heart thankful to the gods.

4. Remember how long thou hast been putting off these things, and how often thou hast received an opportunity from the gods, and yet dost not use it. Thou must now at last perceive of what universe thou art a part, and of what administrator of the universe thy existence is an efflux, and that a limit of time is fixed for thee, which if thou dost not use for clearing away the clouds from thy mind, it will go and thou wilt go, and it will never return.

5. Every moment think steadily as a Roman and a man to do what thou hast in hand with perfect and simple dignity, and feeling of affection, and freedom, and justice, and to give thyself relief from all other thoughts. And thou wilt give thyself relief if thou doest every act of thy life as if it were the last, laying aside all carelessness and passionate aversion from the commands of reason, and all hypocrisy, and self-love, and discontent with the portion which has been given to thee. Thou seest how few the things are, the which if a man lays hold of, he is able to live a life which flows in quiet, and is like the existence of the gods; for the gods on their part will require nothing more from him who observes these things.

6. Do wrong[26] to thyself, do wrong to thyself, my soul; but thou wilt no longer have the opportunity of honoring thyself. Every man's life is sufficient. But thine is nearly finished, though thy soul reverences not itself, but places thy felicity in the souls of others.

7. Do the things external which fall upon thee distract thee? Give thyself time to learn something new and good, and cease to be whirled around. But then thou must also avoid being carried about the other way; for those too are triflers who have wearied themselves in life by their activity, and yet have no object to which to direct every movement, and, in a word, all their thoughts.

8. Through not observing what is in the mind of another a man has seldom been seen to be unhappy; but those who do not observe the movements of their own minds must of necessity be unhappy.

9. This thou must always bear in mind, what is the nature of the whole, and what is my nature, and how this is related to that, and what kind of a part it is of what kind of a whole, and that there is no one who hinders thee from always doing and saying the things which are according to the nature of which thou art a part.

---

[26] Perhaps it should be, "thou art doing violence to thyself." ὑβρίζεις, not ὕβριζε.

10. Theophrastus, in his comparison of bad acts—such a comparison as one would make in accordance with the common notions of mankind—says, like a true philosopher, that the offenses which are committed through desire are more blamable than those which are committed through anger. For he who is excited by anger seems to turn away from reason with a certain pain and unconscious contraction; but he who offends through desire, being overpowered by pleasure, seems to be in a manner more intemperate and more womanish in his offences. Rightly, then, and in a way worthy of philosophy, he said that the offence which is committed with pleasure is more blamable than that which is committed with pain; and on the whole the one is more like a person who has been first wronged and through pain is compelled to be angry, but the other is moved by his own impulse to do wrong, being carried towards doing something by desire.

11. Since it is possible[27] that thou mayest depart from life this very moment, regulate every act and thought accordingly.[28] But to go away from among men, if there are gods, is not a thing to be afraid of, for the gods will not involve thee in evil; but if indeed they do not exist, or if they have no concern about human affairs, what is it to me to live in a universe devoid of gods or devoid of providence? But in truth they do exist, and they do care for human things, and they have put all the means in man's power to enable him not to fall into real evils. And as to the rest, if there was anything evil, they would have provided for this also, that it should be altogether in a man's power not to fall into it. Now that which does not make a man worse, how can it make a man's life worse? But neither through ignorance, nor— having the knowledge but not the power to guard against or correct these things, is it possible that the nature of the universe has overlooked them; nor is it possible that it has made so great a mistake, either through want of power or want of skill, that good and evil should happen indiscriminately to the good and the bad. But death certainly, and life, honor and dishonor, pain and pleasure,—all these things equally happen to good men and bad, being things which make us neither better nor worse. Therefore they are neither good nor evil.

12. How quickly all things disappear,—in the universe the bodies themselves, but in time the remembrance of them. What is the nature of all sensible things, and particularly those which attract with the bait of pleasure or terrify by pain, or are noised abroad by vapory fame; how worthless, and contemptible, and sordid, and perishable, and dead they are,—all this it is the part of the intellectual faculty to observe. To observe too who these are whose

---

[27] Or it may mean, "since it is in thy power to depart;" which gives a meaning somewhat different.
[28] See Cicero, Tuscul., i. 49.

opinions and voices give reputation; what death is, and the fact that, if a man looks at it in itself, and by the abstractive power of reflection resolves into their parts all the things which present themselves to the imagination in it, he will then consider it to be nothing else than an operation of nature; and if any one is afraid of an operation of nature, he is a child. This, however, is not only an operation of nature, but it is also a thing which conduces to the purposes of nature. To observe too how man comes near to the Deity, and by what part of him, and when this part of man is so disposed (vi. 28).

13. Nothing is more wretched than a man who traverses everything in a round, and pries into the things beneath the earth, as the poet[29] says, and seeks by conjecture what is in the minds of his neighbors, without perceiving that it is sufficient to attend to the daemon within him, and to reverence it sincerely. And reverence of the daemon consists in keeping it pure from passion and thoughtlessness, and dissatisfaction with what comes from gods and men. For the things from the gods merit veneration for their excellence; and the things from men should be dear to us by reason of kinship; and sometimes even, in a manner, they move our pity by reason of men's ignorance of good and bad; this defect being not less than that which deprives us of the power of distinguishing things that are white and black.

14. Though thou shouldest be going to live three thousand years and as many times ten thousand years, still remember that no man loses any other life than this which he now lives, nor lives any other than this which he now loses. The longest and shortest are thus brought to the same. For the present is the same to all, though that which perish is not the same;[30] and so that which is lost appears to be a mere moment. For a man cannot lose either the past or the future: for what a man has not, how can any one take this from him? These two things then thou must bear in mind; the one, that all things from eternity are of like forms and come round in a circle, and that it makes no difference whether a man shall see the same things during a hundred years, or two hundred, or an infinite time; and the second, that the longest liver and he who will die soonest lose just the same. For the present is the only thing of which a man can be deprived, if it is true that this is the only thing which he has, and that a man cannot lose a thing if he has it not.

15. Remember that all is opinion. For what was said by the Cynic Monimus is manifest: and manifest too is the use of what was said, if a man receives what may be got out of it as far as it is true.

---

[29] Pindar, in the Theaetetus of Plato. See xi. 1.
[30] See Gataker's note.

16. The soul of man does violence to itself, first of all, when it becomes an abscess, and, as it were, a tumor on the universe, so far as it can. For to be vexed at anything which happens is a separation of ourselves from nature, in some part of which the natures of all other things are contained. In the next place, the soul does violence to itself when it turns away from any man, or even moves towards him with the intention of injuring, such as are the souls of those who are angry. In the third place, the soul does violence to itself when it is overpowered by pleasure or by pain. Fourthly, when it plays a part, and does or says anything insincerely and untruly. Fifthly, when it allows any act of its own and any movement to be without an aim, and does anything thoughtlessly and without considering what it is, it being right that even the smallest things be done with reference to an end; and the end of rational animals is to follow the reason and the law of the most ancient city and polity.

17. Of human life the time is a point, and the substance is in a flux, and the perception dull, and the composition of the whole body subject to putrefaction, and the soul a whirl, and fortune hard to divine, and fame a thing devoid of judgment. And, to say all in a word, everything which belongs to the body is a stream, and what belongs to the soul is a dream and vapor, and life is a warfare and a stranger's sojourn, and after fame is oblivion. What then is that which is able to conduct a man? One thing, and only one, philosophy. But this consists in keeping the daemon within a man free from violence and unharmed, superior to pains and pleasures, doing nothing without a purpose, nor yet falsely and with hypocrisy, not feeling the need of another man's doing or not doing anything; and besides, accepting all that happens, and all that is allotted, as coming from thence, wherever it is, from whence he himself came; and, finally, waiting for death with a cheerful mind, as being nothing else than a dissolution of the elements of which every living being is compounded. But if there is no harm to the elements themselves in each continually changing into another, why should a man have any apprehension about the change and dissolution of all the elements? For it is according to nature, and nothing is evil which is according to nature.

This in Carnuntum.[31]

---

[31] Carnuntum was a town of Pannonia, on the south side of the Danube, about thirty miles east of Vindobona (Vienna). Orosius (vii. 15) and Eutropius (viii. 13) say that Antoninus remained three years at Carmuntum during his war with the Marcomanni.

BOOK III

We ought to consider not only that our life is daily wasting away and a smaller part of it is left, but another thing also must be taken into the account, that if a man should live longer, it is quite uncertain whether the understanding will still continue sufficient for the comprehension of things, and retain the power of contemplation which strives to acquire the knowledge of the divine and the human. For if he shall begin to fall into dotage, perspiration and nutrition and imagination and appetite, and whatever else there is of the kind, will not fail; but the power of making use of ourselves, and filling up the measure of our duty, and clearly separating all appearances, and considering whether a man should now depart from life, and whatever else of the kind absolutely requires a disciplined reason,—all this is already extinguished. We must make haste, then, not only because we are daily nearer to death, but also because the conception of things and the understanding of them cease first.

2. We ought to observe also that even the things which follow after the things which are produced according to nature contain something pleasing and attractive. For instance, when bread is baked some parts are split at the surface, and these parts which thus open, and have a certain fashion contrary to the purpose of the baker's art, are beautiful in a manner, and in a peculiar way excite a desire for eating. And again, figs, when they are quite ripe, gape open; and in the ripe olives the very circumstance of their being near to rottenness adds a peculiar beauty to the fruit. And the ears of corn bending down, and the lion's eyebrows, and the foam which flows from the mouth of wild boars, and many other things,—though they are far from being beautiful if a man should examine them severally,—still, because they are consequent upon the things which are formed by nature, help to adorn them, and they please the mind; so that if a man should have a feeling and deeper insight with respect to the things which are produced in the universe, there is hardly one of those which follow by way of consequence which will not seem to him to be in a manner disposed so as to give pleasure. And so he will see even the real gaping jaws of wild beasts with no less pleasure than those which painters and sculptors show by imitation; and

in an old woman and an old man he will be able to see a certain maturity and comeliness; and the attractive loveliness of young persons he will be able to look on with chaste eyes; and many such things will present themselves, not pleasing to every man, but to him only who has become truly familiar with Nature and her works.

3. Hippocrates, after curing many diseases, himself fell sick and died. The Chaldaei foretold the deaths of many, and then fate caught them too. Alexander and Pompeius, and Caius Caesar, after so often completely destroying whole cities, and in battle cutting to pieces many ten thousands of cavalry and infantry, themselves too at last departed from life. Heraclitus, after so many speculations on the conflagration of the universe, was filled with water internally and died smeared all over with mud. And lice destroyed Democritus; and other lice killed Socrates. What means all this? Thou hast embarked, thou hast made the voyage, thou art come to shore; get out. If indeed to another life, there is no want of gods, not even there; but if to a state without sensation, thou wilt cease to be held by pains and pleasures, and to be a slave to the vessel, which is as much inferior as that which serves it is superior: for the one is intelligence and deity; the other is earth and corruption.

4. Do not waste the remainder of thy life in thoughts about others, when thou dost not refer thy thoughts to some object of common utility. For thou losest the opportunity of doing something else when thou hast such thoughts as these,—What is such a person doing, and why, and what is he saying, and what is he thinking of, and what is he contriving, and whatever else of the kind makes us wander away from the observation of our own ruling power. We ought then to check in the series of our thoughts everything that is without a purpose and useless, but most of all the over-curious feeling and the malignant; and a man should use himself to think of those things only about which if one should suddenly ask, What hast thou now in thy thoughts? with perfect openness thou mightest immediately answer, This or That; so that from thy words it should be plain that everything in thee is simple and benevolent, and such as befits a social animal, and one that cares not for thoughts about pleasure or sensual enjoyments at all, nor has any rivalry or envy and suspicion, or anything else for which thou wouldst blush if thou shouldst say that thou hadst it in thy mind. For the man who is such, and no longer delays being among the number of the best, is like a priest and minister of the gods, using too the [deity] which is planted within him, which makes the man uncontaminated by pleasure, unharmed by any pain, untouched by any insult, feeling no wrong, a fighter in the noblest fight, one who cannot be overpowered by any passion, dyed deep with justice, accepting with all his soul everything which happens and is assigned to him as

his portion; and not often, nor yet without great necessity and for the general interest, imagining what another says, or does, or thinks. For it is only what belongs to himself that he makes the matter for his activity; and he constantly thinks of that which is allotted to himself out of the sum total of things, and he makes his own acts fair, and he is persuaded that his own portion is good. For the lot which is assigned to each man is carried along with him and carries him along with it. And he remembers also that every rational animal is his kinsman, and that to care for all men is according to man's nature; and a man should hold on to the opinion not of all, but of those only who confessedly live according to nature. But as to those who live not so, he always bears in mind what kind of men they are both at home and from home, both by night and by day, and what they are, and with what men they live an impure life. Accordingly, he does not value at all the praise which comes from such men, since they are not even satisfied with themselves.

5. Labor not unwillingly, nor without regard to the common interest, nor without due consideration, nor with distraction; nor let studied ornament set off thy thoughts, and be not either a man of many words, or busy about too many things. And further, let the deity which is in thee be the guardian of a living being, manly and of ripe age, and engaged in matter political, and a Roman, and a ruler, who has taken his post like a man waiting for the signal which summons him from life, and ready to go, having need neither of oath nor of any man's testimony. Be cheerful also, and seek not external help nor the tranquillity which others give. A man then must stand erect, not be kept erect by others.

6. If thou findest in human life anything better than justice, truth, temperance, fortitude, and, in a word, anything better than thy own mind's self-satisfaction in the things which it enables thee to do according to right reason, and in the condition that is assigned to thee without thy own choice; if, I say, thou seest anything better than this, turn to it with all thy soul, and enjoy that which thou hast found to be the best. But if nothing appears to be better than the Deity which is planted in thee, which has subjected to itself all thy appetites, and carefully examines all the impressions, and, as Socrates said, has detached itself from the persuasions of sense, and has submitted itself to the gods, and cares for mankind; if thou findest everything else smaller and of less value than this, give place to nothing else, for if thou dost once diverge and incline to it, thou wilt no longer without distraction be able to give the preference to that good thing which is thy proper possession and thy own; for it is not right that anything of any other kind, such as praise from the many, or power, or enioyment of pleasure, should come into competition with that which is rationally and politically [or, practically] good. All these things, even though they may seem to

adapt themselves [to the better things] in a small degree, obtain the superiority all at once, and carry us away. But do thou, I say, simply and freely choose the better, and hold to it.—But that which is useful is the better.—Well, then, if it is useful to thee as a rational being, keep to it; but if it is only useful to thee as an animal, say so, and maintain thy judgment without arrogance: only take care that thou makest the inquiry by a sure method.

7. Never value anything as profitable to thyself which shall compel thee to break thy promise, to lose thy self-respect, to hate any man, to suspect, to curse, to act the hypocrite, to desire anything which needs walls and curtains: for he who has preferred to everything else his own intelligence and daemon and the worship of its excellence, acts no tragic part, does not groan, will not need either solitude or much company; and, what is chief of all, he will live without either pursuing or flying from [death];[32] but whether for a longer or a shorter time he shall have the soul enclosed in the body, he cares not at all: for even if he must depart immediately, he will go as readily as if he were going to do anything else which can be done with decency and order; taking care of this only all through life, that his thoughts turn not away from anything which belongs to an intelligent animal and a member of a civil community.

8. In the mind of one who is chastened and purified thou wilt find no corrupt matter, nor impurity, nor any sore skinned over. Nor is his life incomplete when fate overtakes him, as one may say of an actor who leaves the stage before ending and finishing the play. Besides, there is in him nothing servile, nor affected, nor too closely bound [to other things], nor yet detached[33] [from other things], nothing worthy of blame, nothing which seeks a hiding-place.

9. Reverence the faculty which produces opinion. On this faculty it entirely depends whether there shall exist in thy ruling part any opinion inconsistent with nature and the constitution of the rational animal. And this faculty promises freedom from hasty judgment, and friendship towards men, and obedience to the gods.

10. Throwing away then all things, hold to these only which are few; and besides, bear in mind that every man lives only this present time, which is an indivisible point, and that all the rest of his life is either past or it is uncertain. Short then is the time which every man lives; and small the nook of the earth where he lives; and short too the longest posthumous fame, and even this only continued by a succession of poor human beings, who will very soon die, and who know not even themselves, much less him who died long ago.

---

[32] Comp. ix. 3.
[33] viii. 34.

11. To the aids which have been mentioned let this one still be added: Make for thyself a definition or description of the thing which is presented to thee, so as to see distinctly what kind of a thing it is in its substance, in its nudity, in its complete entirety, and tell thyself its proper name, and the names of the things of which it has been compounded, and into which it will be resolved. For nothing is so productive of elevation of mind as to be able to examine methodically and truly every object which is presented to thee in life, and always to look at things so as to see at the same time what kind of universe this is, and what kind of use everything performs in it, and what value everything has with reference to the whole, and what with reference to man, who is a citizen of the highest city, of which all other cities are like families; what each thing is, and of what it is composed, and how long it is the nature of this thing to endure which now makes an impression on me, and what virtue I have need of with respect to it, such as gentleness, manliness, truth, fidelity, simplicity, contentment, and the rest. Wherefore, on every occasion a man should say: This comes from god; and this is according to the apportionment and spinning of the thread of destiny, and such-like coincidence and chance; and this is from one of the same stock, and a kinsman and partner, one who knows not, however, what is according to his nature. But I know; for this reason I behave towards him according to the natural law of fellowship with benevolence and justice. At the same time, however, in things indifferent[34] I attempt to ascertain the value of each.

12. If thou workest at that which is before thee, following right reason seriously, vigorously, calmly, without allowing anything else to distract thee, but keeping thy divine part pure, as if thou shouldst be bound to give it back immediately; if thou holdest to this, expecting nothing, fearing nothing, but satisfied with thy present activity according to nature, and with heroic truth in every word and sound which thou utterest, thou wilt live happy. And there is no man who is able to prevent this.

13. As physicians have always their instruments and knives ready for cases which suddenly require their skill, so do thou have principles ready for the understanding of things divine and human, and for doing everything, even the smallest, with a recollection of the bond which unites the divine and human to one another. For neither wilt thou do anything well which pertains to man without at the same time having a reference to things divine; nor the contrary.

14. No longer wander at hazard; for neither wilt thou read thy own memoirs,[35] nor the acts of the ancient Romans and Hellenes, and the selections

---

[34] Est et horum quae media appellamus grande discrimen.—*Seneca*, Ep. 82.
[35] ὑπομνήματα: or memoranda, notes, and the like. See i. 17.

from books which thou wast reserving for thy old age.[36] Hasten then to the end which thou hast before thee, and, throwing away idle hopes, come to thy own aid, if thou carest at all for thyself, while it is in thy power.

15. They know not how many things are signified by the words stealing, sowing, buying, keeping quiet, seeing what ought to be done; for this is not effected by the eyes, but by another kind of vision.

16. Body, soul, intelligence: to the body belong sensation, to the soul appetites, to the intelligence principles. To receive the impressions of forms by means of appearances belongs even to animals; to be pulled by the strings[37] of desire belongs both to wild beasts and to men who have made themselves into women, and to a Phalaris and a Nero: and to have the intelligence that guides to the things which appear suitable belongs also to those who do not believe in the gods, and who betray their country, and do their impure deeds when they have shut the doors. If then everything else is common to all that I have mentioned, there remains that which is peculiar to the good man, to be pleased and content with what happens, and with the thread which is spun for him; and not to defile the divinity which is planted in his breast, nor disturb it by a crowd of images, but to preserve it tranquil, following it obediently as a god, neither saying anything contrary to the truth, nor doing anything contrary to justice. And if all men refuse to believe that he lives a simple, modest, and contented life, he is neither angry with any of them, nor does he deviate from the way which leads to the end of life, to which a man ought to come pure, tranquil, ready to depart, and without any compulsion perfectly reconciled to his lot.

---

[36] Compare Fronto, ii. 9; a letter of Marcus to Fronto, who was then consul: "Feci tamen mihi per hos dies excerpta ex libris sexaginta in quinque tomis." But he says some of them were small books.
[37] Compare Plato, De Legibus, i. p. 644, ὅτι ταῦτα τὰ πάθη etc.; and Antoninus, ii. 2; vii. 3; xii. 19.

BOOK IV

That which rules within, when it is according to nature, is so affected with respect to the events which happened, that it always easily adapts itself to that which is possible and is presented to it. For it requires no definite material, but it moves towards its purpose,[38] under certain conditions, however; and it makes a material for itself out of that which opposes it, as fire lays hold of what falls into it, by which a small light would have been extinguished; but when the fire is strong, it soon appropriates to itself the matter which is heaped on it, and consumes it, and rises higher by means of this very material.

2. Let no act be done without a purpose, nor otherwise than according to the perfect principles of art.

3. Men seek retreats for themselves, houses in the country, sea-shores, and mountains; and thou too art wont to desire such things very much. But this is altogether a mark of the most common sort of men, for it is in thy power whenever thou shalt choose to retire into thyself. For nowhere either with more quiet or more freedom from trouble does a man retire than into his own soul, particularly when he has within him such thoughts that by looking into them he is immediately in perfect tranquillity; and I affirm that tranquillity is nothing else than the good ordering of the mind. Constantly then give to thyself this retreat, and renew thyself; and let thy principles be brief and fundamental, which, as soon as thou shalt recur to them, will be sufficient to cleanse the soul completely, and to send thee back free from all discontent with the things to which thou returnest. For with what art thou discontented? With the badness of men? Recall to thy mind this conclusion, that rational animals exist for one another, and that to endure is a part of justice, and that men do wrong involuntarily; and consider how many already, after mutual enmity, suspicion, hatred, and fighting, have been stretched dead, reduced to ashes; and be quiet at last.—But perhaps thou art dissatisfied with that which is assigned to thee

---

[38] πρὸς τά ἡγούμενα, literally "towards that which leads." The exact translation is doubtful. See Gataker's note.

out of the universe.—Recall to thy recollection this alternative; either there is providence or atoms [fortuitous concurrence of things]; or remember the arguments by which it has been proved that the world is a kind of political community [and be quiet at last].—But perhaps corporeal things will still fasten upon thee.—Consider then further that the mind mingles not with the breath, whether moving gently or violently, when it has once drawn itself apart and discovered its own power, and think also of all that thou hast heard and assented to about pain and pleasure [and be quiet at last].—But perhaps the desire of the thing called fame will torment thee.—See how soon everything is forgotten, and look at the chaos of infinite time on each side of [the present], and the emptiness of applause, and the changeableness and want of judgment in those who pretend to give praise, and the narrowness of the space within which it is circumscribed [and be quiet at last]. For the whole earth is a point, and how small a nook in it is this thy dwelling, and how few are there in it, and what kind of people are they who will praise thee.

This then remains: Remember to retire into this little territory of thy own,[39] and above all do not distract or strain thyself, but be free, and look at things as a man, as a human being, as a citizen, as a mortal. But among the things readiest to thy hand to which thou shalt turn, let there be these, which are two. One is that things do not touch the soul, for they are external and remain immovable; but our perturbations come only from the opinion which is within. The other is that all these things, which thou seest, change immediately and will no longer be; and constantly bear in mind how many of these changes thou hast already witnessed. The universe is transformation: life is opinion.

4. If our intellectual part is common, the reason also, in respect of which we are rational beings, is common: if this is so, common also is the reason which commands us what to do, and what not to do; if this is so, there is a common law also; if this is so, we are fellow-citizens; if this is so, we are members of some political community; if this is so, the world is in a manner a state.[40] For of what other common political community will any one say that the whole human race are members? And from thence, from this common political community, comes also our very intellectual faculty and reasoning faculty and our capacity for law; or whence do they come? For as my earthly part is a portion given to me from certain earth, and that which is watery from another element, and that which is hot and fiery from some peculiar source (for nothing comes out of that which is

---

[39] Tecum habita, noris quam sit tibi curta supellex.—*Persius*, iv. 52.
[40] Compare Cicero De Legibus, i. 7.

nothing, as nothing also returns to non-existence), so also the intellectual part comes from some source.

5. Death is such as generation is, a mystery of nature; composition out of the same elements, and a decomposition into the same; and altogether not a thing of which any man should be ashamed, for it is not contrary to [the nature of] a reasonable animal, and not contrary to the reason of our constitution.

6. It is natural that these things should be done by such persons, it is a matter of necessity; and if a man will not have it so, he will not allow the fig-tree to have juice. But by all means bear this in mind, that within a very short time both thou and he will be dead; and soon not even your names will be left behind.

7. Take away thy opinion, and then there is taken away the complaint, "I have been harmed." Take away the complaint, "I have been harmed," and the harm is taken away.

8. That which does not make a man worse than he was, also does not make his life worse, nor does it harm him either from without or from within.

9. The nature of that which is [universally] useful has been compelled to do this.

10. Consider that everything which happens, happens justly, and if thou observest carefully, thou wilt find it to be so. I do not say only with respect to the continuity of the series of things, but with respect to what is just, and as if it were done by one who assigns to each thing its value. Observe then as thou hast begun; and whatever thou doest, do it in conjunction with this, the being good, and in the sense in which a man is properly understood to be good. Keep to this in every action.

11. Do not have such an opinion of things as he has who does thee wrong, or such as he wishes thee to have, but look at them as they are in truth.

12. A man should always have these two rules in readiness; the one to do only whatever the reason of the ruling and legislating faculty may suggest for the use of men; the other, to change thy opinion, if there is any one at hand who sets thee right and moves thee from any opinion. But this change of opinion must proceed only from a certain persuasion, as of what is just or of common advantage, and the like, not because it appears pleasant or brings reputation.

13. Hast thou reason? I have.—Why then dost not thou use it? For if this does its own work, what else dost thou wish?

14. Thou hast existed as a part. Thou shalt disappear in that which produced thee; but rather thou shalt be received back into its seminal principle by transmutation.

15. Many grains of frankincense on the same altar: one falls before, another falls after; but it makes no difference.

16. Within ten days thou wilt seem a god to those to whom thou art now a beast and an ape, if thou wilt return to thy principles and the worship of reason.

17. Do not act as if thou wert going to live ten thousand years. Death hangs over thee. While thou livest, while it is in thy power, be good.

18. How much trouble he avoids who does not look to see what his neighbor says or does or thinks, but only to what he does himself, that it may be just and pure; or, as Agathon says, look not round at the depraved morals of others, but run straight along the line without deviating from it.

19. He who has a vehement desire for posthumous fame does not consider that every one of those who remember him will himself also die very soon; then again also they who have succeeded them, until the whole remembrance shall have been extinguished as it is transmitted through men who foolishly admire and perish. But suppose that those who will remember are even immortal, and that the remembrance will be immortal, what then is this to thee? And I say not what is it to the dead, but what is it to the living? What is praise, except indeed so far as it has a certain utility? For thou now rejectest unseasonably the gift of nature, clinging to something else . . .

20. Everything which is in any way beautiful is beautiful in itself, and terminates in itself, not having praise as part of itself. Neither worse then nor better is a thing made by being praised. I affirm this also of the things which are called beautiful by the vulgar, for example, material things and works of art. That which is really beautiful has no need of anything; not more than law, not more than truth, not more than benevolence or modesty. Which of these things is beautiful because it is praised, or spoiled by being blamed? Is such a thing as an emerald made worse than it was, if it is not praised? or gold, ivory, purple, a lyre, a little knife, a flower, a shrub?

21. If souls continue to exist, how does the air contain them from eternity?—But how does the earth contain the bodies of those who have been buried from time so remote? For as here the mutation of these bodies after a certain continuance, whatever it may be, and their dissolution, make room for other dead bodies, so the souls which are removed into the air after subsisting for some time are transmuted and diffused, and assume a fiery nature by being received into the seminal intelligence of the universe, and in this way make room for the fresh souls which come to dwell there. And this is the answer which a man might give on the hypothesis of souls continuing to exist. But we must not only think of the number of bodies which are thus buried, but also of the number of animals which are daily eaten by us and the other animals. For what a number is consumed, and thus in a manner buried in the bodies of those who feed on them! And nevertheless this earth receives them by reason of the

changes [of these bodies] into blood, and the transformations into the aerial or the fiery element.

What is the investigation into the truth in this matter? The division into that which is material and that which is the cause of form [the formal]. (vii. 29.)

22. Do not be whirled about, but in every movement have respect to justice, and on the occasion of every impression maintain the faculty of comprehension [or understanding].

23. Everything harmonizes with me, which is harmonious to thee, O Universe. Nothing for me is too early nor too late, which is in due time for thee. Everything is fruit to me which thy seasons bring, O Nature: from thee are all things, in thee are all things, to thee all things return. The poet says, Dear city of Cecrops; and wilt not thou say, Dear city of Zeus?

24. Occupy thyself with few things, says the philosopher, if thou wouldst be tranquil.—But consider if it would not be better to say, Do what is necessary, and whatever the reason of the animal which is naturally social requires, and as it requires. For this brings not only the tranquillity which comes from doing well, but also that which comes from doing few things. For the greatest part of what we say and do being unnecessary, if a man takes this away, he will have more leisure and less uneasiness. Accordingly, on every occasion a man should ask himself, Is this one of the unnecessary things? Now a man should take away not only unnecessary acts, but also unnecessary thoughts, for thus superfluous acts will not follow after.

25. Try how the life of the good man suits thee, the life of him who is satisfied with his portion out of the whole, and satisfied with his own just acts and benevolent disposition.

26. Hast thou seen those things? Look also at these. Do not disturb thyself. Make thyself all simplicity. Does any one do wrong? It is to himself that he does the wrong. Has anything happened to thee? Well; out of the universe from the beginning everything which happens has been apportioned and spun out to thee. In a word, thy life is short. Thou must turn to profit the present by the aid of reason and justice. Be sober in thy relaxation.

27. Either it is a well-arranged universe[41] or a chaos huddled together, but still a universe. But can a certain order subsist in thee, and disorder in the All? And this too when all things are so separated and diffused and sympathetic.

28. A black character, a womanish character, a stubborn character, bestial, childish, animal, stupid, counterfeit, scurrilous, fraudulent, tyrannical.

---

[41] Antoninus here uses the word κόσμος both in the sense of the Universe and of Order; and it is difficult to express his meaning.

29. If he is a stranger to the universe who does not know what is in it, no less is he a stranger who does not know what is going on in it. He is a runaway, who flies from social reason; he is blind, who shuts the eyes of understanding; he is poor, who has need of another, and has not from himself all things which are useful for life. He is an abscess on the universe who withdraws and separates himself from the reason of our common nature through being displeased with the things which happen, for the same nature produces this, and has produced thee too: he is a piece rent asunder from the state, who tears his own soul from that of reasonable animals, which is one.

30. The one is a philosopher without a tunic, and the other without a book: here is another half naked: Bread I have not, he says, and I abide by reason—and I do not get the means of living out of my learning, and I abide [by my reason].

31. Love the art, poor as it may be, which thou hast learned, and be content with it; and pass through the rest of life like one who has intrusted to the gods with his whole soul all that he has, making thyself neither the tyrant nor the slave of any man.

32. Consider, for example, the times of Vespasian. Thou wilt see all these things, people marrying, bringing up children, sick, dying, warring, feasting, trafficking, cultivating the ground, flattering, obstinately arrogant, suspecting, plotting, wishing for some to die, grumbling about the present, loving, heaping up treasure, desiring consulship, kingly power. Well, then, that life of these people no longer exists at all. Again, remove to the times of Trajan. Again, all is the same. Their life too is gone. In like manner view also the other epochs of time and of whole nations, and see how many after great efforts soon fell and were resolved into the elements. But chiefly thou shouldst think of those whom thou hast thyself known distracting themselves about idle things, neglecting to do what was in accordance with their proper constitution, and to hold firmly to this and to be content with it. And herein it is necessary to remember that the attention given to everything has its proper value and proportion. For thus thou wilt not be dissatisfied, if thou appliest thyself to smaller matters no further than is fit.

33. The words which were formerly familiar are now antiquated: so also the names of those who were famed of old, are now in a manner antiquated, Camillus, Caeso, Volesus, Leonnatus, and a little after also Scipio and Cato, then Augustus, then also Hadrianus and Antoninus. For all things soon pass away and become a mere tale, and complete oblivion soon buries them. And I say this of those who have shone in a wondrous way. For the rest, as soon as they have breathed out their breath they are gone, and no man speaks of them.

And, to conclude the matter, what is even an eternal remembrance? A mere nothing. What then is that about which we ought to employ our serious pains? This one thing, thoughts just, and acts social, and words which never lie, and a disposition which gladly accepts all that happens, as necessary, as usual, as flowing from a principle and source of the same kind.

34. Willingly give thyself up to Clotho [one of the fates], allowing her to spin thy thread into whatever things she pleases.

35. Everything is only for a day, both that which remembers and that which is remembered.

36. Observe constantly that all things take place by change, and accustom thyself to consider that the nature of the universe loves nothing so much as to change the things which are and to make new things like them. For everything that exists is in a manner the seed of that which will be. But thou art thinking only of seeds which are cast into the earth or into a womb: but this is a very vulgar notion.

37. Thou wilt soon die, and thou art not yet simple, nor free from perturbations, nor without suspicion of being hurt by external things, nor kindly disposed towards all; nor dost thou yet place wisdom only in acting justly.

38. Examine men's ruling principles, even those of the wise, what kind of things they avoid, and what kind they pursue.

39. What is evil to thee does not subsist in the ruling principle of another; nor yet in any turning and mutation of thy corporeal covering. Where is it then? It is in that part of thee in which subsists the power of forming opinions about evils. Let this power then not form [such] opinions, and all is well. And if that which is nearest to it, the poor body, is cut, burnt, filled with matter and rottenness, nevertheless let the part which forms opinions about these things be quiet; that is, let it judge that nothing is either bad or good which can happen equally to the bad man and the good. For that which happens equally to him who lives contrary to nature and to him who lives according to nature, is neither according to nature nor contrary to nature.

40. Constantly regard the universe as one living being, having one substance and one soul; and observe how all things have reference to one perception, the perception of this one living being; and how all things act with one movement; and how all things are the co-operating causes of all things which exist; observe too the continuous spinning of the thread and the contexture of the web.

41. Thou art a little soul bearing about a corpse, as Epictetus used to say (i. c. 19).

42. It is no evil for things to undergo change, and no good for things to subsist in consequence of change.

43. Time is like a river made up of the events which happen, and a violent stream; for as soon as a thing has been seen, it is carried away, and another comes in its place, and this will be carried away too.

44. Everything which happens is as familiar and well known as the rose in spring and the fruit in summer; for such is disease, and death, and calumny, and treachery, and whatever else delights fools or vexes them.

45. In the series of things, those which follow are always aptly fitted to those which have gone before: for this series is not like a mere enumeration of disjointed things, which has only a necessary sequence, but it is a rational connection: and as all existing things are arranged together harmoniously, so the things which come into existence exhibit no mere succession, but a certain wonderful relationship (vi. 38; vii. 9; vii. 75, note).

46. Always remember the saying of Heraclitus, that the death of earth is to become water, and the death of water is to become air, and the death of air is to become fire, and reversely. And think too of him who forgets whither the way leads, and that men quarrel with that with which they are most constantly in communion, the reason which governs the universe; and the things which they daily meet with seem to them strange: and consider that we ought not to act and speak as if we were asleep, for even in sleep we seem to act and speak; and that we ought not, like children who learn from their parents, simply to act and speak as we have been taught.

47. If any god told thee that thou shalt die to-morrow, or certainly on the day after to-morrow, thou wouldst not care much whether it was on the third day or on the morrow, unless thou wast in the highest degree mean-spirited; for how small is the difference! So think it no great thing to die after as many years as thou canst name rather than to-morrow.

48. Think continually how many physicians are dead after often contracting their eyebrows over the sick; and how many astrologers after predicting with great pretensions the deaths of others; and how many philosophers after endless discourses on death or immortality; how many heroes after killing thousands; and how many tyrants who have used their power over men's lives with terrible insolence, as if they were immortal; and how many cities are entirely dead, so to speak, Helice[42] and Pompeii and Herculaneum, and others innumerable. Add to the reckoning all whom thou hast known, one after another. One man after burying another has been laid out dead, and another buries him; and all this in a short time. To conclude, always observe how ephemeral and worthless human

---

[42] Ovid, Met. xv. 293:—

"Si quaeras Helicen et Burin Achaidas urbes,
Invenies sub aquis.

things are, and what was yesterday a little mucus, to-morrow will be a mummy or ashes. Pass then through this little space of time conformably to nature, and end thy journey in content, as an olive falls off when it is ripe, blessing nature who produced it, and thanking the tree on which it grew.

49. Be like the promontory against which the waves continually break, but it stands firm and tames the fury of the water around it.

Unhappy am I because this has happened to me? Not so, but happy am I, though this has happened to me, because I continue free from pain, neither crushed by the present nor fearing the future. For such a thing as this might have happened to every man; but every man would not have continued free from pain on such an occasion. Why then is that rather a misfortune than this a good fortune? And dost thou in all cases call that a man's misfortune which is not a deviation from man's nature? And does a thing seem to thee to be a deviation from man's nature, when it is not contrary to the will of man's nature? Well, thou knowest the will of nature. Will then this which has happened prevent thee from being just, magnanimous, temperate, prudent, secure against inconsiderate opinions and falsehood; will it prevent thee from having modesty, freedom, and everything else, by the presence of which man's nature obtains all that is its own? Remember too on every occasion which leads thee to vexation to apply this principle; not that this is a misfortune, but that to bear it nobly is good fortune.

50. It is a vulgar, but still a useful help towards contempt of death, to pass in review those who have tenaciously stuck to life. What more then have they gained than those who have died early? Certainly they lie in their tombs somewhere at last, Cadicianus, Fabius, Julianus, Lepidus, or any one else like them, who have carried out many to be buried, and then were carried out themselves. Altogether the interval is small [between birth and death]; and consider with how much trouble, and in company with what sort of people, and in what a feeble body, this interval is laboriously passed. Do not then consider life a thing of any value. For look to the immensity of time behind thee, and to the time which is before thee, another boundless space. In this infinity then what is the difference between him who lives three days and him who lives three generations?[43]

51. Always run to the short way; and the short way is the natural: accordingly say and do everything in conformity with the soundest reason. For such a purpose frees a man from trouble, and warfare, and all artifice and ostentatious display.

---

[43] An allusion to Homer's Nestor, who was living at the war of Troy among the third generation, like old Parr with his hundred and fifty-two years, and some others in modern times who have beaten Parr by twenty or thirty years if it is true; and yet they died at last. The word is τριγερηνίου in Antoninus. Nestor is named τριγέρων by some writers; but here perhaps there is an allusion to Homer's Γερήνος ἱππότα Νεστωα.

BOOK V

In the morning when thou risest unwillingly, let this thought be present,—I am rising to the work of a human being. Why then am I dissatisfied if I am going to do the things for which I exist and for which I was brought into the world? Or have I been made for this, to lie in the bed-clothes and keep myself warm?—But this is more pleasant.—Dost thou exist then to take thy pleasure, and not at all for action or exertion? Dost thou not see the little plants, the little birds, the ants, the spiders, the bees working together to put in order their several parts of the universe? And art thou unwilling to do the work of a human being, and dost thou not make haste to do that which, is according to thy nature? But it is necessary to take rest also.—It is necessary. However, Nature has fixed bounds to this too: she has fixed bounds to eating and drinking, and yet thou goest beyond these bounds, beyond what is sufficient; yet in thy acts it is not so, but thou stoppest short of what thou canst do. So thou lovest not thyself, for if thou didst, thou wouldst love thy nature and her will. But those who love their several arts exhaust themselves in working at them unwashed and without food; but thou valuest thy own nature less than the turner values the turning art, or the dancer the dancing art, or the lover of money values his money, or the vainglorious man his little glory. And such men, when they have a violent affection to a thing, choose neither to eat nor to sleep rather than to perfect the things which they care for. But are the acts which concern society more vile in thy eyes and less worthy of thy labor?

2. How easy it is to repel and to wipe away every impression which is troublesome or unsuitable, and immediately to be in all tranquillity.

3. Judge every word and deed which are according to nature to be fit for thee; and be not diverted by the blame which follows from any people, nor by their words, but if a thing is good to be done or said, do not consider it unworthy of thee. For those persons have their peculiar leading principle and follow their peculiar movement; which things do not thou regard, but go straight on, following thy own nature and the common nature; and the way of both is one.

4. I go through the things which happen according to nature until I shall fall and rest, breathing out my breath into that element out of which I daily draw it in, and falling upon that earth out of which my father collected the seed, and my mother the blood, and my nurse the milk; out of which during so many years I have been supplied with food and drink; which bears me when I tread on it and abuse it for so many purposes.

5. Thou sayest, Men cannot admire the sharpness of thy wits.—Be it so: but there are many other things of which thou canst not say, I am not formed from them by nature. Show those qualities then which are altogether in thy power, sincerity, gravity, endurance of labor, aversion to pleasure, contentment with thy portion and with few things, benevolence, frankness, no love of superfluity, freedom from trifling, magnanimity. Dost thou not see how many qualities thou art immediately able to exhibit, in which there is no excuse of natural incapacity and unfitness, and yet thou still remainest voluntarily below the mark? or art thou compelled through being defectively furnished by nature to murmur, and to be stingy, and to flatter, and to find fault with thy poor body, and to try to please men, and to make great display, and to be so restless in thy mind? No, by the gods; but thou mightest have been delivered from these things long ago. Only if in truth thou canst be charged with being rather slow and dull of comprehension, thou must exert thyself about this also, not neglecting it nor yet taking pleasure in thy dullness.

6. One man, when he has done a service to another, is ready to set it down to his account as a favor conferred. Another is not ready to do this, but still in his own mind he thinks of the man as his debtor, and he knows what he has done. A third in a manner does not even know what he has done, but he is like a vine which has produced grapes, and seeks for nothing more after it has once produced its proper fruit. As a horse when he has run, a dog when he has tackled the game, a bee when it has made the honey, so a man when he has done a good act does not call out for others to come and see, but he goes on to another act, as a vine goes on to produce again the grapes in season.—Must a man then be one of these, who in a manner act thus without observing it?—Yes.—But this very thing is necessary, the observation of what a man is doing: for, it may be said, it is characteristic of the social animal to perceive that he is working in a social manner, and indeed to wish that his social partner also should perceive it.—It is true that thou sayest, but thou dost not rightly understand what is now said: and for this reason thou wilt become one of those of whom I spoke before, for even they are misled by a certain show of reason. But if thou wilt choose to understand the meaning of what is said, do not fear that for this reason thou wilt omit any social act.

7. A prayer of the Athenians: Rain, rain, O dear Zeus, down on the ploughed fields of the Athenians and on the plains.—In truth we ought not to pray at all, or we ought to pray in this simple and noble fashion.

8. Just as we must understand when it is said, That Aesculapius prescribed to this man horse-exercise, or bathing in cold water, or going without shoes, so we must understand it when it is said, That the nature of the universe prescribed to this man disease, or mutilation, or loss, or anything else of the kind. For in the first case Prescribed means something like this: he prescribed this for this man as a thing adapted to procure health; and in the second case it means, That which happens[44] to [or suits] every man is fixed in a manner for him suitably to his destiny. For this is what we mean when we say that things are suitable to us, as the workmen say of squared stones in walls or the pyramids, that they are suitable, when they fit them to one another in some kind of connection. For there is altogether one fitness [harmony]. And as the universe is made up out of all bodies to be such a body as it is, so out of all existing causes necessity [destiny] is made up to be such a cause as it is. And even those who are completely ignorant understand what I mean; for they say, It [necessity, destiny] brought this to such a person.—This then was brought and this was prescribed to him. Let us then receive these things, as well as those which Aesculapius prescribes. Many as a matter of course even among his prescriptions are disagreeable, but we accept them in the hope of health. Let the perfecting and accomplishment of the things which the common nature judges to be good, be judged by thee to be of the same kind as thy health. And so accept everything which happens, even if it seem disagreeable, because it leads to this, to the health of the universe and to the prosperity and felicity of Zeus [the universe]. For he would not have brought on any man what he has brought, if it were not useful for the whole. Neither does the nature of anything, whatever it may be, cause anything which is not suitable to that which is directed by it. For two reasons then it is right to be content with that which happens to thee; the one, because it was done for thee and prescribed for thee, and in a manner had reference to thee, originally from the most ancient causes spun with thy destiny; and the other, because even that which comes severally to every man is to the power which administers the universe a cause of felicity and perfection, nay even of its very continuance. For the integrity of the whole is mutilated, if thou cuttest off anything whatever from the conjunction and the continuity either of the parts or of the causes. And thou dost cut off, as far as it is in thy power, when thou art dissatisfied, and in a manner triest to put anything out of the way.

---

[44] In this section there is a play on the meaning of συμβα᾽νείν.

9. Be not disgusted, nor discouraged, nor dissatisfied, if thou dost not succeed in doing everything according to right principles, but when thou hast failed, return back again, and be content if the greater part of what thou doest is consistent with man's nature, and love this to which thou returnest; and do not return to philosophy as if she were a master, but act like those who have sore eyes and apply a bit of sponge and egg, or as another applies a plaster, or drenching with water. For thus thou wilt not fail to obey reason, and thou wilt repose in it. And remember that philosophy requires only things which thy nature requires; but thou wouldst have something else which is not according to nature.—It may be objected, Why, what is more agreeable than this [which I am doing]? But is not this the very reason why pleasure deceives us? And consider if magnanimity, freedom, simplicity, equanimity, piety, are not more agreeable. For what is more agreeable than wisdom itself, when thou thinkest of the security and the happy course of all things which depend on the faculty of understanding and knowledge?

10. Things are in such a kind of envelopment that they have seemed to philosophers, not a few nor those common philosophers, altogether unintelligible; nay even to the Stoics themselves they seem difficult to understand. And all our assent is changeable; for where is the man who never changes? Carry thy thoughts then to the objects themselves, and consider how short-lived they are and worthless, and that they may be in the possession of a filthy wretch or a whore or a robber. Then turn to the morals of those who live with thee, and it is hardly possible to endure even the most agreeable of them, to say nothing of a man being hardly able to endure himself. In such darkness then and dirt, and in so constant a flux both of substance and of time, and of motion and of things moved, what there is worth being highly prized, or even an object of serious pursuit, I cannot imagine. But on the contrary it is a man's duty to comfort himself, and to wait for the natural dissolution, and not to be vexed at the delay, but to rest in these principles only: the one, that nothing will happen to me which is not conformable to the nature of the universe; and the other, that it is in my power never to act contrary to my god and daemon: for there is no man who will compel me to this.

11. About what am I now employing my own soul? On every occasion I must ask myself this question, and inquire, What have I now in this part of me which they call the ruling principle? and whose soul have I now,—that of a child, or of a young man, or of a feeble woman, or of a tyrant, or of a domestic animal, or of a wild beast?

12. What kind of things those are which appear good to the many, we may learn even from this. For if any man should conceive certain things as being really good, such as prudence, temperance, justice, fortitude, he would not after

having first conceived these endure to listen to anything which should not be in harmony with what is really good. But if a man has first conceived as good the things which appear to the many to be good, he will listen and readily receive as very applicable that which was said by the comic writer. Thus even the many perceive the difference. For were it not so, this saying would not offend and would not be rejected [in the first case], while we receive it when it is said of wealth, and of the means which further luxury and fame, as said fitly and wittily. Go on then and ask if we should value and think those things to be good, to which after their first conception in the mind the words of the comic writer might be aptly applied,—that he who has them, through pure abundance has not a place to ease himself in.

13. I am composed of the formal and the material; and neither of them will perish into non-existence, as neither of them came into existence out of non-existence. Every part of me then will be reduced by change into some part of the universe, and that again will change into another part of the universe, and so on forever. And by consequence of such a change I too exist, and those who begot me, and so on forever in the other direction. For nothing hinders us from saying so, even if the universe is administered according to definite periods [of revolution].

14. Reason and the reasoning art [philosophy] are powers which are sufficient for themselves and for their own works. They move then from a first principle which is their own, and they make their way to the end which is proposed to them; and this is the reason why such acts are named Catorthoseis or right acts, which word signifies that they proceed by the right road.

15. None of these things ought to be called a man's, which do not belong to a man, as man. They are not required of a man, nor does man's nature promise them, nor are they the means of man's nature attaining its end. Neither then does the end of man lie in these things, nor yet that which aids to the accomplishment of this end, and that which aids toward this end is that which is good. Besides, if any of these things did belong to man, it would not be right for a man to despise them and to set himself against them; nor would a man be worthy of praise who showed that he did not want these things, nor would he who stinted himself in any of them be good, if indeed these things were good. But now the more of these things a man deprives himself of, or of other things like them, or even when he is deprived of any of them, the more patiently he endures the loss, just in the same degree he is a better man.

16. Such as are thy habitual thoughts, such also will be the character of thy mind; for the soul is dyed by the thoughts. Dye it then with a continuous series of such thoughts as these: for instance, that where a man can live, there he can

also live well. But he must live in a palace; well then, he can also live well in a palace. And again, consider that for whatever purpose each thing has been constituted, for this it has been constituted, and towards this it is carried; and its end is in that towards which it is carried; and where the end is, there also is the advantage and the good of each thing. Now the good for the reasonable animal is society; for that we are made for society has been shown above.[45] Is it not plain that the inferior exists for the sake of the superior? But the things which have life are superior to those which have not life, and of those which have life the superior are those which have reason.

17. To seek what is impossible is madness: and it is impossible that the bad should not do something of this kind.

18. Nothing happens to any man which he is not formed by nature to bear. The same things happen to another, and either because he does not see that they have happened, or because he would show a great spirit, he is firm and remains unharmed. It is a shame then that ignorance and conceit should be stronger than wisdom.

19. Things themselves touch not the soul, not in the least degree; nor have they admission to the soul, nor can they turn or move the soul: but the soul turns and moves itself alone, and whatever judgments it may think proper to make, such it makes for itself the things which present themselves to it.

20. In one respect man is the nearest thing to me, so far as I must do good to men and endure them. But so far as some men make themselves obstacles to my proper acts, man becomes to me one of the things which are indifferent, no less than the sun or wind or a wild beast. Now it is true that these may impede my action, but they are no impediments to my affects and disposition, which have the power of acting conditionally and changing: for the mind converts and changes every hindrance to its activity into an aid; and so that which is a hindrance is made a furtherance to an act; and that which is an obstacle on the road helps us on this road.

21. Reverence that which is best in the universe; and this is that which makes use of all things and directs all things. And in like manner also reverence that which is best in thyself; and this is of the same kind as that. For in thyself also, that which makes use of everything else is this, and thy life is directed by this.

22. That which does no harm to the state, does no harm to the citizen. In the case of every appearance of harm apply this rule: if the state is not harmed by this, neither am I harmed. But if the state is harmed, thou must not be angry with him who does harm to the state. Show him where his error is.

---

[45] ii. 1.

23. Often think of the rapidity with which things pass by and disappear, both the things which are and the things which are produced. For substance is like a river in a continual flow, and the activities of things are in constant change, and the causes work in infinite varieties; and there is hardly anything which stands still. And consider this which is near to thee, this boundless abyss of the past and of the future in which all things disappear. How then is he not a fool who is puffed up with such things or plagued about them and makes himself miserable? for they vex him only for a time, and a short time.

24. Think of the universal substance, of which thou hast a very small portion; and of universal time, of which a short and indivisible interval has been assigned to thee; and of that which is fixed by destiny, and how small a part of it thou art.

25. Does another do me wrong? Let him look to it. He has his own disposition, his own activity. I now have what the universal nature now wills me to have; and I do what my nature now wills me to do.

26. Let the part of thy soul which leads and governs be undisturbed by the movements in the flesh, whether of pleasure or of pain; and let it not unite with them, but let it circumscribe itself and limit those affects to their parts. But when these affects rise up to the mind by virtue of that other sympathy that naturally exists in a body which is all one, then thou must not strive to resist the sensation, for it is natural: but let not the ruling part of itself add to the sensation the opinion that it is either good or bad.

27. Live with the gods. And he does live with the gods who constantly shows to them that his own soul is satisfied with that which is assigned to him, and that it does all that the daemon wishes, which Zeus hath given to every man for his guardian and guide, a portion of himself. And this is every man's understanding and reason.

28. Art thou angry with him whose armpits stink? art thou angry with him whose mouth smells foul? What good will this anger do thee? He has such a mouth, he has such armpits: it is necessary that such an emanation must come from such things: but the man has reason, it will be said, and he is able, if he takes pains, to discover wherein he offends; I wish thee well of thy discovery. Well then, and thou hast reason: by thy rational faculty stir up his rational faculty; show him his error, admonish him. For if he listens, thou wilt cure him, and there is no need of anger. [Neither tragic actor nor whore.][46]

---

[46] This is imperfect or corrupt, or both. There is also something wrong or incomplete in the beginning of S. 29, where he says ὡς ἐξελθὼν ζῆν διανοῇ, which Gataker translates "as if thou wast about to quit life;" but we cannot translate ἐξελθὼν in that way. Other translations are not much more satisfactory. I have translated it literally and left it imperfect.

29. As thou intendest to live when thou art gone out, . . . so it is in thy power to live here. But if men do not permit thee, then get away out of life, yet so as if thou wert suffering no harm. The house is smoky, and I quit it.[47] Why dost thou think that this is any trouble? But so long as nothing of the kind drives me out, I remain, am free, and no man shall hinder me from doing what I choose; and I choose to do what is according to the nature of the rational and social animal.

30. The intelligence of the universe is social. Accordingly it has made the inferior things for the sake of the superior, and it has fitted the superior to one another. Thou seest how it has subordinated, co-ordinated, and assigned to everything its proper portion, and has brought together into concord with one another the things which are the best.

31. How hast thou behaved hitherto to the gods, thy parents, brethren, children, teachers, to those who looked after thy infancy, to thy friends, kinsfolk, to thy slaves? Consider if thou hast hitherto behaved to all in such a way that this may be said of thee,—

"Never has wronged a man in deed or word."

And call to recollection both how many things thou hast passed through, and how many things thou hast been able to endure, and that the history of thy life is now complete and thy service is ended; and how many beautiful things thou hast seen; and how many pleasures and pains thou hast despised; and how many things called honorable thou hast spurned; and to how many ill-minded folks thou hast shown a kind disposition.

32. Why do unskilled and ignorant souls disturb him who has skill and knowledge? What soul then has skill and knowledge? That which knows beginning and end, and knows the reason which pervades all substance, and though all time by fixed periods [revolutions] administers the universe.

33. Soon, very soon, thou wilt be ashes, or a skeleton, and either a name or not even a name; but name is sound and echo. And the things which are much valued in life are empty and rotten and trifling, and [like] little dogs biting one another, and little children quarreling, laughing, and then straightway weeping. But fidelity and modesty and justice and truth are fled

Up to Olympus from the wide-spread earth.

Hesiod, *Works, etc.* v. 197.

What then is there which still detains thee here, if the objects of sense are easily changed and never stand still, and the organs of perception are dull and easily receive false impressions, and the poor soul itself is an exhalation from blood? But to have good repute amid such a world as this is an empty thing.

---

[47] Epictetus, i. 25, 18.

Why then dost thou not wait in tranquillity for thy end, whether it is extinction or removal to another state? And until that time comes, what is sufficient? Why, what else than to venerate the gods and bless them, and to do good to men, and to practise tolerance and self-restraint;[48] but as to everything which is beyond the limits of the poor flesh and breath, to remember that this is neither thine nor in thy power.

34. Thou canst pass thy life in an equable flow of happiness, if thou canst go by the right way, and think and act in the right way. These two things are common both to the soul of God and to the soul of man, and to the soul of every rational being: not to be hindered by another; and to hold good to consist in the disposition to justice and the practice of it, and in this to let thy desire find its termination.

35. If this is neither my own badness, nor an effect of my own badness, and the common weal is not injured, why am I troubled about it, and what is the harm to the common weal?

36. Do not be carried along inconsiderately by the appearance of things, but give help [to all] according to thy ability and their fitness; and if they should have sustained loss in matters which are indifferent, do not imagine this to be a damage; for it is a bad habit. But as the old man, when he went away, asked back his foster-child's top, remembering that it was a top, so do thou in this case also.

When thou art calling out on the Rostra, hast thou forgotten, man, what these things are?—Yes; but they are objects of great concern to these people—wilt thou too then be made a fool for these things? I was once a fortunate man, but I lost it, I know not how.—But fortunate means that a man has assigned to himself a good fortune: and a good fortune is good disposition of the soul, good emotions, good actions.[49]

---

[48] This is the Stoic precept ἀνέχον καί ἀπέχον. The first part teaches us to be content with men and things as they are. The second part teaches us the virtue of self-restraint, or the government of our passions.

[49] This section is unintelligible. Many of the words may be corrupt, and the general purport of the section cannot be discovered. Perhaps several things have been improperly joined in one section. I have translated it nearly literally. Different translators give the section a different turn, and the critics have tried to mend what they cannot understand.

BOOK VI

The substance of the universe is obedient and compliant; and the reason which governs it has in itself no cause for doing evil, for it has no malice, nor does it do evil to anything, nor is anything harmed by it. But all things are made and perfected according to this reason.

2. Let it make no difference to thee whether thou art cold or warm, if thou art doing thy duty; and whether thou art drowsy or satisfied with sleep; and whether ill-spoken of or praised; and whether dying or doing something else. For it is one of the acts of life, this act by which we die; it is sufficient then in this act also to do well what we have in hand (vi. 22, 28).

3. Look within. Let neither the peculiar quality of anything nor its value escape thee.

4. All existing things soon change, and they will either be reduced to vapor, if indeed all substance is one, or they will be dispersed.

5. The reason which governs knows what its own disposition is, and what it does, and on what material it works.

6. The best way of avenging thyself is not to become like [the wrong-doer].

7. Take pleasure in one thing and rest in it, in passing from one social act to another social act, thinking of God.

8. The ruling principle is that which rouses and turns itself, and while it makes itself such as it is and such as it wills to be, it also makes everything which happens appear to itself to be such as it wills.

9. In conformity to the nature of the universe every single thing is accomplished; for certainly it is not in conformity to any other nature that each thing is accomplished, either a nature which externally comprehends this, or a nature which is comprehended within this nature, or a nature external and independent of this (xi. 1; vi. 40; viii. 50).

10. The universe is either a confusion, and a mutual involution of things, and a dispersion, or it is unity and order and providence. If then it is the former, why do I desire to tarry in a fortuitous combination of things and such a disorder? and why do I care about anything else than how I shall at last become earth? and

why am I disturbed, for the dispersion of my elements will happen whatever I do? But if the other supposition is true, I venerate, and I am firm, and I trust in him who governs (iv. 27).

11. When thou hast been compelled by circumstances to be disturbed in a manner, quickly return to thyself, and do not continue out of tune longer than the compulsion lasts; for thou wilt have more mastery over the harmony by continually recurring to it.

12. If thou hadst a step-mother and a mother at the same time, thou wouldst be dutiful to thy step-mother, but still thou wouldst constantly return to thy mother. Let the court and philosophy now be to thee step-mother and mother: return to philosophy frequently and repose in her, through whom what thou meetest with in the court appears to thee tolerable, and thou appearest tolerable in the court.

13. When we have meat before us and such eatables, we receive the impression that this is the dead body of a fish, and this the dead body of a bird or of a pig; and again, that this Falernian is only a little grape-juice, and this purple robe some sheep's wool dyed with the blood of a shell-fish: such then are these impressions, and they reach the things themselves and penetrate them, and so we see what kind of things they are. Just in the same way ought we to act all through life, and where there are things which appear most worthy of our approbation, we ought to lay them bare and look at their worthlessness and strip them of all the words by which they are exalted. For outward show is a wonderful perverter of the reason, and when thou art most sure that thou art employed about things worth thy pains, it is then that it cheats thee most. Consider then what Crates says of Xenocrates himself.

14. Most of the things which the multitude admire are referred to objects of the most general kind, those which are held together by cohesion or natural organization, such as stones, wood, fig-trees, vines, olives. But those which are admired by men, who are a little more reasonable, are referred to the things which are held together by a living principle, as flocks, herds. Those which are admired by men who are still more instructed are the things which are held together by a rational soul, not however a universal soul, but rational so far as it is a soul skilled in some art, or expert in some other way, or simply rational so far as it possesses a number of slaves. But he who values a rational soul, a soul universal and fitted for political life, regards nothing else except this; and above all things he keeps his soul in a condition and in an activity conformable to reason and social life, and he co-operates to this end with those who are of the same kind as himself.

15. Some things are hurrying into existence, and others are hurrying out of it; and of that which is coming into existence part is already extinguished. Motions

and changes are continually renewing the world, just as the uninterrupted course of time is always renewing the infinite duration of ages. In this flowing stream then, on which there is no abiding, what is there of the things which hurry by on which a man would set a high price? It would be just as if a man should fall in love with one of the sparrows which fly by, but it has already passed out of sight. Something of this kind is the very life of every man, like the exhalation of the blood and the respiration of the air. For such as it is to have once drawn in the air and to have given it back, which we do every moment, just the same is it with the whole respiratory power, which thou didst receive at thy birth yesterday and the day before, to give it back to the element from which thou didst first draw it.

16. Neither is transpiration, as in plants, a thing to be valued, nor respiration, as in domesticated animals and wild beasts, nor the receiving of impressions by the appearances of things, nor being moved by desires as puppets by strings, nor assembling in herds, nor being nourished by food; for this is just like the act of separating and parting with the useless part of our food. What then is worth being valued? To be received with clapping of hands? No. Neither must we value the clapping of tongues; for the praise which comes from the many is a clapping of tongues. Suppose then that thou hast given up this worthless thing called fame, what remains that is worth valuing? This, in my opinion: to move thyself and to restrain thyself in conformity to thy proper constitution, to which end both all employments and arts lead. For every art aims at this, that the thing which has been made should be adapted to the work for which it has been made; and both the vine-planter who looks after the vine, and the horse-breaker, and he who trains the dog, seek this end. But the education and the teaching of youth aim at something. In this then is the value of the education and the teaching. And if this is well, thou wilt not seek anything else. Wilt thou not cease to value many other things too? Then thou wilt be neither free, nor sufficient for thy own happiness, nor without passion. For of necessity thou must be envious, jealous, and suspicious of those who can take away those things, and plot against those who have that which is valued by thee. Of necessity a man must be altogether in a state of perturbation who wants any of these things; and besides, he must often find fault with the gods. But to reverence and honor thy own mind will make thee content with thyself, and in harmony with society, and in agreement with the gods, that is, praising all that they give and have ordered.

17. Above, below, all around are the movements of the elements. But the motion of virtue is in none of these: it is something more divine, and advancing by a way hardly observed, it goes happily on its road.

18. How strangely men act! They will not praise those who are living at the same time and living with themselves; but to be themselves praised by posterity,

by those whom they have never seen nor ever will see, this they set much value on. But this is very much the same as if thou shouldst be grieved because those who have lived before thee did not praise thee.

19. If a thing is difficult to be accomplished by thyself, do not think that it is impossible for man: but if anything is possible for man and conformable to his nature, think that this can be attained by thyself too.

20. In the gymnastic exercises suppose that a man has torn thee with his nails, and by dashing against thy head has inflicted a wound. Well, we neither show any signs of vexation, nor are we offended, nor do we suspect him afterwards as a treacherous fellow; and yet we are on our guard against him, not however as an enemy, nor yet with suspicion, but we quietly get out of his way. Something like this let thy behavior be in all the other parts of life; let us overlook many things in those who are like antagonists in the gymnasium. For it is in our power, as I said, to get out of the way, and to have no suspicion nor hatred.

21. If any man is able to convince me and show me that I do not think or act right, I will gladly change; for I seek the truth, by which no man was ever injured. But he is injured who abides in his error and ignorance.

22. I do my duty: other things trouble me not; for they are either things without life, or things without reason, or things that have rambled and know not the way.

23. As to the animals which have no reason, and generally all things and objects, do thou, since thou hast reason and they have none, make use of them with a generous and liberal spirit. But towards human beings, as they have reason, behave in a social spirit. And on all occasions call on the gods, and do not perplex thyself about the length of time in which thou shalt do this; for even three hours so spent are sufficient.

24. Alexander the Macedonian and his groom by death were brought to the same state; for either they were received among the same seminal principles of the universe, or they were alike dispersed among the atoms.

25. Consider how many things in the same indivisible time take place in each of us,—things which concern the body and things which concern the soul: and so thou wilt not wonder if many more things, or rather all things which come into existence in that which is the one and all, which we call Cosmos, exist in it at the same time.

26. If any man should propose to thee the question, how the name Antoninus is written, wouldst thou with a straining of the voice utter each letter? What then if they grow angry, wilt thou be angry too? Wilt thou not go on with composure and number every letter? Just so then in this life also remember that every duty is made up of certain parts. These it is thy duty to observe, and without being

disturbed or showing anger towards those who are angry with thee, to go on thy way and finish that which is set before thee.

27. How cruel it is not to allow men to strive After the things which appear to them to be suitable to their nature and profitable! And yet in a manner thou dost not allow them to do this, when thou art vexed because they do wrong. For they are certainly moved towards things because they suppose them to be suitable to their nature and profitable to them.—But it is not so.—Teach them then, and show them without being angry.

28. Death is a cessation of the impressions through the senses, and of the pulling of the strings which move the appetites, and of the discursive movements of the thoughts, and of the service to the flesh (ii. 12).

29. It is a shame for the soul to be first to give way in this life, when thy body does not give way.

30. Take care that thou art not made into a Caesar, that thou art not dyed with this dye; for such things happen. Keep thyself then simple, good, pure, serious, free from affectation, a friend of justice, a worshipper of the gods, kind, affectionate, strenuous in all proper acts. Strive to continue to be such as philosophy wished to make thee. Reverence the gods, and help men. Short is life. There is only one fruit of this terrene life—a pious disposition and social acts. Do everything as a disciple of Antoninus. Remember his constancy in every act which was conformable to reason, and his evenness in all things, and his piety, and the serenity of his countenance, and his sweetness, and his disregard of empty fame, and his efforts to understand things; and how he would never let anything pass without having first most carefully examined it and clearly understood it; and how he bore with those who blamed him unjustly without blaming them in return; how he did nothing in a hurry; and how he listened not to calumnies, and how exact an examiner of manners and actions he was; and not given to reproach people, nor timid, nor suspicious, nor a sophist; and with how little he was satisfied, such as lodging, bed, dress, food, servants; and how laborious and patient; and how he was able on account of his sparing diet to hold out to the evening, not even requiring to relieve himself by any evacuations except at the usual hour; and his firmness and uniformity in his friendships; and how he tolerated freedom of speech in those who opposed his opinions; and the pleasure that he had when any man showed him anything better; and how religious he was without superstition. Imitate all this, that thou mayest have as good a conscience, when thy last hour comes, as he had (i. 16).

31. Return to thy sober senses and call thyself back; and when thou hast roused thyself from sleep and hast perceived that they were only dreams which

troubled thee, now in thy waking hours look at these [the things about thee] as thou didst look at those [the dreams].

32. I consist of a little body and a soul. Now to this little body all things are indifferent, for it is not able to perceive differences. But to the understanding those things only are indifferent which are not the works of its own activity. But whatever things are the works of its own activity, all these are in its power. And of these however only those which are done with reference to the present; for as to the future and the past activities of the mind, even these are for the present indifferent.

33. Neither the labor which the hand does nor that of the foot is contrary to nature, so long as the foot does the foot's work and the hand the hand's. So then neither to a man as a man is his labor contrary to nature, so long as it does the things of a man. But if the labor is not contrary to his nature, neither is it an evil to him.

34. How many pleasures have been enjoyed by robbers, patricides, tyrants.

35. Dost thou not see how the handicrafts-men accommodate themselves up to a certain point to those who are not skilled in their craft—nevertheless they cling to the reason [the principles] of their art, and do not endure to depart from it? Is it not strange if the architect and the physician shall have more respect to the reason [the principles] of their own arts than man to his own reason, which is common to him and the gods?

36. Asia, Europe, are corners of the universe; all the sea a drop in the universe; Athos a little clod of the universe: all the present time is a point in eternity. All things are little, changeable, perishable. All things come from thence, from that universal ruling power, either directly proceeding or by way of sequence. And accordingly the lion's gaping jaws, and that which is poisonous, and every harmful thing, as a thorn, as mud, are after-products of the grand and beautiful. Do not then imagine that they are of another kind from that which thou dost venerate, but form a just opinion of the source of all (vii. 75).

37. He who has seen present things has seen all, both everything which has taken place from all eternity and everything which will be for time without end; for all things are of one kin and of one form.

38. Frequently consider the connection of all things in the universe and their relation to one another. For in a manner all things are implicated with one another, and all in this way are friendly to one another; for one thing comes in order after another, and this is by virtue of the active movement and mutual conspiration and the unity of the substance (ix. 1).

39. Adapt thyself to the things with which thy lot has been cast: and the men among whom thou hast received thy portion, love them, but do it truly [sincerely].

40. Every instrument, tool, vessel, if it does that for which it has been made, is well, and yet he who made it is not there. But in the things which are held together by nature there is within, and there abides in them the power which made them; wherefore the more is it fit to reverence this power, and to think, that, if thou dost live and act according to its will, everything in thee is in conformity to intelligence. And thus also in the universe the things which belong to it are in conformity to intelligence.

41. Whatever of the things which are not within thy power thou shalt suppose to be good for thee or evil, it must of necessity be that, if such a bad thing befall thee, or the loss of such a good thing, thou wilt not blame the gods, and hate men too, those who are the cause of the misfortune or the loss, or those who are suspected of being likely to be the cause; and indeed we do much injustice because we make a difference between these things [because we do not regard these things as indifferent].[50] But if we judge only those things which are in our power to be good or bad, there remains no reason either for finding fault with God or standing in a hostile attitude to man.[51]

42. We are all working together to one end, some with knowledge and design, and others without knowing what they do; as men also when they are asleep, of whom it is Heraclitus, I think, who says that they are laborers and co-operators in the things which take place in the universe. But men co-operate after different fashions: and even those co-operate abundantly, who find fault with what happens and those who try to oppose it and to hinder it; for the universe had need even of such men as these. It remains then for thee to understand among what kind of workmen thou placest thyself; for he who rules all things will certainly make a right use of thee, and he will receive thee among some part of the co-operators and of those whose labors conduce to one end. But be not thou such a part as the mean and ridiculous verse in the play, which Chrysippus speaks of.[52]

43. Does the sun undertake to do the work of the rain, or Aesculapius the work of the Fruit-bearer [the earth]? And how is it with respect to each of the stars—are they not different and yet they work together to the same end?

44. If the gods have determined about me and about the things which must happen to me, they have determined well, for it is not easy even to imagine a deity without forethought; and as to doing me harm, why should they have any

---

[50] Gataker translates this "because we strive to get these things," comparing the use of διαφέρεσθαι in v. I, and x. 27, and ix. 38, where it appears that his reference should be xi. 10. He may be right in his interpretation, but I doubt.

[51] Cicero, De Natura Deorum. iii. 32.

[52] Plutarch, adversus Stoicos, c. 14.

desire towards that? for what advantage would result to them from this or to the whole, which is the special object of their providence? But if they have not determined about me individually, they have certainly determined about the whole at least, and the things which happen by way of sequence in this general arrangement I ought to accept with pleasure and to be content with them. But if they determine about nothing,—which it is wicked to believe, or if we do believe it, let us neither sacrifice nor pray nor swear by them, nor do anything else which we do as if the gods were present and lived with us,—but if however the gods determine about none of the things which concern us, I am able to determine about myself, and I can inquire about that which is useful; and that is useful to every man which is conformable to his own constitution and nature. But my nature is rational and social; and my city and country, so far as I am Antoninus, is Rome, but so far as I am a man, it is the world. The things then which are useful to these cities are alone useful to me.

45. Whatever happens to every man, this is for the interest of the universal: this might be sufficient. But further thou wilt observe this also as a general truth, if thou dost observe, that whatever is profitable to any man is profitable also to other men. But let the word profitable be taken here in the common sense as said of things of the middle kind [neither good nor bad].

46. As it happens to thee in the amphitheatre and such places, that the continual sight of the same things, and the uniformity, make the spectacle wearisome, so it is in the whole of life; for all things above, below, are the same and from the same. How long then?

47. Think continually that all kinds of men and all kinds of pursuits and of all nations are dead, so that thy thoughts come down even to Philistion and Phoebus and Origanion. Now turn thy thoughts to the other kinds [of men]. To that place then we must remove, where there are so many great orators, and so many noble philosophers, Heraclitus, Pythagoras, Socrates; so many heroes of former days, and so many generals after them, and tyrants; besides these, Eudoxus, Hipparchus, Archimedes, and other men of acute natural talents, great minds, lovers of labor, versatile, confident, mockers even of the perishable and ephemeral life of man, as Menippus and such as are like him. As to all these consider that they have long been in the dust. What harm then is this to them; and what to those whose names are altogether unknown? One thing here is worth a great deal, to pass thy life in truth and justice, with a benevolent disposition even to liars and unjust men.

48. When thou wishest to delight thyself, think of the virtues of those who live with thee; for instance, the activity of one, and the modesty of another, and the liberality of a third, and some other good quality of a fourth. For nothing

delights so much as the examples of the virtues, when they are exhibited in the morals of those who live with us and present themselves in abundance, as far as is possible. Wherefore we must keep them before us.

49. Thou art not dissatisfied. I suppose, because thou weighest only so many litrae and not three hundred. Be not dissatisfied then that thou must live only so many years and not more; for as thou art satisfied with the amount of substance which has been assigned to thee, so be content with the time.

50. Let us try to persuade them [men]. But act even against their will, when the principles of justice lead that way. If however any man by using force stands in thy way, betake thyself to contentment and tranquillity, and at the same time employ the hindrance towards the exercise of some other virtue; and remember that thy attempt was with a reservation [conditionally], that thou didst not desire to do impossibilities. What then didst thou desire?—Some such effort as this.—But thou attainest thy object, if the things to which thou wast moved are [not] accomplished.

51. He who loves fame considers another man's activity to be his own good; and he who loves pleasure, his own sensations; but he who has understanding considers his own acts to be his own good.

52. It is in our power to have no opinion about a thing, and not to be disturbed in our soul; for things themselves have no natural power to form our judgments.

53. Accustom thyself to attend carefully to what is said by another, and as much as it is possible, be in the speaker's mind.

54. That which is not good for the swarm, neither is it good for the bee.

55. If sailors abused the helmsman, or the sick the doctor, would they listen to anybody else? or how could the helmsman secure the safety of those in the ship, or the doctor the health of those whom he attends?

56. How many together with whom I came into the world are already gone out of it.

57. To the jaundiced honey tastes bitter, and to those bitten by mad dogs water causes fear; and to little children the ball is a fine thing. Why then am I angry? Dost thou think that a false opinion has less power than the bile in the jaundiced or the poison in him who is bitten by a mad dog?

58. No man will hinder thee from living according to the reason of thy own nature: nothing will happen to thee contrary to the reason of the universal nature.

59. What kind of people are those whom men wish to please, and for what objects, and by what kind of acts? How soon will time cover all things, and how many it has covered already.

BOOK VII

What is badness? It is that which thou hast often seen. And on the occasion of everything which happens keep this in mind, that it is that which thou hast often seen. Everywhere up and down thou wilt find the same things, with which the old histories are filled, those of the middle ages and those of our own day; with which cities and houses are filled now. There is nothing new: all things are both familiar and short-lived.

2. How can our principles become dead, unless the impressions [thoughts] which correspond to them are extinguished? But it is in thy power continuously to fan these thoughts into a flame. I can have that opinion about anything which I ought to have. If I can, why am I disturbed? The things which are external to my mind have no relation at all to my mind.—Let this be the state of thy affects, and thou standest erect. To recover thy life is in thy power. Look at things again as thou didst use to look at them; for in this consists the recovery of thy life.

3. The idle business of show, plays on the stage, flocks of sheep, herds, exercises with spears, a bone cast to little dogs, a bit of bread into fishponds, laborings of ants and burden-carrying, runnings about of frightened little mice, puppets pulled by strings—[all alike]. It is thy duty then in the midst of such things to show good humor and not a proud air; to understand however that every man is worth just so much as the things are worth about which he busies himself.

4. In discourse thou must attend to what is said, and in every movement thou must observe what is doing. And in the one thou shouldst see immediately to what end it refers, but in the other watch carefully what is the thing signified.

5. Is my understanding sufficient for this or not? If it is sufficient, I use it for the work as an instrument given by the universal nature. But if it is not sufficient, then either I retire from the work and give way to him who is able to do it better, unless there be some reason why I ought not to do so; or I do it as well as I can, taking to help me the man who with the aid of my ruling principle can do what is now fit and useful for the general good. For what-soever either by myself or with another I can do, ought to be directed to this only, to that which is useful and well suited to society.

6. How many after being celebrated by fame have been given up to oblivion; and how many who have celebrated the fame of others have long been dead.

7. Be not ashamed to be helped; for it is thy business to do thy duty like a soldier in the assault on a town. How then, if being lame thou canst not mount up on the battlements alone, but with the help of another it is possible?

8. Let not future things disturb thee, for thou wilt come to them, if it shall be necessary, having with thee the same reason which now thou usest for present things.

9. All things are implicated with one another, and the bond is holy; and there is hardly anything unconnected with any other thing. For things have been co-ordinated, and they combine to form the same universe [order]. For there is one universe made up of all things, and one god who pervades all things, and one substance,[53] and one law, [one] common reason in all intelligent animals, and one truth; if indeed there is also one perfection for all animals which are of the same stock and participate in the reason.

10. Everything material soon disappears in the substance of the whole; and everything formal [causal] is very soon taken back into the universal reason; and the memory of everything is very soon overwhelmed in time.

11. To the rational animal the same act is according to nature and according to reason.

12. Be thou erect, or be made erect (iii. 5).

13. Just as it is with the members in those bodies which are united in one, so it is with rational beings which exist separate, for they have been constituted for one co-operation. And the perception of this will be more apparent to thee if thou often sayest to thyself that I am a member [μέλος] of the system of rational beings. But if [using the letter r] thou sayest that thou art a part [μέρος], thou dost not yet love men from thy heart; beneficence does not yet delight thee for its own sake;[54] thou still doest it barely as a thing of propriety, and not yet as doing good to thyself.

14. Let there fall externally what will on the parts which can feel the effects of this fall. For those parts which have felt will complain, if they choose. But I, unless I think that what has happened is an evil, am not injured. And it is in my power not to think so.

15. Whatever any one does or says, I must be good; just as if the gold, or the emerald, or the purple, were always saying this. Whatever any one does or says, I must be emerald and keep my color.

---

[53] "One substance," p. 42, note 1.
[54] I have used Gataker's conjecture καταληκτικῶς instead of the common reading καταληπτικῶς: compare iv. 20; ix. 42.

16. The ruling faculty does not disturb itself; I mean, does not frighten itself or cause itself pain. But if any one else can frighten or pain it, let him do so. For the faculty itself will not by its own opinion turn itself into such ways. Let the body itself take care, if it can, that it suffer nothing, and let it speak, if it suffers. But the soul itself, that which is subject to fear, to pain, which has completely the power of forming an opinion about these things, will suffer nothing, for it will never deviate into such a judgment. The leading principle in itself wants nothing, unless it makes a want for itself; and therefore it is both free from perturbation and unimpeded, if it does not disturb and impede itself.

17. Eudaemonia [happiness] is a good daemon, or a good thing. What then art thou doing here, O imagination? Go away, I entreat thee by the gods, as thou didst come, for I want thee not. But thou art come according to thy old fashion. I am not angry with thee: only go away.

18. Is any man afraid of change? Why, what can take place without change? What then is more pleasing or more suitable to the universal nature? And canst thou take a bath unless the wood undergoes a change? and canst thou be nourished, unless the food undergoes a change? And can anything else that is useful be accomplished without change? Dost thou not see then that for thyself also to change is just the same, and equally necessary for the universal nature?

19. Through the universal substance as through a furious torrent all bodies are carried, being by their nature united with and co-operating with the whole, as the parts of our body with one another. How many a Chrysippus, how many a Socrates, how many an Epictetus has time already swallowed up! And let the same thought occur to thee with reference to every man and thing (v. 23; vi. 15).

20. One thing only troubles me, lest I should do something which the constitution of man does not allow, or in the way which it does not allow, or what it does not allow now.

21. Near is thy forgetfulness of all things; and near the forgetfulness of thee by all.

22. It is peculiar to man to love even those who do wrong. And this happens, if when they do wrong it occurs to thee that they are kinsmen, and that they do wrong through ignorance and unintentionally, and that soon both of you will die; and above all, that the wrong-doer has done thee no harm, for he has not made thy ruling faculty worse than it was before.

23. The universal nature out of the universal substance, as if it were wax, now moulds a horse, and when it has broken this up, it uses the material for a tree, then for a man, then for something else; and each of these things subsists for a very short time. But it is no hardship for the vessel to be broken up, just as there was none in its being fastened together (viii. 50).

24. A scowling look is altogether unnatural; when it is often assumed,[55] the result is that all comeliness dies away, and at last is so completely extinguished that it cannot be again lighted up at all. Try to conclude from this very fact that it is contrary to reason. For if even the perception of doing wrong shall depart, what reason is there for living any longer?

25. Nature which governs the whole will soon change all things thou seest, and out of their substance will make other things, and again other things from the substance of them, in order that the world may be ever new (xii. 23).

26. When a man has done thee any wrong, immediately consider with what opinion about good or evil he has done wrong. For when thou hast seen this, thou wilt pity him, and wilt neither wonder nor be angry. For either thou thyself thinkest the same thing to be good that he does, or another thing of the same kind. It is thy duty then to pardon him. But if thou dost not think such things to be good or evil, thou wilt more readily be well disposed to him who is in error.

27. Think not so much of what thou hast not as of what thou hast: but of the things which thou hast select the best, and then reflect how eagerly they would have been sought, if thou hadst them not. At the same time, however, take care that thou dost not through being so pleased with them accustom thyself to overvalue them, so as to be disturbed if ever thou shouldst not have them.

28. Retire into thyself. The rational principle which rules has this nature, that it is content with itself when it does what is just, and so secures tranquillity.

29. Wipe out the imagination. Stop the pulling of the strings. Confine thyself to the present. Understand well what happens either to thee or to another. Divide and distribute every object into the causal [formal] and the material. Think of thy last hour. Let the wrong which is done by a man stay there where the wrong was done (viii. 29).

30. Direct thy attention to what is said. Let thy understanding enter into the things that are doing and the things which do them (vii. 4).

31. Adorn thyself with simplicity and modesty, and with indifference towards the things which lie between virtue and vice. Love mankind. Follow God. The poet says that law rules all— And it is enough to remember that law rules all.[56]

32. About death: whether it is a dispersion, or a resolution into atoms, or annihilation, it is either extinction or change.

---

[55] This is corrupt.
[56] The end of this section is unintelligible.

33. About pain: the pain which is intolerable carries us off; but that which lasts a long time is tolerable; and the mind maintains its own tranquillity by retiring into itself, and the ruling faculty is not made worse. But the parts which are harmed by pain, let them, if they can, give their opinion about it.

34. About fame: look at the minds [of those who seek fame], observe what they are, and what kind of things they avoid, and what kind of things they pursue. And consider that as the heaps of sand piled on one another hide the former sands; so in life the events which go before are soon covered by those which come after.

35. From Plato:[57] The man who has an elevated mind and takes a view of all time and of all substance, dost thou suppose it possible for him to think that human life is anything great? It is not possible, he said.—Such a man then will think that death also is no evil.—Certainly not.

36. From Antisthenes: It is royal to do good and to be abused.

37. It is a base thing for the countenance to be obedient and to regulate and compose itself as the mind commands, and for the mind not to be regulated and composed by itself.

38. It is not right to vex ourselves at things,
For they care nought about it.[58]

39. To the immortal gods and us give joy.

40. Life must be reaped like the ripe ears of corn.
One man is born; another dies.[59]

41. If gods care not for me and my children,
There is a reason for it.

42. For the good is with me, and the just.[60]

43. No joining others in their wailing, no violent emotion.

44. From Plato:[61] But I would make this man a sufficient answer, which is this: Thou sayest not well, if thou thinkest that a man who is good for anything at all ought to compute the hazard of life or death, and should not rather look to this only in all that he does, whether he is doing what is just or unjust, and the works of a good or bad man.

---

[57] Plato, Pol. vi. 486.
[58] From the Bellerophon of Euripides.
[59] From the Hypsipyle of Euripides. Cicero (Tuscul. iii. 25) has translated six lines from Euripides, and among them are these two lines,—

"Reddenda terrae est terra: tum vita omnibus
Metenda ut fruges: Sic jubet necessitas."

[60] See Aristophanes, Acharnenses, v. 661.
[61] From the Apologia, c. 16.

45. For[62] thus it is, men of Athens, in truth: wherever a man has placed himself thinking it the best place for him, or has been placed by a commander, there in my opinion he ought to stay and to abide the hazard, taking nothing into the reckoning, either death or anything else, before the baseness [of deserting his post].

46. But, my good friend, reflect whether that which is noble and good is not something different from saving and being saved; for as to a man living such or such a time, at least one who is really a man, consider if this is not a thing to be dismissed from the thoughts: and there must be no love of life: but as to these matters a man must intrust them to the Deity and believe what the women say, that no man can escape his destiny, the next inquiry being how he may best live the time that he has to live.[63]

47. Look round at the courses of the stars, as if thou wert going along with them; and constantly consider the changes of the elements into one another, for such thoughts purge away the filth of the terrene life.

48. This is a fine saying of Plato:[64] That he who is discoursing about men should look also at earthly things as if he viewed them from some higher place; should look at them in their assemblies, armies, agricultural labors, marriages, treaties, births, deaths, noise of the courts of justice, desert places, various nations of barbarians, feasts, lamentations, markets, a mixture of all things and an orderly combination of contraries.

49. Consider the past,—such great changes of political supremacies; thou mayest foresee also the things which will be. For they will certainly be of like form, and it is not possible that they should deviate from the order of the things which take place now; accordingly to have contemplated human life for forty years is the same as to have contemplated it for ten thousand years. For what more wilt thou see?

50. That which has grown from the earth to the earth,
But that which has sprung from heavenly seed,
Back to the heavenly realms returns.[65]

This is either a dissolution of the mutual involution of the atoms, or a similar dispersion of the unsentient elements.

---

[62] From the Apologia, c. 16.

[63] Plato, Gorgias, c. 68 (512). In this passage the text of Antoninus has ἐατέον, which is perhaps right; but there is a difficulty in the words μὴ γὰρ τοῦτο μέν, τὸ ζῆν ὁποσονδὴ χρόνον τόνγε ὡς ἀληθῶς ἄνδρα ἐατέον ἐστί καὶ οὐ , &c. The conjecture εὐκτέον for ἐατέον does not mend the matter.

[64] It is said that this is not in the extant writings of Plato.

[65] From the Chrysippus of Euripides.

51. With food and drinks and cunning magic arts
Turning the channel's course to 'scape from death.[66]
The breeze which heaven has sent
We must endure, and toil without complaining.

52. Another may be more expert in casting his opponent; but he is not more social, nor more modest, nor better disciplined to meet all that happens, nor more considerate with respect to the faults of his neighbors.

53. Where any work can be done conformably to the reason which is common to gods and men, there we have nothing to fear; for where we are able to get profit by means of the activity which is successful and proceeds according to our constitution, there no harm is to be suspected.

54. Everywhere and at all times it is in thy power piously to acquiesce in thy present condition, and to behave, justly to those who are about thee, and to exert thy skill upon thy present thoughts, that nothing shall steal into them without being well examined.

55. Do not look around thee to discover other men's ruling principles, but look straight to this, to what nature leads thee, both the universal nature through the things which happen to thee, and thy own nature through the acts which must be done by thee. But every being ought to do that which is according to its constitution; and all other things have been constituted for the sake of rational beings, just as among irrational things the inferior for the sake of the superior, but the rational for the sake of one another.

The prime principle then in man's constitution is the social. And the second is not to yield to the persuasions of the body,—for it is the peculiar office of the rational and intelligent motion to circumscribe itself, and never to be overpowered either by the motion of the senses or of the appetites, for both are animal: but the intelligent motion claims superiority, and does not permit itself to be overpowered by the others. And with good reason, for it is formed by nature to use all of them. The third thing in the rational constitution is freedom from error and from deception. Let then the ruling principle holding fast to these things go straight on, and it has what is its own.

56. Consider thyself to be dead, and to have completed thy life up to the present time; and live according to nature the remainder which is allowed thee.

57. Love that only which happens to thee and is spun with the thread of thy destiny. For what is more suitable?

58. In everything which happens keep before thy eyes those to whom the same things happened, and how they were vexed, and treated them as strange

---

[66] The first two lines are from the Supplices of Euripides, v. 1110.

things, and found fault with them: and now where are they? Nowhere. Why then dost thou too choose to act in the same way? and why dost thou not leave these agitations which are foreign to nature to those who cause them and those who are moved by them; and why art thou not altogether intent upon the right way of making use of the things which happen to thee? For then thou wilt use them well, and they will be a material for thee [to work on]. Only attend to thyself, and resolve to be a good man in every act which thou doest: and remember . . .[67]

59. Look within. Within is the fountain of good, and it will ever bubble up, if thou wilt ever dig.

60. The body ought to be compact, and to show no irregularity either in motion or attitude. For what the mind shows in the face by maintaining in it the expression of intelligence and propriety, that ought to be required also in the whole body. But all these things should be observed without affectation.

61. The art of life is more like the wrestler's art than the dancer's, in respect of this, that it should stand ready and firm to meet onsets which are sudden and unexpected.

62. Constantly observe who those are whose approbation thou wishest to have, and what ruling principles they possess. For then thou wilt neither blame those who offend involuntarily, nor wilt thou want their approbation, if thou lookest to the sources of their opinions and appetites.

63. Every soul, the philosopher says, is involuntarily deprived of truth; consequently in the same way it is deprived of justice and temperance and benevolence and everything of the kind. It is most necessary to bear this constantly in mind, for thus thou wilt be more gentle towards all.

64. In every pain let this thought be present, that there is no dishonor in it, nor does it make the governing intelligence worse, for it does not damage the intelligence either so far as the intelligence is rational[68] or so far as it is social. Indeed in the case of most pains let this remark of Epicurus aid thee, that pain is neither intolerable nor everlasting, if thou bearest in mind that it has its limits, and if thou addest nothing to it in imagination: and remember this too, that we do not perceive that many things which are disagreeable to us are the same as pain, such as excessive drowsiness, and the being scorched by heat, and the

---

[67] This section is obscure, and the conclusion is so corrupt that it is impossible to give any probable meaning to it. It is better to leave it as it is than to patch it up, as some critics and translators have done.

[68] The text has ὑλική, which it has been proposed to alter to λογική, and this change is necessary. We shall then have in this section λογική and κοινωνική associated, as we have in s. 68 λογική; and πολιτική, and in s. 72.

having no appetite. When then thou art discontented about any of these things, say to thyself that thou art yielding to pain.

65. Take care not to feel towards the inhuman as they feel towards men.[69]

66. How do we know if Telauges was not superior in character to Socrates? For it is not enough that Socrates died a more noble death, and disputed more skilfully with the sophists, and passed the night in the cold with more endurance, and that when he was bid to arrest Leon[70] of Salamis, he considered it more noble to refuse, and that he walked in a swaggering way in the streets[71]—though as to this fact one may have great doubts if it was true. But we ought to inquire what kind of a soul it was that Socrates possessed, and if he was able to be content with being just towards men and pious towards the gods, neither idly vexed on account of men's villainy, nor yet making himself a slave to any man's ignorance, nor receiving as strange anything that fell to his share out of the universal, nor enduring it as intolerable, nor allowing his understanding to sympathize with the affects of the miserable flesh.

67. Nature has not so mingled [the intelligence] with the composition of the body, as not to have allowed thee the power of circumscribing thyself and of bringing under subjection to thyself all that is thy own; for it is very possible to be a divine man and to be recognized as such by no one. Always bear this in mind; and another thing too, that very little indeed is necessary for living a happy life. And because thou hast despaired of becoming a dialectician and skilled in the knowledge of nature, do not for this reason renounce the hope of being both free and modest, and social and obedient to God.

68. It is in thy power to live free from all compulsion in the greatest tranquillity of mind, even if all the world cry out against thee as much as they choose, and even if wild beasts tear in pieces the members of this kneaded matter which has grown around thee. For what hinders the mind in the midst of all this from maintaining itself in tranquillity and in a just judgment of all surrounding things and in a ready use of the objects which are presented to it, so that the judgment may say to the thing which falls under its observation: This thou art in substance [reality], though in men's opinion thou mayest appear to be of a different kind; and the use shall say to that which falls under the hand: Thou art the thing that I was seeking; for to me that which presents itself is always a material for virtue both rational and political, and in a word, for the exercise of art, which belongs to man or God. For everything which happens has

---

[69] I have followed Gataker's conjecture οἱ ἀπάνθρωποι instead of the MSS. reading οἱ ἄνθρωποι.
[70] Leon of Salamis. See Plato, Epist. 7; Apolog. c, 20; Epictetus, iv. 1, 160; iv. 7, 30.
[71] Aristophan. Nub. 362. ὅτι βρενθύει τ' ἐν ταῖσιν ὁδοῖς καὶ τὼ ὀφθαλμὼ παραβάλλει.

a relationship either to God or man, and is neither new nor difficult to handle, but usual and apt matter to work on.

69. The perfection of moral character consists in this, in passing every day as the last, and in being neither violently excited nor torpid nor playing the hypocrite.

70. The gods who are immortal are not vexed because during so long a time they must tolerate continually men such as they are and so many of them bad; and besides this, they also take care of them in all ways. But thou, who art destined to end so soon, art thou wearied of enduring the bad, and this too when thou art one of them?

71. It is a ridiculous thing for a man not to fly from his own badness, which is indeed possible, but to fly from other men's badness, which is impossible.

72. Whatever the rational and political [social] faculty finds to be neither intelligent nor social, it properly judges to be inferior to itself.

73. When thou hast done a good act and another has received it, why dost thou still look for a third thing besides these, as fools do, either to have the reputation of having done a good act or to obtain a return?

74. No man is tired of receiving what is useful. But it is useful to act according to nature. Do not then be tired of receiving what is useful by doing it to others.

75. The nature of the All moved to make the universe. But now either everything that takes place comes by way of consequence or [continuity]; or even the chief things towards which the ruling power of the universe directs its own movement are governed by no rational principle. If this is remembered, it will make thee more tranquil in many things (vi. 44; ix. 28).[72]

---

[72] It is not easy to understand this section. It has been suggested that there is some error in ἢ ἀλόγιστα, &c. Some of the translators have made nothing of the passage, and they have somewhat perverted the words. The first proposition is, that the universe was made by some sufficient power. A beginning of the universe is assumed, and a power which framed an order. The next question is, How are things produced now? Or, in other words, by what power do forms appear in continuous succession? The answer, according to Antoninus, may be this: It is by virtue of the original constitution of things that all change and succession have been effected and are effected. And this is intelligible in a sense, if we admit that the universe is always one and the same, a continuity of identity; as much one and the same as man is one and the same—which he believes himself to be, though he also believes, and cannot help believing, that both in his body and in his thoughts there is change and succession. There is no real discontinuity then in the universe; and if we say that there was an order framed in the beginning, and that the things which are now produced are a consequence of a previous arrangement, we speak of things as we are compelled to view them, as forming a series of succession, just as we speak of the changes in our own bodies and the sequence of our own thoughts. But as there are no .intervals, not even intervals infinitely small, between any two supposed states of any one thing, so there are no intervals, not even infinitely small, between what we call one thing and any other thing which we speak of as immediately

preceding or following it. What we call time is an idea derived from our notion of a succession of things or events, an idea which is a part of our constitution, but not an idea which we can suppose to belong to an infinite intelligence and power. The conclusion then is certain that the present and the past, the production of present things and the supposed original order, out of which we say that present things now come, are one, and the present productive power and the so-called past arrangement are only different names for one thing. I suppose then that Antoninus wrote here as people sometimes talk now, and that his real meaning is not exactly expressed by his words. There are certainly other passages from which I think that we may collect that he had notions of production something like what I have expressed.

We now come to the alternate: "or even the chief things . . . principle." I do not exactly know what he means by τὰ κυριώτατα "the chief," or "the most excellent," or whatever it is. But as he speaks elsewhere of inferior and superior things, and of the inferior being for the use of the superior, and of rational beings being the highest, he may here mean rational beings. He also in this alternative assumes a governing power of the universe, and that it acts by directing its power towards these chief objects, or making its special, proper motion towards them. And here he uses the noun (ὁρμή) "movement," which contains the same notion as the verb (ὥρμησε) "moved," which he used at the beginning of the paragraph, when he was speaking of the making of the universe. If we do not accept the first hypothesis, he says, we must take the conclusion of the second, that the "chief things towards which the ruling power of the universe directs its own movement are governed by no rational principle." The meaning then is, if there is a meaning in it, that though there is a governing power which strives to give effect to its efforts, we must conclude that there is no rational direction of anything, if the power which first made the universe does not in some way govern it still. Besides, if we assume that anything is now produced or now exists without the action of the supreme intelligence, and yet that this intelligence makes an effort to act, we obtain a conclusion which cannot be reconciled with the nature of a supreme power, whose existence Antoninus always assumes. The tranquillity that a man may gain from these reflections must result from his rejecting the second hypothesis and accepting the first—whatever may be the exact sense in which the emperor understood the first. Or, as he says elsewhere, if there is no Providence which governs the world, man has at least the power of governing himself according to the constitution of his nature; and so he may be tranquil if he does the best that he can.

If there is no error in the passage, it is worth the labor to discover the writer's exact meaning—for I think that he had a meaning, though people may not agree what it was. (Compare ix. 28.) If I have rightly explained the emperor's meaning in this and other passages, he has touched the solution of a great question.

BOOK VIII

This reflection also tends to the removal of the desire of empty fame, that it is no longer in thy power to have lived the whole of thy life, or at least thy life from thy youth upwards, like a philosopher; but both to many others and to thyself it is plain that thou art far from philosophy. Thou hast fallen into disorder then, so that it is no longer easy for thee to get the reputation of a philosopher; and thy plan of life also opposes it. If then thou hast truly seen where the matter lies, throw away the thought, How thou shall seem [to others], and be content if thou shalt live the rest of thy life in such wise as thy nature wills. Observe then what it wills, and let nothing else distract thee; for thou hast had experience of many wanderings without having found happiness anywhere,—not in syllogisms, nor in wealth, nor in reputation, nor in enjoyment, nor anywhere. Where is it then? In doing what man's nature requires. How then shall a man do this? If he has principles from which come his affects and his acts. What principles? Those which relate to good and bad: the belief that there is nothing good for man which does not make him just, temperate, manly, free; and that there is nothing bad which does not do the contrary to what has been mentioned.

2. On the occasion of every act ask thyself, How is this with respect to me? Shall I repent of it? A little time and I am dead, and all is gone. What more do I seek, if what I am now doing is the work of an intelligent living being, and a social being, and one who is under the same law with God?

3. Alexander and Caius[73] and Pompeius, what are they in comparison with Diogenes and Heraclitus and Socrates? For they were acquainted with things, and their causes [forms], and their matter, and the ruling principles of these men were the same [or conformable to their pursuits]. But as to the others, how many things had they to care for, and to how many things were they slaves!

4. [Consider] that men will do the same things nevertheless, even though thou shouldst burst.

---

[73] Caius is C. Julius Caesar, the dictator; and Pompeius is Cn. Pompeius, named Magnus.

5. This is the chief thing: Be not perturbed, for all things are according to the nature of the universal; and in a little time thou wilt be nobody and nowhere, like Hadrianus and Augustus. In the next place, having fixed thy eyes steadily on thy business, look at it, and at the same time remembering that it is thy duty to be a good man, and what man's nature demands, do that without turning aside; and speak as it seems to thee most just, only let it be with a good disposition and with modesty and without hypocrisy.

6. The nature of the universal has this work to do,—to remove to that place the things which are in this, to change them, to take, them away hence, and to carry them there. All things are change, yet we need not fear anything new. All things are familiar [to us]; but the distribution of them still remains the same.

7. Every nature is contented with itself when it goes on its way well; and a rational nature goes on its way well when in its thoughts it assents to nothing false or uncertain, and when it directs its movements to social acts only, and when it confines its desires and aversions to the things which are in its power, and when it is satisfied with everything that is assigned to it by the common nature. For of this common nature every particular nature is a part, as the nature of the leaf is a part of the nature of the plant; except that in the plant the nature of the leaf is part of a nature which has not perception or reason, and is subject to be impeded; but the nature of man is part of a nature which is not subject to impediments, and is intelligent and just, since it gives to everything in equal portions and according to its worth, times, substance, cause [form], activity, and incident. But examine, not to discover that any one thing compared with any other single thing is equal in all respects, but by taking all the parts together of one thing and comparing them with all the parts together of another.

8. Thou hast not leisure [or ability] to read. But thou hast leisure [or ability] to check arrogance: thou hast leisure to be superior to pleasure and pain: thou hast leisure to be superior to love of fame, and not to be vexed at stupid. and ungrateful people, nay even to care for them.

9. Let no man any longer hear thee finding fault with the court life or with thy own (v. 16).

10. Repentance is a kind of self-reproof for having neglected something useful; but that which is good must be something useful, and the perfect good man should look after it. But no such man would ever repent of having refused any sensual pleasure. Pleasure then is neither good nor useful.

11. This thing, what is it in itself, in its own constitution? What is its substance and material? And what its causal nature [or form]? And what is it doing in the world? And how long does it subsist?

12. When thou risest from sleep with reluctance, remember that it is according to thy constitution and according to human nature to perform social acts, but sleeping is common also to irrational animals. But that which is according to each individual's nature is also more peculiarly its own, and more suitable to its nature, and indeed also more agreeable (v. 1).

13. Constantly, and, if it be possible, on the occasion of every impression on the soul, apply to it the principles of Physic, of Ethic, and of Dialectic.

14. Whatever man thou meetest with, immediately say to thyself: What opinions has this man about good and bad? For if with respect to pleasure and pain and the causes of each, and with respect to fame and ignominy, death and life, he has such and such opinions, it will seem nothing wonderful or strange to me if he does such and such things; and I shall bear in mind that he is compelled to do so.[74]

15. Remember that as it is a shame to be surprised if the fig-tree produces figs, so it is to be surprised if the world produces such and such things of which it is productive; and for the physician and the helmsman it is a shame to be surprised if a man has a fever, or if the wind is unfavorable.

16. Remember that to change thy opinion and to follow him who corrects thy error is as consistent with freedom as it is to persist in thy error. For it is thy own, the activity which is exerted according to thy own movement and judgment, and indeed according to thy own understanding too.

17. If a thing is in thy own power, why dost thou do it? but if it is in the power of another, whom dost thou blame,—the atoms [chance] or the gods? Both are foolish. Thou must blame nobody. For if thou canst, correct [that which is the cause]; but if thou canst not do this, correct at least the thing itself; but if thou canst not do even this, of what use is it to thee to find fault? for nothing should be done without a purpose.

18. That which has died falls not out of the universe. If it stays here, it also changes here, and is dissolved into its proper parts, which are elements of the universe and of thyself. And these too change, and they murmur not.

19. Everything exists for some end,—a horse, a vine. Why dost thou wonder? Even the sun will say, I am for some purpose, and the rest of the gods will say the same. For what purpose then art thou,—to enjoy pleasure? See if common sense allows this.

20. Nature has had regard in everything no less to the end than to the beginning and the continuance, just like the man who throws up a ball. What

---

[74] Antoninus v. 16. Thucydides, iii. 10: ἐν γὰρ τῷ διαλλάσσοντι τῆς γνώμης καὶ αἱ διαφοραὶ τῶν ἔργων καθίστανται.

good is it then for the ball to be thrown up, or harm for it to come down, or even to have fallen? and what good is it to the bubble while it holds together, or what harm when it is burst? The same may be said of a light also.

21. Turn it [the body] inside out, and see what kind of thing it is; and when it has grown old, what kind of thing it becomes, and when it is diseased.

Short lived are both the praiser and the praised, and the rememberer and the remembered: and all this in a nook of this part of the world; and not even here do all agree, no, not any one with himself: and the whole earth too is a point.

22. Attend to the matter which is before thee, whether it is an opinion or an act or a word.

Thou sufferest this justly: for thou choosest rather to become good tomorrow than to be good to-day.

23. Am I doing anything? I do it with reference to the good of mankind. Does anything happen to me? I receive it and refer it to the gods, and the source of all things, from which all that happens is derived.

24. Such as bathing appears to thee,—oil, sweat, dirt, filthy water, all things disgusting,—so is every part of life and everything.

25. Lucilla saw Verus die, and then Lucilla died. Secunda saw Maximus die, and then Secunda died. Epitynchanus saw Diotimus die, and then Epitynchanus died. Antoninus saw Faustina die, and then Antoninus died. Such is everything. Celer saw Hadrianus die, and then Celer died. And those sharp-witted men, either seers or men inflated with pride, where are they,—for instance the sharp-witted men, Charax and Demetrius the Platonist, and Eudaemon, and any one else like them? All ephemeral, dead long ago. Some indeed have not been remembered even for a short time, and others have become the heroes of fables, and again others have disappeared even from fables. Remember this then, that this little compound, thyself, must either be dissolved, or thy poor breath must be extinguished, or be removed and placed elsewhere.

26. It is satisfaction to a man to do the proper works of a man. Now it is a proper work of a man to be benevolent to his own kind, to despise the movements of the senses, to form a just judgment of plausible appearances, and to take a survey of the nature of the universe and of the things which happen in it.

27. There are three relations [between thee and other things]: the one to the body[75] which surrounds thee; the second to the divine cause from which all things come to all; and the third to those who live with thee.

---

[75] The text has αἴτιον, which in Antoninus means "form," "formal." Accordingly Schultz recommends either Valkenaer's emendation ἀγγεῖον, "body," or Coraïs' σωμάτιον. Compare xii. 13; x. 38.

28. Pain is either an evil to the body—then let the body say what it thinks of it—or to the soul; but it is in the power of the soul to maintain its own serenity and tranquillity, and not to think that pain is an evil. For every judgment and movement and desire and aversion is within, and no evil ascends so high.

29. Wipe out thy imaginations by often saying to thyself: Now it is in my power to let no badness be in this soul, nor desire, nor any perturbation at all; but looking at all things I see what is their nature, and I use each according to its value.—Remember this power which thou hast from nature.

30. Speak both in the senate and to every man, whoever he may be, appropriately, not with any affectation: use plain discourse.

31. Augustus' court, wife, daughter, descendants, ancestors, sister, Agrippa, kinsmen, intimates, friends; Areius,[76] Maecenas, physicians, and sacrificing priests,—the whole court is dead. Then turn to the rest, not considering the death of a single man [but of a whole race], as of the Pompeii; and that which is inscribed on the tombs,—The last of his race. Then consider what trouble those before them have had that they might leave a successor; and then, that of necessity some one must be the last. Again, here consider the death of a whole race.

32. It is thy duty to order thy life well in every single act; and if every act does its duty as far as is possible, be content; and no one is able to hinder thee so that each act shall not do its duty.—But something external will stand in the way. Nothing will stand in the way of thy acting justly and soberly and considerately.—But perhaps some other active power will be hindered. Well, but by acquiescing in the hindrance and by being content to transfer thy efforts to that which is allowed, another opportunity of action is immediately put before thee in place of that which was hindered, and one which will adapt itself to this ordering of which we are speaking.

33. Receive [wealth or prosperity] without arrogance; and be ready to let it go.

34. If thou didst ever see a hand cut off, or a foot, or a head, lying anywhere apart from the rest of the body, such does a man make himself, as far as he can, who is not content with what happens, and separates himself from others, or does anything unsocial. Suppose that thou hast detached thyself from the natural unity,—for thou wast made by nature a part, but now thou hast cut thyself off,—yet here there is this beautiful provision, that it is in thy power again to unite thyself. God has allowed this to no other part, after it has been

---

[76] Areius ("Αρειος) was a philosopher, who was intimate with Augustus; Sueton. Augustus, c. 89; Plutarch, Antoninus, 80; Dion Cassius, 51, c. 16.

separated and cut asunder, to come together again. But consider the kindness by which he has distinguished man, for he has put it in his power not to be separated at all from the universal; and when he has been separated, he has allowed him to return and to be united and to resume his place as a part.

35. As the nature of the universal has given to every rational being all the other powers that it has, so we have received from it this power also. For as the universal nature converts and fixes in its predestined place everything which stands in the way and opposes it, and makes such things a part of itself, so also the rational animal is able to make every hindrance its own material, and to use it for such purposes as it may have designed.[77]

36. Do not disturb thyself by thinking of the whole of thy life. Let not thy thoughts at once embrace all the various troubles which thou mayest expect to befall thee: but on every occasion ask thyself, What is there in this which is intolerable and past bearing? for thou wilt be ashamed to confess. In the next place remember that neither the future nor the past pains thee, but only the present. But this is reduced to a very little, if thou only circumscribest it, and chidest thy mind if it is unable to hold out against even this.

37. Does Panthea or Fergamus now sit by the tomb of Verus?[78] Does Chaurias or Diotimus sit by the tomb of Hadrianus? That would be ridiculous. Well, suppose they did sit there, would the dead be conscious of it? and if the dead were conscious, would they be pleased? and if they were pleased, would that make them immortal? Was it not in the order of destiny that these persons too should first become old women and old men and then die? What then would those do after these were dead? All this is foul smell and blood in a bag.

38. If thou canst see sharp, look and judge wisely, says the philosopher.

39. In the constitution of the rational animal I see no virtue which is opposed to justice; but I see a virtue which is opposed to love of pleasure, and that is temperance.

40. If thou takest away thy opinion about that which appears to give thee pain, thou thyself standest in perfect security.—Who is this self?—The reason.—But I am not reason.—Be it so. Let then the reason itself not trouble itself. But if any other part of thee suffers, let it have its own opinion about itself (vii. 16).

41. Hindrance to the perceptions of sense is an evil to the animal nature. Hindrance to the movements [desires] is equally an evil to the animal nature. And something else also is equally an impediment and an evil to the constitution

---

[77] The text is corrupt at the beginning of the paragraph, but the meaning will appear if the second λογικῶν is changed into ὅλων: though this change alone will not establish the grammatical completeness of the text.

[78] "Verus" is a conjecture of Saumaise, and perhaps the true reading.

of plants. So then that which is a hindrance to the intelligence is an evil to the intelligent nature. Apply all these things then to thyself. Does pain or sensuous pleasure affect thee? The senses will look to that. Has any obstacle opposed thee in thy efforts towards an object? If indeed thou wast making this effort absolutely [unconditionally, or without any reservation], certainly this obstacle is an evil to thee considered as a rational animal. But if thou takest [into consideration] the usual course of things, thou hast not yet been injured nor even impeded. The things however which are proper to the understanding no other man is used to impede, for neither fire, nor iron, nor tyrant, nor abuse, touches it in any way. When it has been made a sphere, it continues a sphere (xi. 12).

42. It is not fit that I should give myself pain, for I have never intentionally given pain even to another.

43. Different things delight different people; but it is my delight to keep the ruling faculty sound without turning away either from any man or from any of the things which happen to men, but looking at and receiving all with welcome eyes and using everything according to its value.

44. See that thou secure this present time to thyself: for those who rather pursue posthumous fame do not consider that the men of after time will be exactly such as these whom they cannot bear now; and both are mortal. And what is it in any way to thee if these men of after time utter this or that sound, or have this or that opinion about thee?

45. Take me and cast me where thou wilt; for there I shall keep my divine part tranquil, that is, content, if it can feel and act comfortably to its proper constitution. Is this [change of place] sufficient reason why my soul should be unhappy and worse than it was, depressed, expanded, shrinking, affrighted? and what wilt thou find which is sufficient reason for this?[79]

46. Nothing can happen to any man which is not a human accident, nor to an ox which is not according to the nature of an ox, nor to a vine which is not according to the nature of a vine, nor to a stone which is not proper to a stone. If then there happens to each thing both what is usual and natural, why shouldst thou complain? For the common nature brings nothing which may not be borne by thee.

47. If thou art pained by any external thing, it is not this thing that disturbs thee, but thy own judgment about it. And it is in thy power to wipe out this judgment now. But if anything in thy own disposition gives thee pain, who hinders thee from correcting thy opinion? And even if thou art pained because

---

[79] ὀρεγομένη in this passage seems to have a passive sense. It is difficult to find an apt expression for it and some of the other words. A comparison with xi. 12, will help to explain the meaning.

thou art not doing some particular thing which seems to thee to be right, why dost thou not rather act than complain?—But some insuperable obstacle is in the way?—Do not be grieved then, for the cause of its not being done depends not on thee.—But it is not worth while to live, if this cannot be done.—Take thy departure then from life contentedly, just as he dies who is in full activity, and well pleased too with the things which are obstacles.

48. Remember that the ruling faculty is invincible, when self-collected it is satisfied with itself, if it does nothing which it does not choose to do, even if it resist from mere obstinacy. What then will it be when it forms a judgment about anything aided by reason and deliberately? Therefore the mind which is free from passions is a citadel, for man has nothing more secure to which he can fly for refuge and for the future be inexpugnable. He then who has not seen this is an ignorant man; but he who has seen it and does not fly to this refuge is unhappy.

49. Say nothing more to thyself than what the first appearances report. Suppose that it has been reported to thee that a certain person speaks ill of thee. This has been reported; but that thou hast been injured, that has not been reported. I see that my child is sick. I do see; but that he is in danger, I do not see. Thus then always abide by the first appearances, and add nothing thyself from within, and then nothing happens to thee. Or rather add something like a man who knows everything that happens in the world.

50. A cucumber is bitter—Throw it away.—There are briers in the road—Turn aside from them.—This is enough. Do not add, And why were such things made in the world? For thou wilt be ridiculed by a man who is acquainted with nature, as thou wouldst be ridiculed by a carpenter and shoemaker if thou didst find fault because thou seest in their workshop shavings and cuttings from the things which they make. And yet they have places into which they can throw these shavings and cuttings, and the universal nature has no external space; but the wondrous part of her art is that though she has circumscribed herself, everything within her which appears to decay and to grow old and to be useless she changes into herself, and again makes other new things from these very same, so that she requires neither substance from without nor wants a place into which she may cast that which decays. She is content then with her own space, and her own matter, and her own art.

51. Neither in thy actions be sluggish nor in thy conversation without method, nor wandering in thy thoughts, nor let there be in thy soul inward contention nor external effusion, nor in life be so busy as to have no leisure.

Suppose that men kill thee, cut thee in pieces, curse thee. What then can these things do to prevent thy mind from remaining pure, wise, sober, just? For instance, if a man should stand by a limpid pure spring, and curse it, the spring never ceases sending up potable water; and if he should cast clay into it or filth, it will speedily disperse them and wash them out, and will not be at all polluted. How then shalt thou possess a perpetual fountain [and not a mere well]? By forming thyself hourly to freedom conjoined with contentment, simplicity, and modesty.

52. He who does not know what the world is, does not know where he is. And he who does not know for what purpose the world exists, does not know who he is, nor what the world is. But he who has failed in any one of these things could not even say for what purpose he exists himself. What then dost thou think of him who [avoids or] seeks the praise of those who applaud, of men who know not either where they are or who they are?

53. Dost thou wish to be praised by a man who curses himself thrice every hour? wouldst thou wish to please a man who does not please himself? Does a man please himself who repents of nearly everything that he does?

54. No longer let thy breathing only act in concert with the air which surrounds thee, but let thy intelligence also now be in harmony with the intelligence which embraces all things. For the intelligent power is no less diffused in all parts and pervades all things for him who is willing to draw it to him than the aerial power for him who is able to respire it.

55. Generally, wickedness does no harm at all to the universe; and particularly the wickedness [of one man] does no harm to another. It is only harmful to him who has it in his power to be released from it as soon as he shall choose.

56. To my own free will the free will of my neighbor is just as indifferent as his poor breath and flesh. For though we are made especially for the sake of one another, still the ruling power of each of us has its own office, for otherwise my neighbor's wickedness would be my harm, which God has not willed, in order that my unhappiness may not depend on another.

57. The sun appears to be poured down, and in all directions indeed it is diffused, yet it is not effused. For this diffusion is extension: Accordingly its rays are called Extensions [ἀκτῖνες] because they are extended [ἀπὸ τοῦ ἐκτείνεσθαι].[80] But one may judge what kind of a thing a ray is, if he looks at the sun's light passing through a narrow opening into a darkened room, for it is extended in a right line, and as it were is divided when it meets with any solid body which stands in the way and intercepts the air beyond; but there the light remains fixed and does not glide or fall off. Such then ought to be the outpouring

---

[80] A piece of bad etymology.

and diffusion of the understanding, and it should in no way be an effusion, but an extension, and it should make no violent or impetuous collision with the obstacles which are in its way; nor yet fall down, but be fixed, and enlighten that which receives it. For a body will deprive itself of the illumination, if it does not admit it.

58. He who fears death either fears the loss of sensation or a different kind of sensation. But if thou shalt have no sensation, neither wilt thou feel any harm; and if thou shalt acquire another kind of sensation, thou wilt be a different kind of living being and thou wilt not cease to live.

59. Men exist for the sake of one another. Teach them then, or bear with them.

60. In one way an arrow moves, in another way the mind. The mind indeed, both when it exercises caution and when it is employed about inquiry, moves straight onward not the less, and to its object.

61. Enter into every man's ruling faculty; and also let every other man enter into thine.[81]

---

[81] Compare Epictetus, iii. 9, 12.

BOOK IX

He who acts unjustly acts impiously. For since the universal nature has made rational animals for the sake of one another, to help one another according to their deserts, but in no way to injure one another, he who transgresses her will is clearly guilty of impiety towards the highest divinity. And he too who lies is guilty of impiety to the same divinity; for the universal nature is the nature of things that are; and things that are have a relation to all things that come into existence.[82] And further, this universal nature is named truth, and is the prime cause of all things that are true. He then who lies intentionally is guilty of impiety, inasmuch as he acts unjustly by deceiving; and he also who lies unintentionally, inasmuch as he is at variance with the universal nature, and inasmuch as he disturbs the order by fighting against the nature of the world; for he fights against it, who is moved of himself to that which is contrary to truth, for he had received powers from nature through the neglect of which he is not able now to distinguish falsehood from truth. And indeed he who pursues pleasure as good, and avoids pain as evil, is guilty of impiety. For of necessity such a man must often find fault with the universal nature, alleging that it assigns things to the bad and the good contrary to their deserts, because frequently the bad are in the enjoyment of pleasure and possess the things which procure pleasure, but the good have pain for their share and the things which cause pain. And further, he who is afraid of pain will sometimes also be afraid of some of the things which will happen in the world, and even this is impiety. And he who pursues pleasure

---

[82] "As there is not any action or natural event, which we are acquainted with, so single and unconnected as not to have a respect to some other actions and events, so possibly each of them, when it has not an immediate, may yet have a remote, natural relation to other actions and events, much beyond the compass of this present world." Again: "Things seemingly the most insignificant imaginable are perpetually observed to be necessary conditions to other things of the greatest importance, so that any one thing whatever may, for aught we know to the contrary, be a necessary condition to any other."—Butler's Analogy, Chap. 7. See all the chapter. Some critics take τὰ ὑπάρχοντα in this passage of Antoninus to be the same as τὰ ὄντα: but if that were so he might have said πρὸς ἄλληλα instead of πρὸς τὰ ὑπάρχοντα. Perhaps the meaning of πρὸς τὰ ὑπάρχοντα may be "to all prior things." If so, the translation is still correct. See vi. 38.

will not abstain from injustice, and this is plainly impiety. Now with respect to the things towards which the universal nature is equally affected—for it would not have made both, unless it was equally affected towards both—towards these they who wish to follow nature should be of the same mind with it, and equally affected. With respect to pain, then, and pleasure, or death and life, or honor and dishonor, which the universal nature employs equally, whoever is not equally affected is manifestly acting impiously. And I say that the universal nature employs them equally, instead of saying that they happen alike to those who are produced in continuous series and to those who come after them by virtue of a certain original movement of Providence, according to which it moved from a certain beginning to this ordering of things, having conceived certain principles of the things which were to be, and having determined powers productive of beings and of changes and of such like successions (vii. 75).

2. It would be a man's happiest lot to depart from mankind without having had any taste of lying and hypocrisy and luxury and pride. However, to breathe out one's life when a man has had enough of these things is the next best voyage, as the saying is. Hast thou determined to abide with vice, and hast not experience yet induced thee to fly from this pestilence? For the destruction of the understanding is a pestilence, much more, indeed, than any such corruption and change of this atmosphere which surrounds us. For this corruption is a pestilence of animals so far as they are animals; but the other is a pestilence of men so far as they are men.

3. Do not despise death, but be well content with it, since this too is one of those things which nature wills. For such as it is to be young and to grow old, and to increase and to reach maturity, and to have teeth and beard and gray hairs, and to beget and to be pregnant and to bring forth, and all the other natural operations which the seasons of thy life bring, such also is dissolution. This, then, is consistent with the character of a reflecting man—to be neither careless nor impatient nor contemptuous with respect to death, but to wait for it as one of the operations of nature. As thou now waitest for the time when the child shall come out of thy wife's womb, so be ready for the time when thy soul shall fall out of this envelope.[83] But if thou requirest also a vulgar kind of comfort which shall reach thy heart, thou wilt be made best reconciled to death by observing the objects from which thou art going to be removed, and the morals of those with whom thy soul will no longer be mingled. For it is no way right to be offended with men, but it is thy duty to care for them and to bear with them gently; and yet to remember that thy departure will not be from men

---

[83] Note 1 of the Philosophy, p. 76.

who have the same principles as thyself. For this is the only thing, if there be any, which could draw us the contrary way and attach us to life,—to be permitted to live with those who have the same principles as ourselves. But now thou seest how great is the trouble arising from the discordance of those who live together, so that thou mayst say, Come quick, O death, lest perchance I, too, should forget myself.

4. He who does wrong does wrong against himself. He who acts unjustly acts unjustly to himself, because he makes himself bad.

5. He often acts unjustly who does not do a certain thing; not only he who does a certain thing.

6. Thy present opinion founded on understanding, and thy present conduct directed to social good, and thy present disposition of contentment with everything which happens—that is enough.

7. Wipe out imagination; check desire: extinguish appetite: keep the ruling faculty in its own power.

8. Among the animals which have not reason one life is distributed; but among reasonable animals one intelligent soul is distributed: just as there is one earth of all things which are of an earthly nature, and we see by one light, and breathe one air, all of us that have the faculty of vision and all that have life.

9. All things which participate in anything which is common to them all, move towards that which is of the same kind with themselves. Everything which is earthy turns towards the earth, everything which is liquid flows together, and everything which is of an aerial kind does the same, so that they require something to keep them asunder, and the application of force. Fire indeed moves upwards on account of the elemental fire, but it is so ready to be kindled together with all the fire which is here, that even every substance which is somewhat dry is easily ignited, because there is less mingled with it of that which is a hindrance to ignition. Accordingly, then, everything also which participates in the common intelligent nature moves in like manner towards that which is of the same kind with itself, or moves even more. For so much as it is superior in comparison with all other things, in the same degree also is it more ready to mingle with and to be fused with that which is akin to it. Accordingly among animals devoid of reason we find swarms of bees, and herds of cattle, and the nurture of young birds, and in a manner, loves; for even in animals there are souls, and that power which brings them together is seen to exert itself in a superior degree, and in such a way as never has been observed in plants nor in stones nor in trees. But in rational animals there are political communities and friendships, and families and meetings of people; and in wars, treaties, and armistices. But in the things which are still superior,

even though they are separated from one another, unity in a manner exists, as in the stars. Thus the ascent to the higher degree is able to produce a sympathy even in things which are separated. See, then, what now takes place; for only intelligent animals have now forgotten this mutual desire and inclination, and in them alone the property of flowing together is not seen. But still, though men strive to avoid [this union], they are caught and held by it, for their nature is too strong for them; and thou wilt see what I say, if thou only observest. Sooner, then, will one find anything earthy which comes in contact with no earthy thing, than a man altogether separated from other men.

10. Both man and God and the universe produce fruit; at the proper seasons each produces it. But and if usage has especially fixed these terms to the vine and like things, this is nothing. Reason produces fruit both for all and for itself, and there are produced from it other things of the same kind as reason itself.

11. If thou art able, correct by teaching those who do wrong; but if thou canst not, remember that indulgence is given to thee for this purpose. And the gods, too, are indulgent to such persons; and for some purposes they even help them to get health, wealth, reputation; so kind they are. And it is in thy power also; or say, who hinders thee?

12. Labor not as one who is wretched, nor yet as one who would be pitied or admired; but direct thy will to one thing only—to put thyself in motion and to check thyself, as the social reason requires.

13. To-day I have got out of all trouble, or rather I have cast out all trouble, for it was not outside, but within and in my opinions.

14. All things are the same, familiar in experience, and ephemeral in time, and worthless in the matter. Everything now is just as it was in the time of those whom we have buried.

15. Things stand outside of us, themselves by themselves, neither knowing aught of themselves, nor expressing any judgment. What is it, then, which does judge about them? The ruling faculty.

16. Not in passivity but in activity lie the evil and the good of the rational social animal, just as his virtue and his vice lie not in passivity but in activity.[84]

17. For the stone which has been thrown up it is no evil to come down, nor indeed any good to have been carried up (viii. 20).

18. Penetrate inwards into men's leading principles, and thou wilt see what judges thou art afraid of, and what kind of judges they are of themselves.

19. All things are changing: and thou thyself art in continuous mutation and in a manner in continuous destruction, and the whole universe too.

---

[84] Virtutis omnis laus in actione consistit.—*Cicero, De Off.*, i. 6.

20. It is thy duty to leave another man's wrongful act there where it is (vii. 29; ix. 38).

21. Termination of activity, cessation from movement and opinion, and in a sense their death, is no evil. Turn thy thoughts now to the consideration of thy life, thy life as a child, as a youth, thy manhood, thy old age, for in these also every change was a death. Is this anything to fear? Turn thy thoughts now to thy life under thy grandfather, then to thy life under thy mother, then to thy life under thy father; and as thou findest many other differences and changes and terminations, ask thyself, Is this anything to fear? In like manner, then, neither are the termination and cessation and change of thy whole life a thing to be afraid of.

22. Hasten [to examine] thy own ruling faculty and that of the universe and that of thy neighbor: thy own, that thou mayst make it just: and that of the universe, that thou mayst remember of what thou art a part; and that of thy neighbor, that thou mayst know whether he has acted ignorantly or with knowledge, and thou mayst also consider that his ruling faculty is akin to thine.

23. As thou thyself art a component part of a social system, so let every act of thine be a component part of social life. Whatever act of thine then has no reference either immediately or remotely to a social end, this tears asunder thy life, and does not allow it to be one, and it is of the nature of a mutiny, just as when in a popular assembly a man acting by himself stands apart from the general agreement.

24. Quarrels of little children and their sports, and poor spirits carrying about dead bodies [such is everything]; and so what is exhibited in the representation of the mansions of the dead[85] strikes our eyes more clearly.

25. Examine into the quality of the form of an object, and detach it altogether from its material part, and then contemplate it; then determine the time, the longest which a thing of this peculiar form is naturally made to endure.

26. Thou hast endured infinite troubles through not being contented with thy ruling faculty when it does the things which it is constituted by nature to do. But enough [of this].

27. When another blames thee or hates thee, or when men say about thee anything injurious, approach their poor souls, penetrate within, and see what kind of men they are. Thou wilt discover that there is no reason to take any trouble that these men may have this or that opinion about thee. However, thou

---

[85] τὸ τῆς Νεκυίας may be, as Gataker conjectures, a dramatic representation of the state of the dead. Schultz supposes that it may be also a reference to the Νεκυία of the Odyssey (lib. xi.).

must be well disposed towards them, for by nature they are friends. And the gods too aid them in all ways, by dreams, by signs, towards the attainment of those things on which they set a value.

28. The periodic movements of the universe are the same, up and down from age to age. And either the universal intelligence puts itself in motion for every separate effect, and if this is so, be thou content with that which is the result of its activity; or it puts itself in motion once, and everything else comes by way of sequence[86] in a manner; or indivisible elements are the origin of all things.—In a word, if there is a god, all is well; and if chance rules, do not thou also be governed by it (vi. 44; vii. 75).

Soon will the earth cover us all: then the earth, too, will change, and the things also which result from change will continue to change forever, and these again forever. For if a man reflects on the changes and transformations which follow one another like wave after wave and their rapidity, he will despise everything which is perishable (xii. 21).

29. The universal cause is like a winter torrent: it carries everything along with it. But how worthless are all these poor people who are engaged in matters political, and, as they suppose, are playing the philosopher! All drivellers. Well then, man: do what nature now requires. Set thyself in motion, if it is in thy power, and do not look about thee to see if any one will observe it; nor yet expect Plato's Republic:[87] but be content if the smallest thing goes on well, and consider such an event to be no small matter. For who can change men's opinions? and without a change of opinions what else is there than the slavery of men who groan while they pretend to obey? Come now and tell me of Alexander and Philippus and Demetrius of Phalerum. They themselves shall judge whether they discovered what the common nature required, and trained themselves accordingly. But if they acted like tragedy heroes, no one has condemned me to imitate them. Simple and modest is the work of philosophy. Draw me not aside to insolence and pride.

30. Look down from above on the countless herds of men and their countless solemnities, and the infinitely varied voyagings in storms and calms, and the differences among those who are born, who live together, and die. And consider, too, the life lived by others in olden time, and the life of those who will live after thee, and the life now lived among barbarous nations, and how many know not even thy name, and how many will soon forget it, and how they who perhaps

---

[86] The words which immediately follow κατ' ἐπακολούθησιν are corrupt. But the meaning is hardly doubtful. (Compare vii. 75.)

[87] Those who wish to know what Plato's Republic is may now study it in the accurate translation of Davies and Vaughan.

now are praising thee will very soon blame thee, and that neither a posthumous name is of any value, nor reputation, nor anything else.

31. Let there be freedom from perturbations with respect to the things which come from the external cause; and let there be justice in the things done by virtue of the internal cause, that is, let there be movement and action terminating in this, in social acts, for this is according to thy nature.

32. Thou canst remove out of the way many useless things among those which disturb thee, for they lie entirely in thy opinion; and thou wilt then gain for thyself ample space by comprehending the whole universe in thy mind, and by contemplating the eternity of time, and observing the rapid change of every several thing, how short is the time from birth to dissolution, and the illimitable time before birth as well as the equally boundless time after dissolution!

33. All that thou seest will quickly perish, and those who have been spectators of its dissolution will very soon perish too. And he who dies at the extremest old age will be brought into the same condition with him who died prematurely.

34. What are these men's leading principles, and about what kind of things are they busy, and for what kind of reasons do they love and honor? Imagine that thou seest their pool souls laid bare. When they think that they do harm by their blame or good by their praise, what an idea!

35. Loss is nothing else than change. But the universal nature delights in change, and in obedience to her all things are now done well, and from eternity have been in like form, and will be such to time without end. What, then, dost thou say,—that all things have been and all things always will be bad, and that no power has ever been found in so many gods to rectify these things, but the world has been condemned to be bound in never ceasing evil (iv. 45, vii. 18)?

36. The rottenness of the matter which is the foundation of everything! water, dust, bones, filth: or again, marble rocks, the callosities of the earth; and gold and silver, the sediments; and garments, only bits of hair; and purple dye, blood; and everything else is of the same kind. And that which is of the nature of breath is also another thing of the same kind, changing from this to that.

37. Enough of this wretched life and murmuring and apish tricks. Why art thou disturbed? What is there new in this? What unsettles thee? Is it the form of the thing? Look at it. Or is it the matter? Look at it. But besides these there is nothing. Towards the gods then, now become at last more simple and better. It is the same whether we examine these things for a hundred years or three.

38. If a man has done wrong the harm is his own. But perhaps he has not done wrong.

39. Either all things proceed from one intelligent source and come together as in one body, and the part ought not to find fault with what is done for the

benefit of the whole; or there are only atoms, and nothing else than mixture and dispersion. Why, then, art thou disturbed? Say to the ruling faculty, Art thou dead, art thou corrupted, art thou playing the hypocrite, art thou become a beast, dost thou herd and feed with the rest?[88]

40. Either the gods have no power or they have power. If, then, they have no power, why dost thou pray to them? But if they have power, why dost thou not pray for them to give thee the faculty of not fearing any of the things which thou fearest, or of not desiring any of the things which thou desirest, or not being pained at anything, rather than pray that any of these things should not happen or happen? for certainly if they can co-operate with men, they can co-operate for these purposes. But perhaps thou wilt say the gods have placed them in thy power. Well, then, is it not better to use what is in thy power like a free man than to desire in a slavish and abject way what is not in thy power? And who has told thee that the gods do not aid us, even in the things which are in our power? Begin, then, to pray for such things, and thou wilt see. One man prays thus: How shall I be able to lie with that woman? Do thou pray thus: How shall I not desire to lie with her? Another prays thus: How shall I be released from this? Pray thou: How shall I not desire to be released? Another thus: How shall I not lose my little son? Thou thus: How shall I not be afraid to lose him? In fine, turn thy prayers this way, and see what comes.

41. Epicurus says, In my sickness my conversation was not about my bodily sufferings, nor, says he, did I talk on such subjects to those who visited me; but I continued to discourse on the nature of things as before, keeping to this main point, how the mind, while participating in such movements as go on in the poor flesh, shall be free from perturbations and maintain its proper good. Nor did I, he says, give the physicians an opportunity of putting on solemn looks, as if they were doing something great, but my life went on well and happily. Do, then, the same that he did both in sickness, if thou art sick, and in any other circumstances; for never to desert philosophy in any events that may befall us, nor to hold trifling talks either with an ignorant man or with one unacquainted with nature, is a principle of all schools of philosophy; but to be intent only on that which thou art now doing and on the instrument by which thou doest it.

42. When thou art offended with any man's shameless conduct, immediately ask thyself, Is it possible, then, that shameless men should not be in the world? It is not possible. Do not, then, require what is impossible. For this man also

---

[88] There is some corruption at the end of this section, but I think that the translation expresses the emperor's meaning. Whether intelligence rules all things or chance rules, a man must not be disturbed. He must use the power that he has and be tranquil.

is one of those shameless men who must of necessity be in the world. Let the same considerations be present to thy mind in the case of the knave, and the faithless man, and of every man who does wrong in any way. For at the same time that thou dost remind thyself that it is impossible that such kind of men should not exist, thou wilt become more kindly disposed towards every one individually. It is useful to perceive this, too, immediately when the occasion arises, what virtue nature has given to man to oppose to every wrongful act. For she has given to man, as an antidote against the stupid man, mildness, and against another kind of man some other power. And in all cases it is possible for thee to correct by teaching the man who is gone astray; for every man who errs misses his object and is gone astray. Besides, wherein hast thou been injured? For thou wilt find that no one among those against whom thou art irritated has done anything by which thy mind could be made worse; but that which is evil to thee and harmful has its foundation only in the mind. And what harm is done or what is there strange, if the man who has not been instructed does the acts of an uninstructed man? Consider whether thou shouldst not rather blame thyself, because thou didst not expect such a man to err in such a way. For thou hadst means given thee by thy reason to suppose that it was likely that he would commit this error, and yet thou hast forgotten and art amazed that he has erred. But most of all when thou blamest a man as faithless or ungrateful, turn to thyself. For the fault is manifestly thy own, whether thou didst trust that a man who had such a disposition would keep his promise, or when conferring thy kindness thou didst not confer it absolutely, nor yet in such way as to have received from thy very act all the profit. For what more dost thou want when thou hast done a man a service? art thou not content that thou hast done something conformable to thy nature, and dost thou seek to be paid for it? just as if the eye demanded a recompense for seeing, or the feet for walking. For as these members are formed for a particular purpose, and by working according to their several constitutions obtain what is their own;[89] so also as man is formed by nature to acts of benevolence, when he has done anything benevolent or in any other way conducive to the common interest, he has acted conformably to his constitution, and he gets what is his own.

---

[89] Ἀπέχει τὸ ἴδιον. This sense of ἀπέχειν occurs in xi. 1, and iv. 49; also in St. Matthew, vi. 2, ἀπέχουσίτὸν μισθον, and in Epictetus.

BOOK X

Wilt thou, then, my soul, never be good and simple and one and naked, more manifest than the body which surrounds thee? Wilt thou never enjoy an affectionate and contented disposition? Wilt thou never be full and without a want of any kind, longing for nothing more, nor desiring anything, either animate or inanimate, for the enjoyment of pleasures? nor yet desiring time wherein thou shalt have longer enjoyment, or place, or pleasant climate, or society of men with whom thou mayst live in harmony? but wilt thou be satisfied with thy present condition, and pleased with all that is about thee, and wilt thou convince thyself that thou hast everything, and that it comes from the gods, that everything is well for thee, and will be well whatever shall please them, and whatever they shall give for the conservation of the perfect living being,[90] the good and just and beautiful, which generates and holds together all things, and contains and embraces all things which are dissolved for the production of other like things? Wilt thou never be such that thou shalt so dwell in community with gods and men as neither to find fault with them at all, nor to be condemned by them?

2. Observe what thy nature requires, so far as thou art governed by nature only: then do it and accept it, if thy nature, so far as thou art a living being, shall not be made worse by it. And next thou must observe what thy nature requires so far as thou art a living being. And all this thou mayst allow thyself, if thy nature, so far as thou art a rational animal, shall not be made worse by it. But the rational animal is consequently also a political [social] animal. Use these rules, then, and trouble thyself about nothing else.

3. Everything which happens either happens in such wise as thou art formed by nature to bear it, or as thou art not formed by nature to bear it. If, then, it happens to thee in such way as thou art formed by nature to bear it, do not complain, but bear it as thou art formed by nature to bear it. But if it happens in such wise as thou art not formed by nature to bear it, do not complain, for it will

---

[90] That is, God (iv. 40), as he is defined by Zeno. But the confusion between gods and God is strange.

perish after it has consumed thee. Remember, however, that thou art formed by nature to bear everything, with respect to which it depends on thy own opinion to make it endurable and tolerable, by thinking that it is either thy interest or thy duty to do this.

4. If a man is mistaken, instruct him kindly and show him his error. But if thou art not able, blame thyself, or blame not even thyself.

5. Whatever may happen to thee, it was prepared for thee from all eternity; and the implication of causes was from eternity spinning the thread of thy being, and of that which is incident to it (iii. 11; iv. 26).

6. Whether the universe is [a concourse of] atoms, or nature [is a system], let this first be established, that I am a part of the whole which is governed by nature; next, I am in a manner intimately related to the parts which are of the same kind with myself. For remembering this, inasmuch as I am a part, I shall be discontented with none of the things which are assigned to me out of the whole; for nothing is injurious to the part if it is for the advantage of the whole. For the whole contains nothing which is not for its advantage; and all natures indeed have this common principle, but the nature of the universe has this principle besides, that it cannot be compelled even by any external cause to generate anything harmful to itself. By remembering, then, that I am a part of such a whole, I shall be content with everything that happens. And inasmuch as I am in a manner intimately related to the parts which are of the same kind with myself, I shall do nothing unsocial, but I shall rather direct myself to the things which are of the same kind with myself, and I shall turn all my efforts to the common interest, and divert them from the contrary. Now, if these things are done so, life must flow on happily, just as thou mayst observe that the life of a citizen is happy, who continues a course of action which is advantageous to his fellow-citizens, and is content with whatever the state may assign to him.

7. The parts of the whole, everything, I mean, which is naturally comprehended in the universe, must of necessity perish; but let this be understood in this sense, that they must undergo change. But if this is naturally both an evil and a necessity for the parts, the whole would not continue to exist in a good condition, the parts being subject to change and constituted so as to perish in various ways. For whether did Nature herself design to do evil to the things which are parts of herself, and to make them subject to evil and of necessity fall into evil, or have such results happened without her knowing it? Both these suppositions, indeed, are incredible. But if a man should even drop the term Nature [as an efficient power], and should speak of these things as natural, even then it would be ridiculous to affirm at the same time that the parts of the

whole are in their nature subject to change, and at the same time to be surprised or vexed as if something were happening contrary to nature, particularly as the dissolution of things is into those things of which each thing is composed. For there is either a dispersion of the elements out of which everything has been compounded, or a change from the solid to the earthy and from the airy to the aerial, so that these parts are taken back into the universal reason, whether this at certain periods is consumed by fire or renewed by eternal changes. And do not imagine that the solid and the airy part belong to thee from the time of generation. For all this received its accretion only yesterday and the day before, as one may say, from the food and the air which is inspired. This, then, which has received [the accretion], changes, not that which thy mother brought forth. But suppose that this [which thy mother brought forth] implicates thee very much with that other part, which has the peculiar quality [of change], this is nothing in fact in the way of objection to what is said.[91]

8. When thou hast assumed these names, good, modest, true, rational, a man of equanimity, and magnanimous, take care that thou dost not change these names; and if thou shouldst lose them, quickly return to them. And remember that the term Rational was intended to signify a discriminating attention to every several thing, and freedom from negligence; and that Equanimity is the voluntary acceptance of the things which are assigned to thee by the common nature; and that Magnanimity is the elevation of the intelligent part above the pleasurable or painful sensations of the flesh, and above that poor thing called fame, and death, and all such things. If, then, thou maintainest thyself in the possession of these names, without desiring to be called by these names by others, thou wilt be another person and wilt enter on another life. For to continue to be such as thou hast hitherto been, and to be torn in pieces and defiled in such a life, is the character of a very stupid man and one over-fond of his life, and like those half-devoured fighters with wild beasts, who though covered with wounds and gore, still intreat to be kept to the following day, though they will be exposed in the same state to the same claws and bites.[92] Therefore fix thyself in the possession of these few names: and if thou art able to

---

[91] The end of this section is perhaps corrupt. The meaning is very obscure. I have given that meaning which appears to be consistent with the whole argument. The emperor here maintains that the essential part of man is unchangeable, and that the other parts, if they change or perish, do not affect that which really constitutes the man. See the Philosophy of Antoninus, p. 56, note 2. Schultz supposed "thy mother" to mean nature, ἡ φύσις. But I doubt about that.

[92] See Seneca, Epp. 70, on these exhibitions which amused the people of those days. These fighters were the Bestiarri, some of whom may have been criminals; but even if they were, the exhibition was equally characteristic of the depraved habits of the spectators.

abide in them, abide as if thou wast removed to certain islands of the Happy.[93] But if thou shalt perceive that thou fallest out of them and dost not maintain thy hold, go courageously into some nook where thou shalt maintain them, or even depart at once from life, not in passion, but with simplicity and freedom and modesty, after doing this one [laudable] thing at least in thy life, to have gone out of it thus. In order, however to the remembrance of these names, it will greatly help thee if thou rememberest the gods, and that they wish not to be flattered, but wish all reasonable beings to be made like themselves; and if thou rememberest that what does the work of a fig-tree is a fig-tree, and that what does the work of a dog is a dog, and that what does the work of a bee is a bee, and that what does the work of a man is a man.

9. Mimi,[94] war, astonishment, torpor, slavery, will daily wipe out those holy principles of thine. How many things without studying nature dost thou imagine, and how many dost thou neglect?[95] But it is thy duty so to look on and so to do everything, that at the same time the power of dealing with circumstances is perfected, and the contemplative faculty is exercised, and the confidence which comes from the knowledge of each several thing is maintained without showing it, but yet not concealed. For when wilt thou enjoy simplicity, when gravity, and when the knowledge of every several thing, both what it is in substance, and what place it has in the universe, and how long it is formed to exist, and of what things it is compounded, and to whom it can belong, and who are able both to give it and take it away?

10. A spider is proud when it has caught a fly, and another when he has caught a poor hare, and another when he has taken a little fish in a net, and

---

[93] The islands of the Happy, or the Fortunatae Insulae, are spoken of by the Greek and Roman writers. They were the abode of Heroes, like Achilles and Diomedes, as we see in the Scolion of Harmodius and Aristogiton. Sertorius heard of the islands at Cadiz from some sailors who had been there; and he had a wish to go and live in them and rest from his troubles (Plutarch, Sertorius, c. 8). In the Odyssey, Proteus told Menelaus that he should not die in Argos, but be removed to a place at the boundary of the earth where Rhadamanthus dwelt (Odyssey, iv. 565):—

"For there in sooth man's life is easiest:
Nor snow nor raging storm nor rain is there
But ever gently breathing gales of Zephyr
Oceanus sends up to gladden man."

It is certain that the writer of the Odyssey only follows some old legend, without having any knowledge of any place which corresponds to his description. The two islands which Sertorius heard of may be Madeira and the adjacent island. Compare Pindar, Ol. ii. 129.
[94] Corais conjectured μῖσος "hatred" in place of Mimi, Roman plays in which action and gesticulation were all or nearly all.
[95] This is corrupt. See the addition of Schultz.

another when he has taken wild boars, and another when he has taken bears, and another when he has taken Sarmatians. Are not these robbers, if thou examinest their opinions?[96]

11. Acquire the contemplative way of seeing how all things change into one another, and constantly attend to it, and exercise thyself about this part [of philosophy]. For nothing is so much adapted to produce magnanimity. Such a man has put off the body, and as he sees that he must, no one knows how soon, go away from among men and leave everything here, he gives himself up entirely to just doing in all his actions, and in everything else that happens he resigns himself to the universal nature. But as to what any man shall say or think about him or do against him, he never even thinks of it, being himself contented with these two things—with acting justly in what he now does, and being satisfied with what is now assigned to him; and he lays aside all distracting and busy pursuits, and desires nothing else than to accomplish the straight course through the law[97] and by accomplishing the straight course to follow God.

12. What need is there of suspicious fear, since it is in thy power to inquire what ought to be done? And if thou seest clear, go by this way content, without turning back; but if thou dost not see clear, stop and take the best advisers. But if any other things oppose thee, go on according to thy powers with due consideration, keeping to that which appears to be just. For it is best to reach this object, and if thou dost fail, let thy failure be in attempting this. He who follows reason in all things is both tranquil and active at the same time, and also cheerful and collected.

13. Inquire of thyself as soon as thou wakest from sleep whether it will make any difference to thee if another does what is just and right. It will make no difference (vi. 32; viii. 55).

Thou hast not forgotten, I suppose, that those who assume arrogant airs in bestowing their praise or blame on others are such as they are at bed and at board, and thou hast not forgotten what they do, and what they avoid, and what they pursue, and how they steal and how they rob, not with hands and feet, but with their most valuable part, by means of which there is produced, when a man chooses, fidelity, modesty, truth, law, a good daemon [happiness] (vii. 17)?

14. To her who gives and takes back all, to nature, the man who is instructed and modest says, Give what thou wilt; take back what thou wilt. And he says this not proudly, but obediently, and well pleased with her.

---

[96] Marcus means to say that conquerors are robbers. He himself warred against Sarmatians, and was a robber, as he says, like the rest. But compare the life of Avidius Cassius, c. 4, by Vulcatius.
[97] By the law he means the divine law, obedience to the will of God.

15. Short is the little which remains to thee of life. Live as on a mountain. For it makes no difference whether a man lives there or here, if he lives everywhere in the world as in a state [political community]. Let men see, let them know a real man who lives according to nature. If they cannot endure him, let them kill him. For that is better than to live thus [as men do].

16. No longer talk at all about the kind of man that a good man ought to be, but be such.

17. Constantly contemplate the whole of time and the whole of substance, and consider that all individual things as to substance are a grain of a fig, and as to time the turning of a gimlet.

18. Look at everything that exists, and observe that it is already in dissolution and in change, and as it were putrefaction or dispersion, or that everything is so constituted by nature as to die.

19. Consider what men are when they are eating, sleeping, generating, easing themselves, and so forth. Then what kind of men they are when they are imperious and arrogant, or angry and scolding from their elevated place. But a short time ago to how many they were slaves and for what things; and after a little time consider in what a condition they will be.

20. That is for the good of each thing, which the universal nature brings to each. And it is for its good at the time when nature brings it.

21. "The earth loves the shower;" and "the solemn ether loves;" and the universe loves to make whatever is about to be. I say then to the universe, that I love as thou lovest. And is not this too said that "this or that loves [is wont] to be produced?"[98]

22. Either thou livest here and hast already accustomed thyself to it, or thou art going away, and this was thy own will; or thou art dying and hast discharged thy duty. But besides these things there is nothing. Be of good cheer, then.

23. Let this always be plain to thee, that this piece of land is like any other; and that all things here are the same with things on the top of a mountain, or on the sea-shore, or wherever thou choosest to be. For thou wilt find just what Plato says, Dwelling within the walls of a city as in a shepherd's fold on a mountain. [The three last words are omitted in the translation.][99]

---

[98] These words are from Euripides. They are cited by Aristotle, Ethic. Nicom. viii. 1. Athenaeus (xiii. 296) and Stobaeus quote seven complete lines beginning ἐρᾷ μὲν ὄμβρου γαῖα. There is a similar fragment of Aeschylus, Danaides, also quoted by Athenaeus.

It was the fashion of the Stoics to work on the meanings of words. So Antoninus here takes the verb φιλεῖ, "loves," which has also the sense of "is wont," "uses," and the like. He finds in the common language of mankind a philosophical truth, and most great truths are expressed in the common language of life; some understand them, but most people utter them without knowing how much they mean.

[99] Plato, Theaet. 174 D. E. But compare the original with the use that Antoninus has made of it.

24. What is my ruling faculty now to me? and of what nature am I now making it? and for what purpose am I now using it? is it void of understanding? is it loosed and rent asunder from social life? is it melted into and mixed with the poor flesh so as to move together with it?

25. He who flies from his master is a runaway; but the law is master, and he who breaks the law is a runaway. And he also who is grieved or angry or afraid, is dissatisfied because something has been or is or shall be of the things which are appointed by him who rules all things, and he is Law and assigns to every man what is fit. He then who fears or is grieved or is angry is a runaway.[100]

26. A man deposits seed in a womb and goes away, and then another cause takes it and labors on it, and makes a child. What a thing from such a material! Again, the child passes food down through the throat, and then another cause takes it and makes perception and motion, and in fine, life and strength and other things; how many and how strange! Observe then the things which are produced in such a hidden way, and see the power, just as we see the power which carries things downwards and upwards, not with the eyes, but still no less plainly (vii. 85).

27. Constantly consider how all things such as they now are, in time past also were; and consider that they will be the same again. And place before thy eyes entire dramas and stages of the same form, whatever thou hast learned from thy experience or from older history; for example, the whole court of Hadrianus, and the whole court of Antoninus, and the whole court of Philippus, Alexander, Croesus; for all those were such dramas as we see now, only with different actors.

28. Imagine every man who is grieved at anything or discontented to be like a pig which is sacrificed and kicks and screams.

Like this pig also is he who on his bed in silence laments the bonds in which we are held. And consider that only to the rational animal is it given to follow voluntarily what happens; but simply to follow is a necessity imposed on all.

29. Severally on the occasion of everything that thou dost, pause and ask thyself if death is a dreadful thing because it deprives thee of this.

30. When thou art offended at any man's fault, forthwith turn to thyself and reflect in what like manner thou dost err thyself; for example, in thinking that money is a good thing, or pleasure, or a bit of reputation, and the like. For by attending to this thou wilt quickly forget thy anger, if this consideration also is added, that the man is compelled: for what else could he do? or, if thou art able, take away from him the compulsion.

---

[100] Antoninus is here playing on the etymology, of νόμος, law, assignment, that which assigns νέμει to every man his portion.

31. When thou hast seen Satyron[101] the Socratic, think of either Eutyches or Hymen, and when thou hast seen Euphrates, think of Eutychion or Silvanus, and when thou hast seen Alciphron think of Tropaeophorus, and when thou hast seen Xenophon, think of Crito[102] or Severus, and when thou hast looked on thyself, think of any other Caesar, and in the case of every one do in like manner. Then let this thought be in thy mind, Where then are those men? Nowhere, or nobody knows where. For thus continuously thou wilt look at human things as smoke and nothing at all; especially if thou reflectest at the same time that what has once changed will never exist again in the infinite duration of time. But thou, in what a brief space of time is thy existence? And why art thou not content to pass through this short time in an orderly way? What matter and opportunity [for thy activity] art thou avoiding? For what else are all these things, except exercises for the reason, when it has viewed carefully and by examination into their nature the things which happen in life? Persevere then until thou shalt have made these things thy own, as the stomach which is strengthened makes all things its own, as the blazing fire makes flame and brightness out of everything that is thrown into it.

32. Let it not be in any man's power to say truly of thee that thou are not simple or that thou art not good; but let him be a liar whoever shall think anything of this kind about thee; and this is altogether in thy power. For who is he that shall hinder thee from being good and simple? Do thou only determine to live no longer unless thou shalt be such. For neither does reason allow [thee to live], if thou art not such.[103]

33. What is that which as to this material [our life] can be done or said in the way most conformable to reason? For whatever this may be, it is in thy power to do it or to say it, and do not make excuses that thou art hindered. Thou wilt not cease to lament till thy mind is in such a condition that what luxury is to those who enjoy pleasure, such shall be to thee, in the matter which is subjected and presented to thee, the doing of the things which are conformable to man's constitution; for a man ought to consider as an enjoyment everything which it is in his power to do according to his own nature. And it is in his power everywhere. Now, it is not given to a cylinder to move everywhere by its own

---

[101] Nothing is known of Satyron or Satyrion; nor, I believe, of Eutyches or Hymen. Euphrates is honorably mentioned by Epictetus (iii. 15, 8; iv. 8, 17). Pliny (Epp. i. 10) speaks very highly of him. He obtained the permission of the Emperor Hadrian to drink poison, because he was old and in bad health (Dion Cassius, 69, c. 8).

[102] Crito is the friend of Socrates; and he was, it appears, also a friend of Xenophon. When the emperor says "seen" (ἰδών), he does not mean with the eyes.

[103] Compare Epictetus, i. 29, 28.

motion, nor yet to water nor to fire, nor to anything else which is governed by nature or an irrational soul, for the things which check them and stand in the way are many. But intelligence and reason are able to go through everything that opposes them, and in such manner as they are formed by nature and as they choose. Place before thy eyes this facility with which the reason will be carried through all things, as fire upwards, as a stone downwards, as a cylinder down an inclined surface, and seek for nothing further. For all other obstacles either affect the body only, which is a dead thing; or, except through opinion and the yielding of the reason itself, they do not crush nor do any harm of any kind; for if they did, he who felt it would immediately become bad. Now, in the case of all things which have a certain constitution, whatever harm may happen to any of them, that which is so affected becomes consequently worse; but in the like case, a man becomes both better, if one may say so, and more worthy of praise by making a right use of these accidents. And finally remember that nothing harms him who is really a citizen, which does not harm the state; nor yet does anything harm the state, which does not harm law [order]; and of these things which are called misfortunes not one harms law. What then does not harm law does not harm either state or citizen.

34. To him who is penetrated by true principles even the briefest precept is sufficient, and any common precept, to remind him that he should be free from grief and fear. For example:—

"Leaves, some the wind scatters on the ground—
So is the race of men."[104]

Leaves, also, are thy children; and leaves, too, are they who cry out as if they were worthy of credit and bestow their praise, or on the contrary curse, or secretly blame and sneer; and leaves, in like manner, are those who shall receive and transmit a man's fame to after-times. For all such things as these "are produced in the season of spring," as the poet says; then the wind casts them down; then the forest produces other leaves in their places. But a brief existence is common to all things, and yet thou avoidest and pursuest all things as if they would be eternal. A little time, and thou shalt close thy eyes; and him who has attended thee to thy grave another soon will lament.

35. The healthy eye ought to see all visible things and not to say, I wish for green things; for this is the condition of a diseased eye. And the healthy hearing and smelling ought to be ready to perceive all that can be heard and smelled. And the healthy stomach ought to be with respect to all food just as the

---

[104] Homer, Il., vi. 146.

mill with respect to all things which it is formed to grind. And accordingly the healthy understanding ought to be prepared for everything which happens; but that which says, Let my dear children live, and let all men praise whatever I may do, is an eye which seeks for green things, or teeth which seek for soft things.

36. There is no man so fortunate that there shall not be by him when he is dying some who are pleased with what is going to happen.[105] Suppose that he was a good and wise man, will there not be at least some one to say to himself, Let us at last breathe freely, being relieved from this schoolmaster? It is true that he was harsh to none of us, but I perceived that he tacitly condemns us.—This is what is said of a good man. But in our own case how many other things are there for which there are many who wish to get rid of us? Thou wilt consider this, then, when thou art dying, and thou wilt depart more contentedly by reflecting thus: I am going away from such a life, in which even my associates in behalf of whom I have striven so much, prayed, and cared, themselves wish me to depart, hoping perchance to get some little advantage by it. Why then should a man cling to a longer stay here? Do not, however, for this reason go away less kindly disposed to them, but preserving thy own character, and friendly and benevolent and mild, and on the other hand not as if thou wast torn away; but as when a man dies a quiet death, the poor soul is easily separated from the body, such also ought thy departure from men to be, for nature united thee to them and associated thee. But does she now dissolve the union? Well, I am separated as from kinsmen, not however dragged resisting, but without compulsion; for this, too, is one of the things according to nature.

37. Accustom thyself as much as possible on the occasion of anything being done by any person to inquire with thyself, For what object is this man doing this? But begin with thyself, and examine thyself first.

38. Remember that this which pulls the strings is the thing which is hidden within: this is the power of persuasion, this is life, this, if one may so say, is man. In contemplating thyself never include the vessel which surrounds thee and these instruments which are attached about it. For they are like to an axe, differing only in this, that they grow to the body. For indeed there is no more use in these parts without the cause which moves and checks them than in the weaver's shuttle, and the writer's pen, and the driver's whip.[106]

---

[105] He says κακόν, but as he affirms in other places that death is no evil, he must mean what others may call an evil, and he means only "what is going to happen."
[106] See the Philosophy of Antoninus, p. 72, note.

BOOK XI

These are the properties of the rational soul: it sees itself, analyzes itself, and makes itself such as it chooses; the fruit which it bears itself enjoys—for the fruits of plants and that in animals which corresponds to fruits others enjoy—it obtains its own end, wherever the limit of life may be fixed. Not as in a dance and in a play and in such like things, where the whole action is incomplete if anything cuts it short; but in every part, and wherever it may be stopped, it makes what has been set before it full and complete, so that it can say, I have what is my own. And further it traverses the whole universe, and the surrounding vacuum, and surveys its form, and it extends itself into the infinity of time, and embraces and comprehends the[107] periodical renovation of all things, and it comprehends that those who come after us will see nothing new, nor have those before us seen anything more, but in a manner he who is forty years old, if he has any understanding at all, has seen by virtue of the uniformity that prevails all things which have been and all that will be. This too is a property of the rational soul, love of one's neighbor, and truth and modesty, and to value nothing more than itself, which is also the property of Law.[108] Thus the right reason differs not at all from the reason of justice.

2. Thou wilt set little value on pleasing song and dancing and the pancratium, if thou wilt distribute the melody of the voice into its several sounds, and ask thyself as to each, if thou art mastered by this; for thou wilt be prevented by shame from confessing it: and in the matter of dancing, if at each movement and attitude thou wilt do the same; and the like also in the matter of the pancratium. In all things, then, except virtue and the acts of virtue, remember to apply thyself to their several parts, and by this division to come to value them little: and apply this rule also to thy whole life.

3. What a soul that is which is ready, if at any moment it must be separated from the body, and ready either to be extinguished or dispersed or continue to

---

[107] Τὴν περιοδικὴν παλιγγενεσίαν. See v. 13, 32; x. 7.
[108] Law is the order by which all things are governed.

exist; but so that this readiness comes from a man's own judgment, not from mere obstinacy, as with the Christians,[109] but considerately and with dignity and in a way to persuade another, without tragic show.

4. Have I done something for the general interest? Well then, I have had my reward. Let this always be present to thy mind, and never stop [doing such good].

5. What is thy art? To be good. And how is this accomplished well except by general principles, some about the nature of the universe, and others about the proper constitution of man?

6. At first tragedies were brought on the stage as means of reminding men of the things which happen to them, and that it is according to nature for things to happen so, and that, if you are delighted with what is shown on the stage, you should not be troubled with that which takes place on the larger stage. For you see that these things must be accomplished thus, and that even they bear them who cry out,[110] "O Cithaeron." And, indeed, some things are said well by the dramatic writers, of which kind is the following especially:—

"Me and my children if the gods neglect,
This has its reason too."[111]

And again,—

"We must not chafe and fret at that which happens."

And,—

"Life's harvest reap like the wheat's fruitful ear."
And other things of the same kind.

After tragedy the old comedy was introduced, which had a magisterial freedom of speech, and by its very plainness of speaking was useful in reminding men to beware of insolence; and for this purpose too Diogenes used to take from these writers.

But as to the middle comedy, which came next, observe what it was, and again, for what object the new comedy was introduced, which gradually sank down into a mere mimic artifice. That some good things are said even by these writers, everybody knows: but the whole plan of such poetry and dramaturgy, to what end does it look?

---

[109] See the Life of Antoninus. This is the only passage in which the emperor speaks of the Christians. Epictetus (iv. 7, 6) names them Galilaei.
[110] Sophocles, Oedipus Rex.
[111] See vii. 41, 38, 40.

7. How plain does it appear that there is not another condition of life so well suited for philosophizing as this in which thou now happenest to be.

8. A branch cut off from the adjacent branch must of necessity be cut off from the whole tree also. So too a man when he is separated from another man has fallen off from the whole social community. Now as to a branch, another cuts it off; but a man by his own act separates himself from his neighbor when he hates him and turns away from him, and he does not know that he has at the same time cut himself off from the whole social system. Yet he has this privilege certainly from Zeus, who framed society, for it is in our power to grow again to that which is near to us, and again to become a part which helps to make up the whole. However, if it often happens, this kind of separation, it makes it difficult for that which detaches itself to be brought to unity and to be restored to its former condition. Finally, the branch, which from the first grew together with the tree, and has continued to have one life with it, is not like that which after being cut off is then ingrafted, for this is something like what the gardeners mean when they say that it grows with the rest of the tree, but that it has not the same mind with it.

9. As those who try to stand in thy way when thou art proceeding according to right reason will not be able to turn thee aside from thy proper action, so neither let them drive thee from thy benevolent feelings toward them, but be on thy guard equally in both matters, not only in the matter of steady judgment and action, but also in the matter of gentleness to those who try to hinder or otherwise trouble thee. For this also is a weakness, to be vexed at them, as well as to be diverted from thy course of action and to give way through fear; for both are equally deserters from their post,—the man who does it through fear, and the man who is alienated from him who is by nature a kinsman and a friend.

10. There is no nature which is inferior to art, for the arts imitate the natures of things. But if this is so, that nature which is the most perfect and the most comprehensive of all natures, cannot fall short of the skill of art Now all arts do the inferior things for the sake of the superior; therefore the universal nature does so too. And, indeed, hence is the origin of justice, and in justice the other virtues have their foundation: for justice will not be observed, if we either care for middle things [things indifferent], or are easily deceived and careless and changeable (v. 16, 30; vii. 55).

11. If the things do not come to thee, the pursuits and avoidances of which disturb thee, still in a manner thou goest to them. Let then thy judgment about them be at rest, and they will remain quiet, and thou wilt not be seen either pursuing or avoiding.

12. The spherical form of the soul maintains its figure when it is neither extended towards any object, nor contracted inwards, nor dispersed, nor sinks down, but is illuminated by light, by which it sees the truth,—the truth of all things and the truth that is in itself (viii. 41, 45; xii. 3).

13. Suppose any man shall despise me. Let him look to that himself. But I will look to this, that I be not discovered doing or saying anything deserving of contempt. Shall any man hate me? Let him look to it. But I will be mild and benevolent towards every man, and ready to show even him his mistake, not reproachfully, nor yet as making a display of my endurance, but nobly and honestly, like the great Phocion, unless indeed he only assumed it. For the interior [parts] ought to be such, and a man ought to be seen by the gods neither dissatisfied with anything nor complaining. For what evil is it to thee, if thou art now doing what is agreeable to thy own nature, and art satisfied with that which at this moment is suitable to the nature of the universe, since thou art a human being placed at thy post in order that what is for the common advantage may be done in some way?

14. Men despise one another and flatter one another; and men wish to raise themselves above one another, and crouch before one another.

15. How unsound and insincere is he who says, I have determined to deal with thee in a fair way!—What are thou doing, man? There is no occasion to give this notice. It will soon show itself by acts. The voice ought to be plainly written on the forehead. Such as a man's character is, he immediately shows it in his eyes, just as he who is beloved forthwith reads everything in the eyes of lovers. The man who is honest and good ought to be exactly like a man who smells strong, so that the bystander as soon as he comes near him must smell whether he choose or not. But the affectation of simplicity is like a crooked stick.[112] Nothing is more disgraceful than a wolfish friendship [false friendship].[113] Avoid this most of all. The good and simple and benevolent show all these things in the eyes, and there is no mistaking.

16. As to living in the best way, this power is in the soul, if it be indifferent to things which are indifferent. And it will be indifferent, if it looks on each of these things separately and all together, and if it remembers that not one of them produces in us an opinion about itself, nor comes to us; but these things remain immovable, and it is we ourselves who produce the judgments about them, and, as we may say, write them in ourselves, it being in our power not to write them,

---

[112] Instead of σκάλμη Saumaise reads σκαμβή. There is a Greek proverb, σκαμβὸν ξύλον οὐδέποτ᾽ ὀρθόν: "You cannot make a crooked stick straight."
[113] The wolfish friendship is an allusion to the fable of the sheep and the wolves.

and it being in our power, if perchance these judgments have imperceptibly got admission to our minds, to wipe them out; and if we remember also that such attention will only be for a short time, and then life will be at an end. Besides, what trouble is there at all in doing this? For if these things are according to nature, rejoice in them and they will be easy to thee: but if contrary to nature, seek what is conformable to thy own nature, and strive towards this, even if it bring no reputation; for every man is allowed to seek his own good.

17. Consider whence each thing is come, and of what it consists, and into what it changes, and what kind of a thing it will be when it has changed, and that it will sustain no harm.

18. [If any have offended against thee, consider first]: What is my relation to men, and that we are made for one another; and in another respect I was made to be set over them, as a ram over the flock or a bull over the herd. But examine the matter from first principles, from this. If all things are not mere atoms, it is nature which orders all things: if this is so, the inferior things exist for the sake of the superior, and these for the sake of one another (ii. 1; ix. 39; v. 16; iii. 4).

Second, consider what kind of men they are at table, in bed, and so forth; and particularly, under what compulsions in respect of opinions they are; and as to their acts, consider with what pride they do what they do (viii. 14; ix. 34).

Third, that if men do rightly what they do, we ought not to be displeased: but if they do not right, it is plain that they do so involuntarily and in ignorance. For as every soul is unwillingly deprived of the truth, so also is it unwillingly deprived of the power of behaving to each man according to his deserts. Accordingly men are pained when they are called unjust, ungrateful, and greedy, and in a word wrong-doers to their neighbors (vii. 62, 63; ii. 1; vii. 26; viii. 29).

Fourth, consider that thou also doest many things wrong, and that thou art a man like others; and even if thou dost abstain from certain faults, still thou hast the disposition to commit them, though either through cowardice, or concern about reputation, or some such mean motive, thou dost abstain from such faults (i. 17).

Fifth, consider that thou dost not even understand whether men are doing wrong or not, for many things are done with a certain reference to circumstances. And in short, a man must learn a great deal to enable him to pass a correct judgment on another man's acts (ix. 38; iv. 51).

Sixth, consider when thou art much vexed or grieved, that man's life is only a moment, and after a short time we are all laid out dead (vii. 58; iv. 48).

Seventh, that it is not men's acts which disturb us, for those acts have their foundation in men's ruling principles, but it is our own opinions which disturb us. Take away these opinions then, and resolve to dismiss thy judgment about an act as if it were something grievous, and thy anger is gone. How then shall I take away these opinions? By reflecting that no wrongful act of another brings shame on thee: for unless that which is shameful is alone bad, thou also must of necessity do many things wrong, and become a robber and everything else (v. 25; vii. 16).

Eighth, consider how much more pain is brought on us by the anger and vexation caused by such acts than by the acts themselves, at which we are angry and vexed (iv. 39, 49; vii. 24).

Ninth, consider that a good disposition is invincible if it be genuine, and not an affected smile and acting a part. For what will the most violent man do to thee, if thou continuest to be of a kind disposition towards him, and if, as opportunity offers, thou gently admonishest him and calmly correctest his errors at the very time when he is trying to do thee harm, saying, Not so, my child: we are constituted by nature for something else: I shall certainly not be injured, but thou art injuring thyself, my child.—And show him with gentle tact and by general principles that this is so, and that even bees do not do as he does, nor any animals which are formed by nature to be gregarious. And thou must do this neither with any double meaning nor in the way of reproach, but affectionately and without any rancor in thy soul; and not as if thou wert lecturing him, nor yet that any bystander may admire, but either when he is alone, and if others are present . . .[114]

Remember these nine rules, as if thou hadst received them as a gift from the Muses, and begin at last to be a man while thou livest. But thou must equally avoid nattering men and being vexed at them, for both are unsocial and lead to harm. And let this truth be present to thee in the excitement of anger, that to be moved by passion is not manly, but that mildness and gentleness, as they are more agreeable to human nature, so also are they more manly; and he who possesses these qualities possesses strength, nerves, and courage, and not the man who is subject to fits of passion and discontent. For in the same degree in which a man's mind is nearer to freedom from all passion, in the same degree also is it nearer to strength: and as the sense of pain is a characteristic of weakness, so also is anger. For he who yields to pain and he who yields to anger, both are wounded and both submit.

But if thou wilt, receive also a tenth present from the leader of the Muses [Apollo], and it is this,—that to expect bad men not to do wrong is madness, for he who expects this desires an impossibility. But to allow men to behave so to others, and to expect them not to do thee any wrong, is irrational and tyrannical.

---

[114] It appears that there is a defect in the text here.

19. There are four principal aberrations of the superior faculty against which thou shouldst be constantly on thy guard, and when thou hast detected them, thou shouldst wipe them out and say on each occasion thus: This thought is not necessary: this tends to destroy social union: this which thou art going to say comes not from the real thoughts; for thou shouldst consider it among the most absurd of things for a man not to speak from his real thoughts. But the fourth is when thou shalt reproach thyself for anything, for this is an evidence of the diviner part within thee being overpowered and yielding to the less honorable and to the perishable part, the body, and to its gross pleasures (iv. 24; ii. 16).

20. Thy aerial part and all the fiery parts which are mingled in thee, though by nature they have an upward tendency, still in obedience to the disposition of the universe they are overpowered here in the compound mass [the body]. And also the whole of the earthy part in thee and the watery, though their tendency is downward, still are raised up and occupy a position which is not their natural one. In this manner then the elemental parts obey the universal; for when they have been fixed in any place, perforce they remain there until again the universal shall sound the signal for dissolution. Is it not then strange that thy intelligent part only should be disobedient and discontented with its own place? And yet no force is imposed on it, but only those things which are conformable to its nature: still it does not submit, but is carried in the opposite direction. For the movement towards injustice and intemperance and to anger and grief and fear is nothing else than the act of one who deviates from nature. And also when the ruling faculty is discontented with anything that happens, then too it deserts its post: for it is constituted for piety and reverence towards the gods no less than for justice. For these qualities also are comprehended under the generic term of contentment with the constitution of things, and indeed they are prior[115] to acts of justice.

---

[115] The word πρεσβύτερα, which is here translated "prior," may also mean "superior;" but Antoninus seems to say that piety and reverence of the gods precede all virtues, and that other virtues are derived from them, even justice, which in another passage (xi. 10) he makes the foundation of all virtues. The ancient notion of justice is that of giving to every one his due. It is not a legal definition, as some have supposed, but a moral rule which law cannot in all cases enforce. Besides, law has its own rules, which are sometimes moral and sometimes immoral; but it enforces them all simply because they are general rules, and if it did not or could not enforce them, so far Law would not be Law. Justice, or the doing what is just, implies a universal rule and obedience to it; and as we all live under universal Law, which commands both our body and our intelligence, and is the law of our nature, that is, the law of the whole constitution of a man, we must endeavor to discover what this supreme Law is. It is the will of the power that rules all. By acting in obedience to this will, we do justice, and by consequence everything else that we ought to do.

21. He who has not one and always the same object in life, cannot be one and the same all through his life. But what I have said is not enough, unless this also is added, what this object ought to be. For as there is not the same opinion about all the things which in some way or other are considered by the majority to be good, but only about some certain things, that is, things which concern the common interest, so also ought we to propose to ourselves an object which shall be of a common kind [social] and political. For he who directs all his own efforts to this object, will make all his acts alike, and thus will always be the same.

22. Think of the country mouse and of the town mouse, and of the alarm and trepidation of the town mouse.[116]

23. Socrates used to call the opinions of the many by the name of Lamiae,—bugbears to frighten children.

24. The Lacedaemonians at their public spectacles used to set seats in the shade for strangers, but themselves sat down anywhere.

25. Socrates excused himself to Perdiccas[117] for not going to him, saying, It is because I would not perish by the worst of all ends; that is, I would not receive a favor and then be unable to return it.

26. In the writings of the [Ephesians][118] there was this precept, constantly to think of some one of the men of former times who practiced virtue.

27. The Pythagoreans bid us in the morning look to the heavens that we may be reminded of those bodies which continually do the same things and in the same manner perform their work, and also be reminded of their purity and nudity. For there is no veil over a star.

28. Consider what a man Socrates was when he dressed himself in a skin, after Xanthippe had taken his cloak and gone out, and what Socrates said to his friends who were ashamed of him and drew back from him when they saw him dressed thus.

29. Neither in writing nor in reading wilt thou be able to lay down rules for others before thou shalt have first learned to obey rules thyself. Much more is this so in life.

30. A slave thou art: free speech is not for thee.

31. And my heart laughed within.

Odyssey, ix. 413.

32. And virtue they will curse, speaking harsh words.

Hesiod, *Works and Days*, 184.

---

[116] The story is told by Horace in his Satires (ii. 6), and by others since but not better.

[117] Perhaps the emperor made a mistake here, for other writers say that it was Archelaus, the son of Perdiccas, who invited Socrates to Macedonia.

[118] Gataker suggested Ἐπικουρείων for Ἐφεσίων.

33. To look for the fig in winter is a mad-man's act: such is he who looks for his child when it is no longer allowed (Epictetus, iii. 24, 87).

34. When a man kisses his child, said Epictetus, he should whisper to himself, "To-morrow perchance thou wilt die."—But those are words of bad omen.—"No word is a word of bad omen," said Epictetus, "which expresses any work of nature; or if it is so, it is also a word of bad omen to speak of the ears of corn being reaped" (Epictetus, iii. 24, 88).

35. The unripe grape, the ripe bunch, the dried grape, are all changes, not into nothing, but into something which exists not yet (Epictetus, iii. 24).

36. No man can rob us of our free will (Epictetus, iii. 22, 105).

37. Epictetus also said, a man must discover an art [or rules] with respect to giving his assent; and in respect to his movements he must be careful that they be made with regard to circumstances, that they be consistent with social interests, that they have regard to the value of the object; and as to sensual desire, he should altogether keep away from it; and as to avoidance [aversion], he should not show it with respect to any of the things which are not in our power.

38. The dispute then, he said, is not about any common matter, but about being mad or not.

39. Socrates used to say, What do you want, souls of rational men or irrational?—Souls of rational men.—Of what rational men, sound or unsound?—Sound.—Why then do you not seek for them?—Because we have them.—Why then do you fight and quarrel?

BOOK XII

All those things at which thou wishest to arrive by a circuitous road thou canst have now, if thou dost not refuse them to thyself. And this means, if thou wilt take no notice of all the past, and trust the future to providence, and direct the present only conformably to piety and justice. Conformably to piety that thou mayest be content with the lot which is assigned to thee, for nature designed it for thee and thee for it. Conformably to justice, that thou mayst always speak the truth freely and without disguise, and do the things which are agreeable to law and according to the worth of each. And let neither another man's wickedness hinder thee, nor opinion nor voice, nor yet the sensations of the poor flesh which has grown about thee; for the passive part will look to this. If, then, whatever the time may be when thou shalt be near to thy departure, neglecting everything else thou shalt respect only thy ruling faculty and the divinity within thee, and if thou shalt be afraid not because thou must some time cease to live, but if thou shalt fear never to have begun to live according to nature—then thou wilt be a man worthy of the universe which has produced thee, and thou wilt cease to be a stranger in thy native land, and to wonder at things which happen daily as if they were something unexpected, and to be dependent on this or that.

2. God sees the minds [ruling principles] of all men bared of the material vesture and rind and impurities. For with his intellectual part alone he touches the intelligence only which has flowed and been derived from himself into these bodies. And if thou also usest thyself to do this, thou wilt rid thyself of thy much trouble. For he who regards not the poor flesh which envelops him, surely will not trouble himself by looking after raiment and dwelling and fame and such like externals and show.

3. The things are three of which thou art composed: a little body, a little breath [life], intelligence. Of these the first two are thine, so far as it is thy duty to take care of them; but the third alone is properly thine. Therefore if thou shalt separate from thyself, that is, from thy understanding, whatever others do or say, and whatever thou hast done or said thyself, and whatever future things trouble thee because they may happen, and whatever in the body which envelops thee

or in the breath [life], which is by nature associated with the body, is attached to thee independent of thy will, and whatever the external circumfluent vortex whirls round, so that the intellectual power exempt from the things of fate can live pure and free by itself, doing what is just and accepting what happens and saying the truth: if thou wilt separate, I say, from this ruling faculty the things which are attached to it by the impressions of sense, and the things of time to come and of time that is past, and wilt make thyself like Empedocles' sphere,

"All round and in its joyous rest reposing;"[119]

and if thou shalt strive to live only what is really thy life, that is, the present,— then thou wilt be able to pass that portion of life which remains for thee up to the time of thy death free from perturbations, nobly, and obedient to thy own daemon [to the god that is within thee] (ii. 13, 17; iii. 5, 6; xi. 12).

4. I have often wondered how it is that every man loves himself more than all the rest of men, but yet sets less value on his own opinion of himself than on the opinion of others. If then a god or a wise teacher should present himself to a man and bid him to think of nothing and to design nothing which he would not express as soon as he conceived it, he could not endure it even for a single day.[120] So much more respect have we to what our neighbors shall think of us than to what we shall think of ourselves.

5. How can it be that the gods, after having arranged all things well and benevolently for mankind, have overlooked this alone, that some men, and very good men, and men who, as we may say, have had most communion with the divinity, and through pious acts and religious observances have been most intimate with the divinity, when they have once died should never exist again, but should be completely extinguished?

But if this is so, be assured that if it ought to have been otherwise, the gods would have done it. For if it were just, it would also be possible; and if it were according to nature, nature would have had it so. But because it is not so, if in fact it is not so, be thou convinced that it ought not to have been so: for thou seest even of thyself that in this inquiry thou art disputing with the Deity; and we should not thus dispute with the gods, unless they were most excellent and most just; but if this is so, they would not have allowed anything in the ordering of the universe to be neglected unjustly and irrationally.

---

[119] The verse of Empedocles is corrupt in Antoninus. It has been restored by Peyron from a Turin manuscript, thus:—

Σφαῖρος κυκοτερὴς μονίῃ περιγηθέϊ γαίων.

[120] iii. 4.

6. Practise thyself even in the things which thou despairest of accomplishing. For even the left hand, which is ineffectual for all other things for want of practice, holds the bridle more vigorously than the right hand; for it has been practised in this.

7. Consider in what condition both in body and soul a man should be when he is overtaken by death; and consider the shortness of life, the boundless abyss of time past and future, the feebleness of all matter.

8. Contemplate the formative principles [forms] of things bare of their coverings; the purposes of actions; consider what pain is, what pleasure is, and death, and fame; who is to himself the cause of his uneasiness; how no man is hindered by another; that everything is opinion.

9. In the application of thy principles thou must be like the pancratiast, not like the gladiator; for the gladiator lets fall the sword which he uses and is killed; but the other always has his hand, and needs to do nothing else than use it.

10. See what things are in themselves, dividing them into matter, form, and purpose.

11. What a power man has to do nothing except what God will approve, and to accept all that God may give him.

12. With respect to that which happens conformably to nature, we ought to blame neither gods, for they do nothing wrong either voluntarily or involuntarily, nor men, for they do nothing wrong except involuntarily. Consequently we should blame nobody (ii. 11, 12, 13; vii. 62; 18 viii. 17).

13. How ridiculous and what a stranger he is who is surprised at anything which happens in life.

14. Either there is a fatal necessity and invincible order, or a kind providence, or a confusion without a purpose and without a director (iv. 27). If then there is an invincible necessity, why dost thou resist? But if there is a providence which allows itself to be propitiated, make thyself worthy of the help of the divinity. But if there is a confusion without a governor, be content that in such a tempest thou hast in thyself a certain ruling intelligence. And even if the tempest carry thee away, let it carry away the poor flesh, the poor breath, everything else; for the intelligence at least it will not carry away.

15. Does the light of the lamp shine without losing its splendor until it is extinguished? and shall the truth which is in thee and justice and temperance be extinguished [before thy death]?

16. When a man has presented the appearance of having done wrong [say], How then do I know if this is a wrongful act? And even if he has done wrong, how do I know that he has not condemned himself? And so this is like tearing his own face. Consider that he who would not have the bad man do wrong, is

like the man who would not have the fig-tree to bear juice in the figs, and infants to cry, and the horse to neigh, and whatever else must of necessity be. For what must a man do who has such a character? If then thou art irritable, cure this man's disposition.[121]

17. If it is not right, do not do it: if it is not true, do not say it. [For let thy efforts be—][122]

18. In everything always observe what the thing is which produces for thee an appearance, and resolve it by dividing it into the formal, the material, the purpose, and the time within which it must end.

19. Perceive at last that thou hast in thee something better and more divine than the things which cause the various affects, and as it were pull thee by the strings. What is there now in my mind,—is it fear, or suspicion, or desire, or anything of the kind (v. 11)?

20. First, do nothing inconsiderately, nor without a purpose. Second, make thy acts refer to nothing else than to a social end.

21. Consider that before long thou wilt be nobody and nowhere, nor will any of the things exist which thou now seest, nor any of those who are now living. For all things are formed by nature to change and be turned and to perish, in order that other things in continuous succession may exist (ix. 28).

22. Consider that everything is opinion, and opinion is in thy power. Take away then, when thou choosest, thy opinion, and like a mariner who has doubled the promontory, thou wilt find calm, everything stable, and a waveless bay.

23. Any one activity, whatever it may be, when it has ceased at its proper time, suffers no evil because it has ceased; nor he who has done this act, does he suffer any evil for this reason, that the act has ceased. In like manner then the whole, which consists of all the acts, which is our life, if it cease at its proper time, suffers no evil for this reason, that it has ceased; nor he who has terminated this series at the proper time, has he been ill dealt with. But the proper time and the limit nature fixes, sometimes as in old age the peculiar nature of man, but always the universal nature, by the change of whose parts the whole universe continues ever young and perfect[123]. And everything which is useful to the universal is always good and in season. Therefore the termination of life for every man is no evil, because neither is it shameful, since it is both independent of the will and not opposed to the general interest, but it is good, since it is seasonable, and

---

[121] The interpreters translate γοργός by the words "acer, validusque," and "skilful." But in Epictetus (ii. 16, 20; iii. 12, 10) γοργός means "vehement," "prone to anger," "irritable."

[122] There is something wrong here, or incomplete.

[123] vii. 25.

profitable to and congruent with the universal. For thus too he is moved by the Deity who is moved in the same manner with the Deity, and moved towards the same thing in his mind.

24. These three principles thou must have in readiness: In the things which thou doest, do nothing either inconsiderately or otherwise than as justice herself would act; but with respect to what may happen to thee from without, consider that it happens either by chance or according to providence, and thou must neither blame chance nor accuse providence. Second, consider what every being is from the seed to the time of its receiving a soul, and from the reception of a soul to the giving back of the same, and of what things every being is compounded, and into what things it is resolved. Third, if thou shouldst suddenly be raised up above the earth, and shouldst look down on human things, and observe the variety of them how great it is, and at the same time also shouldst see at a glance how great is the number of beings who dwell all around in the air and the ether, consider that as often as thou shouldst be raised up, thou wouldst see the same things, sameness of form and shortness of duration. Are these things to be proud of?

25. Cast away opinion: thou art saved. Who then hinders thee from casting it away?

26. When thou art troubled about anything, thou hast forgotten this, that all things happen according to the universal nature; and forgotten this, that a man's wrongful act is nothing to thee; and further thou hast forgotten this, that everything which happens, always happened so and will happen so, and now happens so everywhere; forgotten this too, how close is the kinship between a man and the whole human race, for it is a community, not of a little blood or seed, but of intelligence. And thou hast forgotten this too, that every man's intelligence is a god and is an efflux of the Deity;[124] and forgotten this, that nothing is a man's own, but that his child and his body and his very soul came from the Deity; forgotten this, that everything is opinion; and lastly thou hast forgotten that every man lives the present time only, and loses only this.

27. Constantly bring to thy recollection those who have complained greatly about anything, those who have been most conspicuous by the greatest fame or misfortunes or enmities or fortunes of any kind: then think where are they all now? Smoke and ash and a tale, or not even a tale. And let there be present to thy mind also everything of this sort, how Fabius Catellinus lived in the country, and Lucius Lupus in his gardens, and Stertinius at Briae, and Tiberius at Capreae, and Velius Rufus [or Rufus at Velia]; and in fine think of the eager pursuit of

---

[124] See Epictetus, ii. 8, 9, etc.

anything conjoined with pride;[125] and how worthless everything is after which men violently strain; and how much more philosophical it is for a man in the opportunities presented to him to show himself just, temperate, obedient to the gods, and to do this with all simplicity: for the pride which is proud of its want of pride is the most intolerable of all.

28. To those who ask, Where hast thou seen the gods, or how dost thou comprehend that they exist and so worshippest them, I answer, in the first place, they may be seen even with the eyes;[126] in the second place, neither have I seen even my own soul, and yet I honor it. Thus then with respect to the gods, from what I constantly experience of their power, from this I comprehend that they exist, and I venerate them.

29. The safety of life is this, to examine everything all through, what it is itself, that is its material, what the formal part; with all thy soul to do justice and to say the truth. What remains, except to enjoy life by joining one good thing to another so as not to leave even the smallest intervals between?

30. There is one light of the sun, though it is interrupted by walls, mountains, and other things infinite. There is one common substance,[127] though it is distributed among countless bodies which have their several qualities. There is one soul, though it is distributed among infinite natures and individual circumscriptions [or individuals]. There is one intelligent soul, though it seems to be divided. Now in the things which have been mentioned, all the other parts, such as those which are air and matter, are without sensation and have no fellowship: and yet even these parts the intelligent principle holds together and the gravitation towards the same. But intellect in a peculiar manner tends to that

---

[125] μετ' οἰήσεως. Οἴησις καὶ τῦφος, Epict. i. 8, 6.
[126] "Seen even with the eyes." It is supposed that this may be explained by the Stoic doctrine, that the universe is a god or living being (iv. 40), and that the celestial bodies are gods (viii. 19). But the emperor may mean that we know that the gods exist, as he afterwards states it, because we see what they do; as we know that man has intellectual powers, because we see what he does, and in no other way do we know it. This passage then will agree with the passage in the Epistle to the Romans (i. v. 20), and with the Epistle to the Colossians (i. v. 15), in which Jesus Christ is named "the image of the invisible god;" and with the passage in the Gospel of St. John (xiv. v. 9).

Gataker, whose notes are a wonderful collection of learning, and all of it sound and good, quotes a passage of Calvin which is founded on St. Paul's language (Rom. i. v. 20): "God by creating the universe [or world, mundum], being himself invisible, has presented himself to our eyes conspicuously in a certain visible form." He also quotes Seneca (De Benef. iv. c. 8): "Quocunque te flexeris, ibi illum videbis occurrentem tibi: nihil ab illo vacat, opus suum ipse implet." Compare also Cicero, De Senectute (c. 22), Xenophon's Cyropaedia (viii. 7), and Mem. iv. 3; also Epictetus, i. 6, de Providentia. I think that my interpretation of Antoninus is right.
[127] iv. 40.

which is of the same kin, and combines with it, and the feeling for communion is not interrupted.

31. What dost thou wish—to continue to exist? Well, dost thou wish to have sensation, movement, growth, and then again to cease to grow, to use thy speech, to think? What is there of all these things which seems to thee worth desiring? But if it is easy to set little value on all these things, turn to that which remains, which is to follow reason and God. But it is inconsistent with honoring reason and God to be troubled because by death a man will be deprived of the other things.

32. How small a part of the boundless and unfathomable time is assigned to every man, for it is very soon swallowed up in the eternal! And how small a part of the whole substance; and how small a part of the universal soul; and on what a small clod of the whole earth thou creepest! Reflecting on all this, consider nothing to be great, except to act as thy nature leads thee, and to endure that which the common nature brings.

33. How does the ruling faculty make use of itself? for all lies in this. But everything else, whether it is in the power of thy will or not, is only lifeless ashes and smoke.

34. This reflection is most adapted to move us to contempt of death, that even those who think pleasure to be a good and pain an evil still have despised it.

35. The man to whom that only is good which comes in due season, and to whom it is the same thing whether he has done more or fewer acts conformable to right reason, and to whom it makes no difference whether he contemplates the world for a longer or a shorter time—for this man neither is death a terrible thing (iii. 7; vi. 23; x. 20; xii. 23).

36. Man, thou hast been a citizen in this great state [the world];[128] what difference does it make to thee whether for five years [or three]? for that which is conformable to the laws is just for all. Where is the hardship then, if no tyrant nor yet an unjust judge sends thee away from the state, but nature, who brought thee into it? the same as if a praetor who has employed an actor dismisses him from the stage.[129]—"But I have not finished the five acts, but only three of them."—Thou sayest well, but in life the three acts are the whole drama; for what shall be a complete drama is determined by him who was once the cause of its composition, and now of its dissolution: but thou art the cause of neither. Depart then satisfied, for he also who releases thee is satisfied.

---

[128] ii. 16; iii. 11; iv. 29.
[129] iii. 8; xi. 1.

ENCHIRIDION

Epictetus

Translated by
George Long

ENCHIRIDION

I

Of things some are in our power, and others are not. In our power are opinion (ὑπόληψις), movement towards a thing (ὁρμή), desire, aversion (ἔκκλισις, turning from a thing); and in a word, whatever are our own acts: not in our power are the body, property, reputation, offices (magisterial power), and in a word, whatever are not our own acts. And the things in our power are by nature free, not subject to restraint nor hindrance: but the things not in our power are weak, slavish, subject to restraint, in the power of others. Remember then that if you think the things which are by nature slavish to be free, and the things which are in the power of others to be your own, you will be hindered, you will lament, you will be disturbed, you will blame both gods and men: but if you think that only which is your own to be your own, and if you think that what is another's, as it really is, belongs to another, no man will ever compel you, no man will hinder you, you will never blame any man, you will accuse no man, you will do nothing involuntarily (against your will), no man will harm you, you will have no enemy, for you will not suffer any harm.

If then you desire (aim at) such great things, remember that you must not (attempt to) lay hold of them with a small effort; but you must leave alone some things entirely, and postpone others for the present. But if you wish for these things also (such great things), and power (office) and wealth, perhaps you will not gain even these very things (power and wealth) because you aim also at those former things (such great things):[130] certainly you will fail in those things through which alone happiness and freedom are secured. Straightway then practise saying to every harsh appearance,[131] You are an appearance, and

---

[130] This passage will be obscure in the original, unless it is examined well. I have followed the explanation of Simplicius, iv. (i 4.)
[131] Appearances are named "harsh" or "rough" when they are "contrary to reason and overexciting and in fact make life rough (uneven) by the want of symmetry and by inequality in the movements.

in no manner what you appear to be. Then examine it by the rules which you possess, and by this first and chiefly, whether it relates to the things which are in our power or to things which are not in our power: and if it relates to anything which is not in our power, be ready to say, that it does not concern you.

II

Remember that desire contains in it the profession (hope) of obtaining that which you desire; and the profession (hope) in aversion (turning from a thing) is that you will not fall into that which you attempt to avoid: and he who fails in his desire is unfortunate; and he who falls into that which he would avoid, is unhappy. If then you attempt to avoid only the things contrary to nature which are within your power, you will not be involved in any of the things which you would avoid. But if you attempt to avoid disease or death or poverty, you will be unhappy. Take away then aversion from all things which are not in our power, and transfer it to the things contrary to nature which are in our power. But destroy desire completely for the present. For if you desire anything which is not in our power, you must be unfortunate: but of the things in our power, and which it would be good to desire, nothing yet is before you. But employ only the power of moving towards an object and retiring from it; and these powers indeed only slightly and with exceptions and with remission.[132]

III

In everything which pleases the soul, or supplies a want, or is loved, remember to add this to the (description, notion); what is the nature of each thing, beginning from the smallest? If you love an earthen vessel, say it is an earthen vessel which you love; for when it has been broken, you will not be disturbed. If you are kissing your child or wife, say that it is a human being whom you are kissing, for when the wife or child dies, you will not be disturbed.

IV

When you are going to take in hand any act, remind yourself what kind of an act it is. If you are going to bathe, place before yourself what happens in the bath: some splashing the water, others pushing against one another, others abusing

---

Simplicius, v. (i 5.)
[132] See the notes in Schweig.'s edition.

one another, and some stealing: and thus with more safety you will undertake the matter, if you say to yourself, I now intend to bathe, and to maintain my will in a manner conformable to nature. And so you will do in every act: for thus if any hindrance to bathing shall happen, let this thought be ready: it was not this only that I intended, but I intended also to maintain my will in a way conformable to nature; but I shall not maintain it so, if I am vexed at what happens.

V

Men are disturbed not by the things which happen, but by the opinions about the things: for example, death is nothing terrible, for if it were, it would have seemed so to Socrates; for the opinion about death, that it is terrible, is the terrible thing. When then we are impeded or disturbed or grieved, let us never blame others, but ourselves, that is, our opinions. It is the act of an ill-instructed man to blame others for his own bad condition; it is the act of one who has begun to be instructed, to lay the blame on himself; and of one whose instruction is completed, neither to blame another, nor himself.

VI

Be not elated at any advantage (excellence), which belongs to another. If a horse when he is elated should say, I am beautiful, one might endure it. But when you are elated, and say, I have a beautiful horse, you must know that you are elated at having a good horse.[133] What then is your own? The use of appearances. Consequently when in the use of appearances you are conformable to nature, then be elated, for then you will be elated at something good which is your own.

VII

As on a voyage when the vessel has reached a port, if you go out to get water, it is an amusement by the way to pick up a shellfish or some bulb, but your thoughts ought to be directed to the ship, and you ought to be constantly watching if the captain should call, and then you must throw away all those things, that you may not be bound and pitched into the ship like sheep: so in life also, if there be given to you instead of a little bulb and a shell a wife

---

[133] Upton proposes to read ἐφ' ἵππου ἀγαφῷ *instead of* ἐπὶ ἵππῳ ἀγαφῷ. The meaning then will be "elated at something good which is in the horse." I think that he is right.

and child, there will be nothing to prevent (you from taking them). But if the captain should call, run to the ship, and leave all those things without regard to them. But if you are old, do not even go far from the ship, lest when you are called you make default.

VIII

Seek not that the things which happen[134] should happen as you wish; but wish the things which happen to be as they are, and you will have a tranquil flow of life.

IX

Disease is an impediment to the body, but not to the will, unless the will itself chooses. Lameness is an impediment to the leg, but not to the will. And add this reflection on the occasion of everything that happens; for you will find it an impediment to something else, but not to yourself.

X

On the occasion of every accident (event) that befalls you, remember to turn to yourself and inquire what power you have for turning it to use. If you see a fair man or a fair woman, you will find that the power to resist is temperance (continence). If labour (pain) be presented to you, you will find that it is endurance. If it be abusive words, you will find it to be patience. And if you have been thus formed to the (proper) habit, the appearances will not carry you along with them.

XI

Never say about anything, I have lost it, but say I have restored it. Is your child dead? It has been restored. Is your wife dead? She has been restored. Has your estate been taken from you? Has not then this also been restored? But he who has taken it from me is a bad man. But what is it to you, by whose hands the giver demanded it back? So long as he may allow you, take care of it as a thing which belongs to another, as travellers do with their inn.

---

[134] The text has τὰ γενόμενα: but it should be τὰ γινόμενα. See Upton's note.

XII

If you intend to improve, throw away such thoughts as these: if I neglect my affairs, I shall not have the means of living: unless I chastise my slave, he will be bad. For it is better to die of hunger and so to be released from grief and fear than to live in abundance with perturbation; and it is better for your slave to be bad than for you to be unhappy.[135] Begin then from little things. Is the oil spilled? Is a little wine stolen? Say on the occasion, at such price is sold freedom from perturbation; at such price is sold tranquillity, but nothing is got for nothing. And when you call your slave, consider that it is possible that he does not hear; and if he does hear, that he will do nothing which you wish. But matters are not so well with him, but altogether well with you, that it should be in his power for you to be not disturbed.[136]

XIII

If you would improve, submit to be considered without sense and foolish with respect to externals. Wish to be considered to know nothing: and if you shall seem to some to be a person of importance, distrust yourself. For you should know that it is not easy both to keep your will in a condition conformable to nature and (to secure) external things: but if a man is careful about the one, it is an absolute necessity that he will neglect the other.

XIV

If you would have your children and your wife and your friends to live forever, you are silly; for you would have the things which are not in your power to be in your power, and the things which belong to others to be yours. So if you would have your slave to be free from faults, you are a fool; for you would have badness not to be badness, but something else.[137] But if you wish not to fail in

---

[135] He means, Do not chastise your slave while you are in a passion, lest, while you are trying to correct him, and it is very doubtful whether you will succeed, you fall into a vice which is a man's great and only calamity. Schweig.

[136] The passage seems to mean, that your slave has not the power of disturbing you, because you have the power of not being disturbed. See Upton's note on the text.

[137] Τέλειν is used here, as it often is among the Stoics, to "wish absolutely," "to will." When Epictetus says "you would have badness not to be badness," he means that "badness" is in the will of him who has the badness, and as you wish to subject it to your will, you are a fool. It is your business, as far as you can, to improve the slave: you may wish this. It is his business to obey your instruction: this is what he ought to wish to do; but for him to will to do this, that lies in himself, not in you. Schweig.

your desires, you are able to do that. Practise then this which you are able to do. He is the master of every man who has the power over the things, which another person wishes or does not wish, the power to confer them on him or to take them away. Whoever then wishes to be free, let him neither wish for anything nor avoid anything which depends on others: if he does not observe this rule, he must be a slave.

XV

Remember that in life you ought to behave as at a banquet. Suppose that something is carried round and is opposite to you. Stretch out your hand and take a portion with decency. Suppose that it passes by you. Do not detain it. Suppose that it is not yet come to you. Do not send your desire forward to it, but wait till it is opposite to you. Do so with respect to children, so with respect to a wife, so with respect to magisterial offices, so with respect to wealth, and you will be some time a worthy partner of the banquets of the gods. But if you take none of the things which are set before you, and even despise them, then you will be not only a fellow banqueter with the gods, but also a partner with them in power. For by acting thus Diogenes and Heracleitus and those like them were deservedly divine, and were so called.

XVI

When you see a person weeping in sorrow either when a child goes abroad or when he is dead, or when the man has lost his property, take care that the appearance do not hurry you away with it, as if he were suffering in external things.[138] But straightway make a distinction in your own mind, and be in readiness to say, it is not that which has happened that afflicts this man, for it does not afflict another, but it is the opinion about this thing which afflicts the man. So far as words then do not be unwilling to show him sympathy,[139] and even if it happens so, to lament with him. But take care that you do not lament internally also.

---

[138] This is obscure. "It is true that the man is wretched, not because of the things external which have happened to him, but through the fact that he allows himself to be affected so much by external things which are placed out of his power." Schweig.

[139] It has been objected to Epictetus that he expresses no sympathy with those who suffer sorrow. But here he tells you to show sympathy, a thing which comforts most people. But it would be contrary to his teaching, if he told you to suffer mentally with another.

XVII

Remember that thou art an actor in a play,[140] of such a kind as the teacher (author)[141] may choose; if short, of a short one; if long, of a long one: if he wishes you to act the part of a poor man, see that you act the part naturally; if the part of a lame man, of a magistrate, of a private person, (do the same). For this is your duty, to act well the part that is given to you; but to select the part, belongs to another.

XVIII

When a raven has croaked inauspiciously, let not the appearance hurry you away with it; but straightway make a distinction in your mind and say, None of these things is signified to me, but either to my poor body, or to my small property, or to my reputation, or to my children or to my wife: but to me all significations are auspicious if I choose. For whatever of these things results, it is in my power to derive benefit from it.

XIX

You can be invincible, if you enter into no contest in which it is not in your power to conquer. Take care then when you observe a man honoured before others or possessed of great power or highly esteemed for any reason, not to suppose him happy, and be not carried away by the appearance. For if the nature of the good is in our power, neither envy nor jealousy will have a place in us. But you yourself will not wish to be a general or senator (πρύτανις) or consul, but a free man: and there is only one way to this, to despise (care not for) the things which are not in our power.

XX

Remember that it is not he who reviles you or strikes you, who insults you, but it is your opinion about these things as being insulting. When then a man irritates you, you must know that it is your own opinion which has irritated you. Therefore especially try not to be carried away by the appearance. For if you once gain time and delay, you will more easily master yourself.

---

[140] Compare Antoninus, xi 6, xii 36.
[141] Note, ed. Schweig.

XXI

Let death and exile and every other thing which appears dreadful be daily before your eyes; but most of all death: and you will never think of anything mean nor will you desire anything extravagantly.

XXII

If you desire philosophy, prepare yourself from the beginning to be ridiculed, to expect that many will sneer at you, and say, He has all at once returned to us as a philosopher; and whence does he get this supercilious look for us? Do you not show a supercilious look; but hold on to the things which seem to you best as one appointed by God to this station. And remember that if you abide in the same principles, these men who first ridiculed will afterwards admire you: but if you shall have been overpowered by them, you will bring on yourself double ridicule.

XXIII

If it should ever happen to you to be turned to externals in order to please some person, you must know that you have lost your purpose in life.[142] Be satisfied then in everything with being a philosopher; and if you wish to seem also to any person to be a philosopher, appear so to yourself, and you will be able to do this.

XXIV

Let not these thoughts afflict you, I shall live unhonoured and be nobody nowhere. For if want of honour (ἀτιμία) is an evil, you cannot be in evil through the means (fault) of another any more than you can be involved in anything base. Is it then your business to obtain the rank of a magistrate, or to be received at a banquet? By no means. How then can this be want of honor (dishonor)? And how will you be nobody nowhere, when you ought to be somebody in those things only which are in your power, in which indeed it is permitted to you to be a man of the greatest worth? But your friends will be without assistance! What do you mean by being without assistance? They will not receive money from you, nor will you make them Roman citizens. Who then told you that these are

---

[142] "If I yet pleased men, I should not be the servant of Christ." Gal. 1:10. Mrs. Carter.

among the things which are in our power, and not in the power of others? And who can give to another what he has not himself? Acquire money then, your friends say, that we also may have something. If I can acquire money and also keep myself modest, and faithful and magnanimous, point out the way, and I will acquire it. But if you ask me to lose the things which are good and my own, in order that you may gain the things which are not good, see how unfair and silly you are. Besides, which would you rather have, money or a faithful and modest friend? For this end then rather help me to be such a man, and do not ask me to do this by which I shall lose that character. But my country, you say, as far as it depends on me, will be without my help. I ask again, what help do you mean? It will not have porticoes or baths through you. And what does this mean? For it is not furnished with shoes by means of a smith, nor with arms by means of a shoemaker. But it is enough if every man fully discharges the work that is his own: and if you provided it with another citizen faithful and modest, would you not be useful to it? Yes. Then you also cannot be useless to it. What place then, you say, shall I hold in the city? Whatever you can, if you maintain at the same time your fidelity and modesty. But if when you wish to be useful to the state, you shall lose these qualities, what profit could you be to it, if you were made shameless and faithless?

XXV

Has any man been preferred before you at a banquet, or in being saluted, or in being invited to a consultation? If these things are good, you ought to rejoice that he has obtained them: but if bad, be not grieved because you have not obtained them; and remember that you cannot, if you do not the same things in order to obtain what is not in our own power, be considered worthy of the same (equal) things. For how can a man obtain an equal share with another when he does not visit a man's doors as that other man does, when he does not attend him when he goes abroad, as the other man does; when he does not praise (flatter) him as another does? You will be unjust then and insatiable, if you do not part with the price, in return for which those things are sold, and if you wish to obtain them for nothing. Well, what is the price of lettuces? An obolus[143] perhaps. If then a man gives up the obolus, and receives the lettuces, and if you do not give up the obolus and do not obtain the lettuces, do not suppose that you receive less than he who has got the lettuces; for as he has the lettuces, so you have the obolus which you did not give. In the same way

---

[143] The sixth part of a drachma.

then in the other matter also you have not been invited to a man's feast, for you did not give to the host the price at which the supper is sold; but he sells it for praise (flattery), he sells it for personal attention. Give then the price,[144] if it is for your interest, for which it is sold. But if you wish both not to give the price and to obtain the things, you are insatiable and silly. Have you nothing then in place of the supper? You have indeed, you have the not flattering of him, whom you did not choose to flatter; you have the not enduring[145] of the man when he enters the room.

XXVI

We may learn the wish (will) of nature from the things in which we do not differ from one another: for instance, when your neighbour's slave has broken his cup, or anything else, we are ready to say forthwith, that it is one of the things which happen. You must know then that when your cup also is broken, you ought to think as you did when your neighbour's cup was broken. Transfer this reflection to greater things also. Is another man's child or wife dead? There is no one who would not say, this is an event incident to man. But when a man's own child or wife is dead, forthwith he calls out, Woe to me, how wretched I am. But we ought to remember how we feel when we hear that it has happened to others.

XXVII

As a mark is not set up for the purpose of missing the aim, so neither does the nature of evil exist in the world.[146]

---

[144] "Price" is here τὸ διαφέρον.
[145] See Schweig.'s note.
[146] This passage is explained in the commentary of Simplicius, (xxxiv, in Schweig.'s ed. xxvii p. 264), and Schweighaeuser agrees with the explanation, which is this: Nothing in the world (universe) can exist or be done (happen) which in its proper sense, in itself and in its nature is bad; for everything is and is done by the wisdom and will of God and for the purpose which he intended: but to miss a mark is to fail in an intention; and as a man does not set up a mark, or does not form a purpose for the purpose of missing the mark or the purpose, so it is absurd (inconsistent) to say that God has a purpose or design, and that he purposed or designed anything which in itself and in its nature is bad. The commentary of Simplicius is worth reading. But how many will read it? Perhaps one in a million.

XXVIII

If any person was intending to put your body in the power of any man whom you fell in with on the way, you would be vexed: but that you put your understanding in the power of any man whom you meet, so that if he should revile you, it is disturbed and troubled, are you not ashamed at this?

XXIX[147]

In every act observe the things which come first, and those which follow it; and so proceed to the act. If you do not, at first you will approach it with alacrity, without having thought of the things which will follow; but afterwards, when certain base (ugly) things have shown themselves, you will be ashamed. A man wishes to conquer at the Olympic games. I also wish indeed, for it is a fine thing. But observe both the things which come first, and the things which follow; and then begin the act. You must do everything according to rule, eat according to strict orders, abstain from delicacies, exercise yourself as you are bid at appointed times, in heat, in cold, you must not drink cold water, nor wine as you choose; in a word, you must deliver yourself up to the exercise master as you do to the physician, and then proceed to the contest. And sometimes you will strain the hand, put the ankle out of joint, swallow much dust, sometimes be flogged, and after all this be defeated. When you have considered all this, if you still choose, go to the contest: if you do not, you will behave like children, who at one time play at wrestlers, another time as flute players, again as gladiators, then as trumpeters, then as tragic actors: so you also will be at one time an athlete, at another a gladiator, then a rhetorician, then a philosopher, but with your whole soul you will be nothing at all; but like an ape you imitate everything that you see, and one thing after another pleases you. For you have not undertaken anything with consideration, nor have you surveyed it well; but carelessly and with cold desire. Thus some who have seen a philosopher and having heard one speak, as Euphrates speaks—and who can speak as he does?—they wish to be philosophers themselves also. My man, first of all consider what kind of thing it is: and then examine your own nature, if you are able to sustain the character. Do you wish to be a pentathlete or a wrestler? Look at your arms, your thighs, examine your loins. For different men are formed by nature for different things.

---

[147] "Compare iii 15, from which all this passage has been transferred to the Enchiridion by the copyists." Upton. On which Schweighaeuser remarks, "Why should we not say by Arrian, who composed the Enchiridion from the Discourses of Epictetus?" See the notes of Upton and Schweig. on some differences in the readings of the passage in iii 15, and in this passage.

Do you think that if you do these things, you can eat in the same manner, drink in the same manner, and in the same manner loathe certain things? You must pass sleepless nights, endure toil, go away from your kinsmen, be despised by a slave, in everything have the inferior part, in honour, in office, in the courts of justice, in every little matter. Consider these things, if you would exchange for them, freedom from passions, liberty, tranquillity. If not, take care that, like little children, you be not now a philosopher, then a servant of the publicani, then a rhetorician, then a procurator (manager) for Caesar. These things are not consistent. You must be one man, either good or bad. You must either cultivate your own ruling faculty, for external things; you must either exercise your skill on internal things or on external things; that is you must either maintain the position of a philosopher or that of a common person.

XXX

Duties are universally measured by relations (ταῖς σχέσεσι). Is a man a father? The precept is to take care of him, to yield to him in all things, to submit when he is reproachful, when he inflicts blows. But suppose that he is a bad father. Were you then by nature made akin to a good father? No; but to a father. Does a brother wrong you? Maintain then your own position towards him, and do not examine what he is doing, but what you must do that your will shall be conformable to nature. For another will not damage you, unless you choose: but you will be damaged then when you shall think that you are damaged. In this way then you will discover your duty from the relation of a neighbour, from that of a citizen, from that of a general, if you are accustomed to contemplate the relations.

XXXI

As to piety towards the Gods you must know that this is the chief thing, to have right opinions about them, to think that they exist, and that they administer the All well and justly; and you must fix yourself in this principle (duty), to obey them, and to yield to them in everything which happens, and voluntarily to follow it as being accomplished by the wisest intelligence. For if you do so, you will never either blame the Gods, nor will you accuse them of neglecting you. And it is not possible for this to be done in any other way than by withdrawing from the things which are not in our power, and by placing the good and the evil only in those things which are in our power. For if you think that any of the things which are not in our power is good or bad, it is absolutely necessary that, when you do not obtain what you wish, and when you fall into those things which you do not wish, you will find fault and hate those who are the cause of them; for every animal is formed by nature to this, to fly from, and to turn from the things which appear harmful and the things which are the cause of the harm, but to follow and admire the things which are useful and the causes of the useful. It is impossible then for a person who thinks that he is harmed to be delighted with that which he thinks to be the cause of the harm, as it is also impossible to be pleased with the harm itself. For this reason also a father is reviled by his son, when he gives no part to his son of the things which are considered to be good: and it was this which made Polynices and Eteocles[148] enemies, the opinion that royal power was a good. It is for this reason that the cultivator of the earth reviles the Gods, for this reason the sailor does, and the merchant, and for this reason those who lose their wives and their children. For where the useful (your interest) is, there also piety is.[149] Consequently he who takes care to desire as he ought and to avoid (ἐκκλίνειν) as he ought, at the same time also cares after piety. But to make libations and to sacrifice and to offer first fruits according to the custom of our fathers, purely and not meanly nor carelessly nor scantily nor above our ability, is a thing which belongs to all to do.

XXXII

When you have recourse to divination, remember that you do not know how it will turn out, but that you are come to inquire from the diviner. But of what kind it is, you know when you come, if indeed you are a philosopher. For if it is any of the things which are not in our power, it is absolutely necessary that it must be neither good nor bad. Do not then bring to the diviner desire or aversion (ἔκκλισιν): if you do, you will approach him with fear. But having determined in your mind that everything which shall turn out (result) is indifferent, and does not concern you, and whatever it may be, for it will be in your power to use it well, and no man will hinder this, come then with

---

[148] See ii 22, 13, iv 5, 9.

[149] "It is plain enough that the philosopher does not say this, that the reckoning of our private advantage ought to be the sole origin and foundation of piety towards God." Schweig., and he proceeds to explain the sentence, which at first appears rather obscure. Perhaps Arrian intends to say that the feeling of piety coincides with the opinion of the useful, the profitable; and that the man who takes care to desire as he ought to do and to avoid as he ought to do, thus also cares after piety, and so he will secure his interest (the profitable) and he will not be discontented.
In i 27, 14 (p. 81) it is said ἐὰν μὴ ἐν τῷ αὐτῷ ᾖ τὸ εὐσεβὲς καὶ συμφέρον, οὐ δύναται σωφῆναι τὸ εὐσεβὲς ἔν τινι. This is what is said here (s. 31).

confidence to the Gods as your advisers. And then when any advice shall have been given, remember whom you have taken as advisers, and whom you will have neglected, if you do not obey them. And go to divination, as Socrates said that you ought, about those matters in which all the inquiry has reference to the result, and in which means are not given either by reason nor by any other art for knowing the thing which is the subject of the inquiry. Wherefore when we ought to share a friend's danger or that of our country, you must not consult the diviner whether you ought to share it. For even if the diviner shall tell you that the signs of the victims are unlucky, it is plain that this is a token of death or mutilation of part of the body or of exile. But reason prevails that even with these risks we should share the dangers of our friend and of our country. Therefore attend to the greater diviner, the Pythian God, who ejected from the temple him who did not assist his friend when he was being murdered.[150]

XXXIII

Immediately prescribe some character and some form to yourself, which you shall observe both when you are alone and when you meet with men.

And let silence be the general rule, or let only what is necessary be said, and in few words. And rarely and when the occasion calls we shall say something; but about none of the common subjects, not about gladiators, nor horse races, nor about athletes, nor about eating or drinking, which are the usual subjects; and especially not about men, as blaming them or praising them, or comparing them. If then you are able, bring over by your conversation the conversation of your associates to that which is proper; but if you should happen to be confined to the company of strangers, be silent.

Let not your laughter be much, nor on many occasions, nor excessive.

Refuse altogether to take an oath, if it is possible: if it is not, refuse as far as you are able.

Avoid banquets which are given by strangers[151] and by ignorant persons. But if ever there is occasion to join in them, let your attention be carefully fixed, that you slip not into the manners of the vulgar (the uninstructed). For you must

---

[150] The story is told by Aelian (iii c. 44), and by Simplicius in his commentary on the Enchiridion (p. 411, ed. Schweig.). Upton.
[151] "*Convivia cum hominibus extraneis et rudibus, discipline non imbutis*" is the Latin version.

know, that if your companion be impure, he also who keeps company with him must become impure, though he should happen to be pure.

Take (apply) the things which relate to the body as far as the bare use, as food, drink, clothing, house, and slaves: but exclude everything which is for show or luxury.

As to pleasure with women, abstain as far as you can before marriage: but if you do indulge in it, do it in the way which is conformable to custom.[152] Do not however be disagreeable to those who indulge in these pleasures, or reprove them; and do not often boast that you do not indulge in them yourself.

If a man has reported to you, that a certain person speaks ill of you, do not make any defence (answer) to what has been told you: but reply, The man did not know the rest of my faults, for he would not have mentioned these only.

It is not necessary to go to the theatres often: but if there is ever a proper occasion for going, do not show yourself as being a partisan of any man except yourself, that is, desire only that to be done which is done, and for him only to gain the prize who gains the prize; for in this way you will meet with no hindrance. But abstain entirely from shouts and laughter at any (thing or person), or violent emotions. And when you are come away, do not talk much about what has passed on the stage, except about that which may lead to your own improvement. For it is plain, if you do talk much that you admired the spectacle (more than you ought).[153]

Do not go to the hearing of certain persons' recitations nor visit them readily.[154] But if you do attend, observe gravity and sedateness, and also avoid making yourself disagreeable.

When you are going to meet with any person, and particularly one of those who are considered to be in a superior condition, place before yourself what Socrates or Zeno would have done in such circumstances, and you will have no difficulty in making a proper use of the occasion.

When you are going to any of those who are in great power, place before yourself that you will not find the man at home, that you will be excluded, that the door

---

[152] The text is ὡς νόμιμον: and the Latin explanation is *"qua fas eat uti; qua uti absque flagitio licet."*
[153] To admire (φαυμάζειν) is contrary to the precept of Epictetus; i 29, ii 6, iii 20. Upton.
[154] Such recitations were common at Rome, when authors read their works and invited persons to attend. These recitations are often mentioned in the letters of the younger Pliny. See Epictetus, iii 23.

will not be opened to you, that the man will not care about you. And if with all this it is your duty to visit him, bear what happens, and never say to yourself that it was not worth the trouble. For this is silly, and marks the character of a man who is offended by externals.

In company take care not to speak much and excessively about your own acts or dangers: for as it is pleasant to you to make mention of your own dangers, it is not so pleasant to others to hear what has happened to you. Take care also not to provoke laughter; for this is a slippery way towards vulgar habits, and is also adapted to diminish the respect of your neighbours. It is a dangerous habit also to approach obscene talk. When then anything of this kind happens, if there is a good opportunity, rebuke the man who has proceeded to this talk: but if there is not an opportunity, by your silence at least, and blushing and expression of dissatisfaction by your countenance, show plainly that you are displeased at such talk.

XXXIV

If you have received the impression (φαντασίαν) of any pleasure, guard yourself against being carried away by it; but let the thing wait for you, and allow yourself a certain delay on your own part. Then think of both times, of the time when you will enjoy the pleasure, and of the time after the enjoyment of the pleasure when you will repent and will reproach yourself. And set against these things how you will rejoice if you have abstained from the pleasure, and how you will commend yourself. But if it seem to you seasonable to undertake (do) the thing, take care that the charm of it, and the pleasure, and the attraction of it shall not conquer you: but set on the other side the consideration how much better it is to be conscious that you have gained this victory.

XXXV

When you have decided that a thing ought to be done and are doing it, never avoid being seen doing it, though the many shall form an unfavourable opinion about it. For if it is not right to do it, avoid doing the thing; but if it is right, why are you afraid of those who shall find fault wrongly?

XXXVI

As the proposition it is either day or it is night is of great importance for the disjunctive argument, but for the conjunctive is of no value,[155] so in a symposium (entertainment) to select the larger share is of great value for the body, but for the maintenance of the social feeling is worth nothing. When then you are eating with another, remember to look not only to the value for the body of the things set before you, but also to the value of the behaviour towards the host which ought to be observed.[156]

XXXVII

If you have assumed a character above your strength, you have both acted in this matter in an unbecoming way, and you have neglected that which you might have fulfilled.

XXXVIII

In walking about as you take care not to step on a nail or to sprain your foot, so take care not to damage your own ruling faculty: and if we observe this rule in every act, we shall undertake the act with more security.

XXXIX

The measure of possession (property) is to every man the body, as the foot is of the shoe.[157] If then you stand on this rule (the demands of the body), you will maintain the measure: but if you pass beyond it, you must then of necessity be hurried as it were down a precipice. As also in the matter of the shoe, if you go beyond the (necessities of the) foot, the shoe is gilded, then of a purple colour, then embroidered:[158] for there is no limit to that which has once passed the true measure.

---

[155] Compare i 25, 11, etc.

[156] See the note of Schweig. on xxxvi.

[157] *Cui non conveniet sua res, ut calceus olim,*
Si pede major erit, subvertet; si minor, uret.
Horat. Epp. i 10, 42, and Epp. i 7, 98.

[158] The word is κεντητόν "acu pictum," ornamented by needlework.

XL

Women forthwith from the age of fourteen[159] are called by the men mistresses (κυρίαι, dominae). Therefore since they see that there is nothing else that they can obtain, but only the power of lying with men, they begin to decorate themselves, and to place all their hopes in this. It is worth our while then to take care that they may know that they are valued (by men) for nothing else than appearing (being) decent and modest and discreet.

XLI

It is a mark of a mean capacity to spend much time on the things which concern the body, such as much exercise, much eating, much drinking, much easing of the body, much copulation. But these things should be done as subordinate things: and let all your care be directed to the mind.

XLII[160]

When any person treats you ill or speaks ill of you, remember that he does this or says this because he thinks that it is his duty. It is not possible then for him to follow that which seems right to you, but that which seems right to himself. Accordingly if he is wrong in his opinion, he is the person who is hurt, for he is the person who has been deceived; for if a man shall suppose the true conjunction[161] to be false, it is not the conjunction which is hindered, but the man who has been deceived about it. If you proceed then from these opinions, you will be mild in temper to him who reviles you: for say on each occasion, It seemed so to him.

XLIII

Everything has two handles, the one by which it may be borne, the other by which it may not. If your brother acts unjustly, do not lay hold of the act by that handle wherein he acts unjustly, for this is the handle which cannot be

---

[159] Fourteen was considered the age of puberty in Roman males, but in females the age of twelve (Justin. inst. I tit. 22). Compare Gaius, i 196.

[160] See Mrs. C.'s note, in which she says "Epictetus seems to be in part mistaken here," etc.; and I think that he is.

[161] τὸ ἀληφὲς συμπεπλεγμένον is rendered in the Latin by "verum conjunctum." Mrs. Carter renders it by "a true proposition," which I suppose to be the meaning.

borne: but lay hold of the other, that he is your brother, that he was nurtured with you, and you will lay hold of the thing by that handle by which it can be borne.

XLIV

These reasonings do not cohere: I am richer than you, therefore I am better than you; I am more eloquent than you, therefore I am better than you. On the contrary these rather cohere, I am richer than you, therefore my possessions are greater than yours: I am more eloquent than you, therefore my speech is superior to yours. But you are neither possession nor speech.

XLV

Does a man bathe quickly (early)? do not say that he bathes badly, but that he bathes quickly. Does a man drink much wine? do not say that he does this badly, but say that he drinks much. For before you shall have determined the opinion,[162] how do you know whether he is acting wrong? Thus it will not happen to you to comprehend some appearances which are capable of being comprehended, but to assent to others.

XLVI

On no occasion call yourself a philosopher, and do not speak much among the uninstructed about theorems (philosophical rules, precepts): but do that which follows from them. For example at a banquet do not say how a man ought to eat, but eat as you ought to eat. For remember that in this way Socrates[163] also altogether avoided ostentation: persons used to come to him and ask to be recommended by him to philosophers, and he used to take them to philosophers: so easily did he submit to being overlooked. Accordingly if any conversation should arise among uninstructed persons about any theorem, generally be silent; for there is great danger that you will immediately vomit up what you have not digested. And when a man shall say to you, that you know nothing, and you are not vexed, then be sure that you have begun the work (of philosophy). For even sheep do not vomit up their grass and show to the shepherds how

---

[162] Mrs. Carter translates this, "Unless you perfectly understand the principle [from which anyone acts]."
[163] See iii 23, 22; iv 8, 2.

much they have eaten; but when they have internally digested the pasture, they produce externally wool and milk. Do you also show not your theorems to the uninstructed, but show the acts which come from their digestion.

XLVII

When at a small cost you are supplied with everything for the body, do not be proud of this; nor, if you drink water, say on every occasion, I drink water. But consider first how much more frugal the poor are than we, and how much more enduring of labour. And if you ever wish to exercise yourself in labour and endurance, do it for yourself, and not for others: do not embrace statues.[164] But if you are ever very thirsty, take a draught of cold water, and spit it out, and tell no man.

XLVIII

The condition and characteristic of an uninstructed person is this: he never expects from himself profit (advantage) nor harm, but from externals. The condition and characteristic of a philosopher is this: he expects all advantage and all harm from himself. The signs (marks) of one who is making progress are these: he censures no man, he praises no man, he blames no man, he accuses no man, he says nothing about himself as if he were somebody or knew something; when he is impeded at all or hindered, he blames himself: if a man praises him, he ridicules the praiser to himself: if a man censures him, he makes no defence: he goes about like weak persons, being careful not to move any of the things which are placed, before they are firmly fixed: he removes all desire from himself, and he transfers aversion (ἔκκλισιν) to those things only of the things within our power which are contrary to nature: he employs a moderate movement towards everything: whether he is considered foolish or ignorant, he cares not: and in a word he watches himself as if he were an enemy and lying in ambush.

XLIX

When a man is proud because he can understand and explain the writings of Chrysippus, say to yourself, If Chrysippus had not written obscurely, this man would have had nothing to be proud of. But what is it that I wish? To understand

---

[164] See iii 12.

Nature and to follow it. I inquire therefore who is the interpreter: and when I have heard that it is Chrysippus, I come to him (the interpreter). But I do not understand what is written, and therefore I seek the interpreter. And so far there is yet nothing to be proud of. But when I shall have found the interpreter, the thing that remains is to use the precepts (the lessons). This itself is the only thing to be proud of. But if I shall admire the exposition, what else have I been made unless a grammarian instead of a philosopher? except in one thing, that I am explaining Chrysippus instead of Homer. When then any man says to me, Read Chrysippus to me, I rather blush, when I cannot show my acts like to and consistent with his words.

L

Whatever things (rules) are proposed[165] to you [for the conduct of life] abide by them, as if they were laws, as if you would be guilty of impiety if you transgressed any of them. And whatever any man shall say about you, do not attend to it: for this is no affair of yours.

LI

How long will you then still defer thinking yourself worthy of the best things, and in no matter transgressing the distinctive reason?[166] Have you accepted the theorems (rules), which it was your duty to agree to, and have you agreed to them? what teacher then do you still expect that you defer to him the correction of yourself? You are no longer a youth, but already a full-grown man. If then you are negligent and slothful, and are continually making procrastination after procrastination, and proposal (intention) after proposal, and fixing day after day, after which you will attend to yourself, you will not know that you are not making improvement, but you will continue ignorant (uninstructed) both while you live and till you die. Immediately then think it right to live as a full-grown man, and one who is making proficiency, and let everything which appears to you to be the best be to you a law which must not be transgressed. And if anything laborious, or pleasant or glorious or inglorious be presented to you, remember that now is the contest, now are the Olympic games, and

---

[165] This may mean "what is proposed to you by philosophers," and especially in this little book. Schweighaeuser thinks that it may mean "what you have proposed to yourself:" but he is inclined to understand it simply, "what is proposed above, or taught above."

[166] τὸν διαιροῦντα λόγον. "Eam partitioned rationis intelligo, qua initio dixit, Quaedam in potestate nostra esse, quaedam non esse." Wolf.

they cannot be deferred; and that it depends on one defeat and one giving way that progress is either lost or maintained. Socrates in this way became perfect, in all things improving himself, attending to nothing except to reason. But you, though you are not yet a Socrates, ought to live as one who wishes to be a Socrates.

LII

The first and most necessary place (part, τόπος) in philosophy is the use of theorems (precepts, φεωρήματα), for instance, that we must not lie: the second part is that of demonstrations, for instance, How is it proved that we ought not to lie: the third is that which is confirmatory of these two and explanatory, for example, How is this a demonstration? For what is demonstration, what is consequence, what is contradiction, what is truth, what is falsehood? The third part (topic) is necessary on account of the second, and the second on account of the first; but the most necessary and that on which we ought to rest is the first. But we do the contrary. For we spend our time on the third topic, and all our earnestness is about it: but we entirely neglect the first. Therefore we lie; but the demonstration that we ought not to lie we have ready to hand.

LIII

In everything (circumstance) we should hold these maxims ready to hand:

> Lead me, O Zeus, and thou O Destiny,
> The way that I am bid by you to go:
> To follow I am ready. If I choose not,
> I make myself a wretch, and still must follow.[167]

> But whoso nobly yields unto necessity,
> We hold him wise, and skill'd in things divine.[168]

---

[167] The first four verses are by the Stoic Cleanthes, the pupil of Zeno, and the teacher of Chrysippus. He was a native of Assus in Mysia; and Simplicius, who wrote his commentary on the Enchiridion in the sixth century, AD, saw even at this late period in Assus a beautiful statue of Cleanthes erected by a decree of the Roman senate in honour of this excellent man. (Simplicius, ed. Schweig. p. 522.)
[168] The two second verses are from a play of Euripides, a writer who has supplied more verses for quotation than any ancient tragedian.

And the third also:

> O Crito, if so it pleases the Gods, so let it be;
> Anytus and Melitus are able indeed to kill me, but they cannot harm me.[169]

---

[169] The third quotation is from the Criton of Plato. Socrates is the speaker. The last part is from the Apology of Plato, and Socrates is also the speaker. The words "and the third also," Schweighaeuser says, have been introduced from the commentary of Simplicius. Simplicius concludes his commentary thus: Epictetus connects the end with the beginning, which reminds us of what was said in the beginning, that the man who places the good and the evil among the things which are in our power, and not in externals, will neither be compelled by any man nor ever injured.

ON A HAPPY LIFE
ON THE SHORTNESS OF LIFE
ON PEACE OF MIND
ON PROVIDENCE

Lucius Annaeus Seneca

Translated by
Aubrey Stewart

ON A HAPPY LIFE

1

All men, brother Gallio, wish to live happily, but are dull at perceiving exactly what it is that makes life happy: and so far is it from being easy to attain the happiness that the more eagerly a man struggles to reach it the further he departs from it, if he takes the wrong road; for, since this leads in the opposite direction, his very swiftness carries him all the further away. We must therefore first define clearly what it is at which we aim: next we must consider by what path we may most speedily reach it, for on our journey itself, provided it be made in the right direction, we shall learn how much progress we have made each day, and how much nearer we are to the goal towards which our natural desires urge us. But as long as we wander at random, not following any guide except the shouts and discordant clamours of those who invite us to proceed in different directions, our short life will be wasted in useless roamings, even if we labour both day and night to get a good understanding. Let us not therefore decide whither we must tend, and by what path, without the advice of some experienced person who has explored the region which we are about to enter, because this journey is not subject to the same conditions as others; for in them some distinctly understood track and inquiries made of the natives make it impossible for us to go wrong, but here the most beaten and frequented tracks are those which lead us most astray. Nothing, therefore, is more important than that we should not, like sheep, follow the flock that has gone before us, and thus proceed not whither we ought, but whither the rest are going. Now nothing gets us into greater troubles than our subservience to common rumour, and our habit of thinking that those things are best which are most generally received as such, of taking many counterfeits for truly good things, and of living not by reason but by imitation of others. This is the cause of those great heaps into which men rush till they are piled one upon another. In a great crush of people, when the crowd presses upon itself, no one can fall without drawing someone else down upon him, and those who go before cause the destruction of those who follow them. You may observe the same thing in human life: no one can merely go wrong by himself, but he must become both the cause and adviser of another's wrong doing. It is harmful to follow the march of those who go before us, and since everyone had rather believe another than form his own opinion, we never pass a deliberate judgment upon life, but some traditional error always entangles us and brings us to ruin, and we perish because we follow other men's examples: we should be cured of this if we were to disengage ourselves from the herd; but as it is, the mob is ready to fight against reason in defence of its own mistake. Consequently the same thing happens as at elections, where, when the fickle breeze of popular favour has veered round, those who have been chosen consuls and praetors are viewed with admiration by the very men who made them so. That we should all approve and disapprove of the same things is the end of every decision which is given according to the voice of the majority.

2

When we are considering a happy life, you cannot answer me as though after a division of the House, "This view has most supporters;" because for that very reason it is the worse of the two: matters do not stand so well with mankind that the majority should prefer the better course: the more people do a thing the worse it is likely to be. Let us therefore inquire, not what is most commonly done, but what is best for us to do, and what will establish us in the possession of undying happiness, not what is approved of by the vulgar, the worst possible exponents of truth. By "the vulgar" I mean both those who wear woollen cloaks and those who wear crowns;[170] for I do not regard the colour of the clothes with which they are covered: I do not trust my eyes to tell me what a man is: I have a better and more trustworthy light by which I can distinguish what is true from what is false: let the mind find out what is good for the mind. If a man ever allows his mind some breathing space and has leisure for communing with himself, what truths he will confess to himself, after having been put to the torture by his own self! He will say, "Whatever I have hitherto done I wish were undone: when I think over what I have said, I envy dumb people: whatever I have longed for seems to have been what my enemies would pray might befall me: good heaven, how far more endurable what I have feared seems to be than what I have lusted after. I have been at enmity with many men, and have changed my dislike of them into friendship, if friendship can exist between bad men: yet

---

[170] Lipsius's conjecture, "those who are dressed in white as well as those who are dressed in coloured clothes," alluding to the white robes of candidates for office, seems reasonable.

I have not yet become reconciled to myself. I have striven with all my strength to raise myself above the common herd, and to make myself remarkable for some talent: what have I effected save to make myself a mark for the arrows of my enemies, and show those who hate me where to wound me? Do you see those who praise your eloquence, who covet your wealth, who court your favour, or who vaunt your power? All these either are, or, which comes to the same thing, may be your enemies: the number of those who envy you is as great as that of those who admire you; why do I not rather seek for some good thing which I can use and feel, not one which I can show? these good things which men gaze at in wonder, which they crowd to see, which one points out to another with speechless admiration, are outwardly brilliant, but within are miseries to those who possess them."

3

Let us seek for some blessing, which does not merely look fine, but is sound and good throughout alike, and most beautiful in the parts which are least seen: let us unearth this. It is not far distant from us; it can be discovered: all that is necessary is to know whither to stretch out your hand: but, as it is, we behave as though we were in the dark, and reach out beyond what is nearest to us, striking as we do so against the very things that we want. However, that I may not draw you into digressions, I will pass over the opinions of other philosophers, because it would take a long time to state and confute them all: take ours. When, however, I say "ours," I do not bind myself to any one of the chiefs of the Stoic school, for I too have a right to form my own opinion. I shall, therefore, follow the authority of some of them, but shall ask some others to discriminate their meaning:[171] perhaps, when after having reported all their opinions, I am asked for my own, I shall impugn none of my predecessors' decisions, and shall say, "I will also add somewhat to them." Meanwhile I follow nature, which is a point upon which every one of the Stoic philosophers are agreed: true wisdom consists in not departing from nature and in moulding our conduct according to her laws and model. A happy life, therefore, is one which is in accordance with its own nature,

---

[171] The Latin words are literally "to divide" their vote, that is, "to separate things of different kinds comprised in a single vote so that they might be voted for separately."—Andrews.
"Sénèque fait allusion ici à une coutume pratiquée dans les assemblés du Sénat; et il nous explique lui-même ailleurs d'un manière très claire: 'Si quelqu'un dans le Sénat,' dit il, 'ouvre un avis, dont une partie me convienne, je le somme de la détacher du reste, et j'y adhère.'"
Ep. 21—La Grange.

and cannot be brought about unless in the first place the mind be sound and remain so without interruption, and next, be bold and vigorous, enduring all things with most admirable courage, suited to the times in which it lives, careful of the body and its appurtenances, yet not troublesomely careful. It must also set due value upon all the things which adorn our lives, without overestimating any one of them, and must be able to enjoy the bounty of Fortune without becoming her slave. You understand without my mentioning it that an unbroken calm and freedom ensue, when we have driven away all those things which either excite us or alarm us: for in the place of sensual pleasures and those slight perishable matters which are connected with the basest crimes, we thus gain an immense, unchangeable, equable joy, together with peace, calmness and greatness of mind, and kindliness: for all savageness is a sign of weakness.

4

Our highest good may also be defined otherwise; that is to say, the same idea may be expressed in different language. Just as the same army may at one time be extended more widely, at another contracted into a smaller compass, and may either be curved towards the wings by a depression in the line of the centre, or drawn up in a straight line, while, in whatever figure it be arrayed, its strength and loyalty remain unchanged; so also our definition of the highest good may in some cases be expressed diffusely and at great length, while in others it is put into a short and concise form. Thus, it will come to the same thing, if I say, "The highest good is a mind which despises the accidents of fortune, and takes pleasure in virtue": or, "It is an unconquerable strength of mind, knowing the world well, gentle in its dealings, showing great courtesy and consideration for those with whom it is brought into contact." Or we may choose to define it by calling that man happy who knows good and bad only in the form of good or bad minds: who worships honour, and is satisfied with his own virtue, who is neither puffed up by good fortune nor cast down by evil fortune, who knows no other good than that which he is able to bestow upon himself, whose real pleasure lies in despising pleasures. If you choose to pursue this digression further, you can put this same idea into many other forms, without impairing or weakening its meaning: for what prevents our saying that a happy life consists in a mind which is free, upright, undaunted, and steadfast, beyond the influence of fear or desire, which thinks nothing good except honour, and nothing bad except shame, and regards everything else as a mass of mean details which can neither add anything to nor take anything away from the happiness of life, but which come and go without either increasing or diminishing the highest good? A man of these principles, whether he will or no, must be accompanied by a continual cheerfulness, a high happiness, which comes indeed from on high because he delights in what he has, and desires no greater pleasures than those which his home affords. Is he not right in allowing these to turn the scale against petty, ridiculous and shortlived movements of his wretched body? on the day on which he becomes proof against pleasure he also becomes proof against pain. See, on the other hand, how evil and guilty a slavery the man is forced to serve who is dominated in turn by pleasures and pains, those most untrustworthy and passionate of masters. We must, therefore, escape from them into freedom. This nothing will bestow upon us save contempt of fortune: but if we attain to this, then there will dawn upon us those invaluable blessings, the repose of a mind that is at rest in a safe haven, its lofty imaginings, its great and steady delight at casting out errors and learning to know the truth, its courtesy, and its cheerfulness, in all of which we shall take delight, not regarding them as good things, but as proceeding from the proper good of man.

5

Since I have begun to make my definitions without a too strict adherence to the letter, a man may be called "happy" who, thanks to reason, has ceased either to hope or to fear: but rocks also feel neither fear nor sadness, nor do cattle, yet no one would call those things happy which cannot comprehend what happiness is. With them you may class men whose dull nature and want of self-knowledge reduces them to the level of cattle, mere animals: there is no difference between the one and the other, because the latter have no reason, while the former have only a corrupted form of it, crooked and cunning to their own hurt. For no one can be styled happy who is beyond the influence of truth: and consequently a happy life is unchangeable, and is founded upon a true and trustworthy discernment; for the mind is uncontaminated and freed from all evils only when it is able to escape not merely from wounds but also from scratches, when it will always be able to maintain the position which it has taken up, and defend it even against the angry assaults of Fortune: for with regard to sensual pleasures, though they were to surround one on every side, and use every means of assault, trying to win over the mind by caresses and making trial of every conceivable stratagem to attract either our entire selves or our separate parts, yet what mortal that retains any traces of human origin would wish to be tickled day and night, and, neglecting his mind, to devote himself to bodily enjoyments?

6

"But," says our adversary, "the mind also will have pleasures of its own." Let it have them, then, and let it sit in judgment over luxury and pleasures; let it indulge itself to the full in all those matters which give sensual delights: then let it look back upon what it enjoyed before, and with all those faded sensualities fresh in its memory let it rejoice and look eagerly forward to those other pleasures which it experienced long ago, and intends to experience again, and while the body lies in helpless repletion in the present, let it send its thoughts onward towards the future, and take stock of its hopes: all this will make it appear, in my opinion, yet more wretched, because it is insanity to choose evil instead of good: now no insane person can be happy, and no one can be sane if he regards what is injurious as the highest good and strives to obtain it. The happy man, therefore, is he who can make a right judgment in all things: he is happy who in his present circumstances, whatever they may be, is satisfied and on friendly terms with the conditions of his life. That man is happy, whose reason recommends to him the whole posture of his affairs.

7

Even those very people who declare the highest good to be in the belly, see what a dishonourable position they have assigned to it: and therefore they say that pleasure cannot be parted from virtue, and that no one can either live honourably without living cheerfully, nor yet live cheerfully without living honourably. I do not see how these very different matters can have any connection with one another. What is there, I pray you, to prevent virtue existing apart from pleasure? of course the reason is that all good things derive their origin from virtue, and therefore even those things which you cherish and seek for come originally from its roots. Yet, if they were entirely inseparable, we should not see some things to be pleasant, but not honourable, and others most honourable indeed, but hard and only to be attained by suffering. Add to this, that pleasure visits the basest lives, but virtue cannot coexist with an evil life; yet some unhappy people are not without pleasure, nay, it is owing to pleasure itself that they are unhappy; and this could not take place if pleasure had any connection with virtue, whereas virtue is often without pleasure, and never stands in need of it. Why do you put together two things which are unlike and even incompatible one with another? virtue is a lofty quality, sublime, royal, unconquerable, untiring: pleasure is low, slavish, weakly, perishable; its haunts and homes are the brothel and the tavern. You will meet virtue in the temple, the marketplace, the senate house, manning the walls, covered with dust, sunburnt, horny-handed: you will find pleasure skulking out of sight, seeking for shady nooks at the public baths, hot chambers, and places which dread the visits of the aedile, soft, effeminate, reeking of wine and perfumes, pale or perhaps painted and made up with cosmetics. The highest good is immortal: it knows no ending, and does not admit of either satiety or regret: for a right-thinking mind never alters or becomes hateful to itself, nor do the best things ever undergo any change: but pleasure dies at the very moment when it charms us most: it has no great scope, and therefore it soon cloys and wearies us, and fades away as soon as its first impulse is over: indeed, we cannot depend upon anything whose nature is to change. Consequently it is not even possible that there should be any solid substance in that which comes and goes so swiftly, and which perishes by the very exercise of its own functions, for it arrives at a point at which it ceases to be, and even while it is beginning always keeps its end in view.

8

What answer are we to make to the reflection that pleasure belongs to good and bad men alike, and that bad men take as much delight in their shame as good men in noble things? This was why the ancients bade us lead the highest, not the most pleasant life, in order that pleasure might not be the guide but the companion of a right-thinking and honourable mind; for it is Nature whom we ought to make our guide: let our reason watch her, and be advised by her. To live happily, then, is the same thing as to live according to Nature: what this may be, I will explain. If we guard the endowments of the body and the advantages of nature with care and fearlessness, as things soon to depart and given to us only for a day; if we do not fall under their dominion, nor allow ourselves to become the slaves of what is no part of our own being; if we assign to all bodily pleasures and external delights the same position which is held by auxiliaries and light-armed troops in a camp; if we make them our servants, not our masters—then and then only are they of value to our minds. A man should be unbiased and not to be conquered by external things: he ought to admire himself alone, to feel confidence in his own spirit, and so to order his life as to be ready alike for good or for bad fortune. Let not his confidence be without knowledge, nor his knowledge without steadfastness: let him always abide by what he has once determined, and let there be no erasure in his doctrines. It will be understood, even though I append it not, that such a man will be tranquil and composed in his demeanour, high-minded and courteous in his actions. Let reason be encouraged by the senses to seek for the truth, and draw its first principles from thence: indeed it has no other base of operations or place from which to start in pursuit of truth: it must fall back upon itself. Even the all-embracing universe and God who is its guide extends himself forth into outward things, and yet altogether returns from all sides back to himself. Let our mind do the same thing: when, following its bodily senses it has by means of them sent itself forth into the things of the outward world, let it remain still their master and its own. By this means we shall obtain a strength and an ability which are united and allied together, and shall derive from it that reason which never halts between two opinions, nor is dull in forming its perceptions, beliefs, or convictions. Such a mind, when it has ranged itself in order, made its various parts agree together, and, if I may so express myself, harmonized them, has attained to the highest good: for it has nothing evil or hazardous remaining, nothing to shake it or make it stumble: it will do everything under the guidance of its own will, and nothing unexpected will befall it, but whatever may be done by it will turn out well, and that, too, readily and easily, without the doer having recourse to any underhand devices: for slow and hesitating action are the signs of discord and want of settled purpose. You may, then, boldly declare that the highest good is singleness of mind: for where agreement and unity are, there must the virtues be: it is the vices that are at war one with another.

9

"But," says our adversary, "you yourself only practise virtue because you hope to obtain some pleasure from it." In the first place, even though virtue may afford us pleasure, still we do not seek after her on that account: for she does not bestow this, but bestows this to boot, nor is this the end for which she labours, but her labour wins this also, although it be directed to another end. As in a tilled-field, when ploughed for corn, some flowers are found amongst it, and yet, though these posies may charm the eye, all this labour was not spent in order to produce them—the man who sowed the field had another object in view, he gained this over and above it—so pleasure is not the reward or the cause of virtue, but comes in addition to it; nor do we choose virtue because she gives us pleasure, but she gives us pleasure also if we choose her. The highest good lies in the act of choosing her, and in the attitude of the noblest minds, which when once it has fulfilled its function and established itself within its own limits has attained to the highest good, and needs nothing more: for there is nothing outside of the whole, any more than there is anything beyond the end. You are mistaken, therefore, when you ask me what it is on account of which I seek after virtue: for you are seeking for something above the highest. Do you ask what I seek from virtue? I answer, Herself: for she has nothing better; she is her own reward. Does this not appear great enough, when I tell you that the highest good is an unyielding strength of mind, wisdom, magnanimity, sound judgment, freedom, harmony, beauty? Do you still ask me for something greater, of which these may be regarded as the attributes? Why do you talk of pleasures to me? I am seeking to find what is good for man, not for his belly; why, cattle and whales have larger ones than he.

10

"You purposely misunderstand what I say," says he, "for I too say that no one can live pleasantly unless he lives honorably also, and this cannot be the case with dumb animals who measure the extent of their happiness by that of their food. I loudly and publicly proclaim that what I call a pleasant life cannot exist without the addition of virtue." Yet who does not know that the greatest fools drink the deepest of those pleasures of yours? or that vice is full of enjoyments, and that the mind itself suggests to itself many perverted, vicious forms of pleasure?— in the first place arrogance, excessive self-esteem, swaggering precedence over other men, a shortsighted, nay, a blind devotion to his own interests, dissolute luxury, excessive delight springing from the most trifling and childish causes, and also talkativeness, pride that takes a pleasure in insulting others, sloth, and the decay of a dull mind which goes to sleep over itself. All these are dissipated by virtue, which plucks a man by the ear, and measures the value of pleasures before she permits them to be used; nor does she set much store by those which she allows to pass current, for she merely allows their use, and her cheerfulness is not due to her use of them, but to her moderation in using them. "Yet when moderation lessens pleasure, it impairs the highest good." You devote yourself to pleasures, I check them; you indulge in pleasure, I use it; you think that it is the highest good, I do not even think it to be good: for the sake of pleasure I do nothing, you do everything.

11

When I say that I do nothing for the sake of pleasure, I allude to that wise man, whom alone you admit to be capable of pleasure: now I do not call a man wise who is overcome by anything, let alone by pleasure: yet, if engrossed by pleasure, how will he resist toil, danger, want, and all the ills which surround and threaten the life of man? How will he bear the sight of death or of pain? How will he endure the tumult of the world, and make head against so many most active foes, if he be conquered by so effeminate an antagonist? He will do whatever pleasure advises him: well, do you not see how many things it will advise him to do? "It will not," says our adversary, "be able to give him any bad advice, because it is combined with virtue?" Again, do you not see what a poor kind of highest good that must be which requires a guardian to ensure its being good at all? and how is virtue to rule pleasure if she follows it, seeing that to follow is the duty of a subordinate, to rule that of a commander? do you put that which commands in the background? According to your school, virtue has the dignified office of preliminary tester of pleasures. We shall, however, see whether virtue still remains virtue among those who treat her with such contempt, for if she leaves her proper station she can no longer keep her proper name: in the meanwhile, to keep to the point, I will show you many men beset by pleasures, men upon whom Fortune has showered all her gifts, whom you must needs admit to be bad men. Look at Nomentanus and Apicius, who digest all the good things, as they call them, of the sea and land, and review upon their tables the whole animal kingdom. Look at them as they lie on beds of roses gloating over their banquet, delighting their ears with music, their eyes with exhibitions, their palates with flavours: their whole bodies are titillated with soft and soothing applications, and lest even their nostrils should be idle, the very place in which they solemnized[172] the rites of luxury is scented with various perfumes. You will say that these men live in the midst of pleasures. Yet they are ill at ease, because they take pleasure in what is not good.

12

"They are ill at ease," replies he, "because many things arise which distract their thoughts, and their minds are disquieted by conflicting opinions." I admit that this is true: still these very men, foolish, inconsistent, and certain to feel remorse as they are, do nevertheless receive great pleasure, and we must allow that in so doing they are as far from feeling any trouble as they are from forming a right judgment, and that, as is the case with many people, they are possessed by a merry madness, and laugh while they rave. The pleasures of wise men, on the other hand, are mild, decorous, verging on dullness, kept under restraint and scarcely noticeable, and are neither invited to come nor received with honour when they come of their own accord, nor are they welcomed with any delight by those whom they visit, who mix them up with their lives and fill up empty spaces

---

[172] *Parentatur* seems to mean where an offering is made to luxury—where they sacrifice to luxury. Perfumes were used at funerals. Lipsius suggests that these feasts were like funerals because the guests were carried away from them dead drunk.

with them, like an amusing farce in the intervals of serious business. Let them no longer, then, join incongruous matters together, or connect pleasure with virtue, a mistake whereby they court the worst of men. The reckless profligate, always in liquor and belching out the fumes of wine, believes that he lives with virtue, because he knows that he lives with pleasure, for he hears it said that pleasure cannot exist apart from virtue; consequently he dubs his vices with the title of wisdom and parades all that he ought to conceal. So, men are not encouraged by Epicurus to run riot, but the vicious hide their excesses in the lap of philosophy, and flock to the schools in which they hear the praises of pleasure. They do not consider how sober and temperate—for so, by Hercules, I believe it to be—that "pleasure" of Epicurus is, but they rush at his mere name, seeking to obtain some protection and cloak for their vices. They lose, therefore, the one virtue which their evil life possessed, that of being ashamed of doing wrong: for they praise what they used to blush at, and boast of their vices. Thus modesty can never reassert itself, when shameful idleness is dignified with an honourable name. The reason why that praise which your school lavishes upon pleasure is so hurtful, is because the honourable part of its teaching passes unnoticed, but the degrading part is seen by all.

13

I myself believe, though my Stoic comrades would be unwilling to hear me say so, that the teaching of Epicurus was upright and holy, and even, if you examine it narrowly, stern: for this much talked of pleasure is reduced to a very narrow compass, and he bids pleasure submit to the same law which we bid virtue do—I mean, to obey nature. Luxury, however, is not satisfied with what is enough for nature. What is the consequence? Whoever thinks that happiness consists in lazy sloth, and alternations of gluttony and profligacy, requires a good patron for a bad action, and when he has become an Epicurean, having been led to do so by the attractive name of that school, he follows, not the pleasure which he there hears spoken of, but that which he brought thither with him, and, having learned to think that his vices coincide with the maxims of that philosophy, he indulges in them no longer timidly and in dark corners, but boldly in the face of day. I will not, therefore, like most of our school, say that the sect of Epicurus is the teacher of crime, but what I say is: it is ill spoken of, it has a bad reputation, and yet it does not deserve it. "Who can know this without having been admitted to its inner mysteries?" Its very outside gives opportunity for scandal, and encourages men's baser desires: it is like a brave man dressed in a woman's gown: your chastity is assured, your manhood is safe, your body is submitted to nothing disgraceful, but your hand holds a drum (like a priest of Cybele). Choose, then, some honourable superscription for your school, some writing which shall in itself arouse the mind: that which at present stands over your door has been invented by the vices. He who ranges himself on the side of virtue gives thereby a proof of a noble disposition: he who follows pleasure appears to be weakly, worn out, degrading his manhood, likely to fall into infamous vices unless someone discriminates his pleasures for him, so that he may know which remain within the bounds of natural desire, which are frantic and boundless, and become all the more insatiable the more they are satisfied. But come! let virtue lead the way: then every step will be safe. Too much pleasure is hurtful: but with virtue we need fear no excess of any kind, because moderation is contained in virtue herself. That which is injured by its own extent cannot be a good thing: besides, what better guide can there be than reason for beings endowed with a reasoning nature? so if this combination pleases you, if you are willing to proceed to a happy life thus accompanied, let virtue lead the way, let pleasure follow and hang about the body like a shadow: it is the part of a mind incapable of great things to hand over virtue, the highest of all qualities, as a handmaid to pleasure.

14

Let virtue lead the way and bear the standard: we shall have pleasure for all that, but we shall be her masters and controllers; she may win some concessions from us, but will not force us to do anything. On the contrary, those who have permitted pleasure to lead the van, have neither one nor the other: for they lose virtue altogether, and yet they do not possess pleasure, but are possessed by it, and are either tortured by its absence or choked by its excess, being wretched if deserted by it, and yet more wretched if overwhelmed by it, like those who are caught in the shoals of the Syrtes and at one time are left on dry ground and at another tossed on the flowing waves. This arises from an exaggerated want of self-control, and a hidden love of evil: for it is dangerous for one who seeks after evil instead of good to attain his object. As we hunt wild beasts with toil and peril, and even when they are caught find them an anxious possession, for they often tear their keepers to pieces, even so are great pleasures: they turn out to be great evils and take their owners prisoner. The more numerous and the greater they are, the more inferior and the slave of more masters does that man become whom the vulgar call a happy man. I may even press this analogy further: as the man who tracks wild animals to their lairs, and who sets great store on—

"Seeking with snares the wandering brutes to noose,"

and

"Making their hounds the spacious glade surround,"

that he may follow their tracks, neglects far more desirable things, and leaves many duties unfulfilled, so he who pursues pleasure postpones everything to it, disregards that first essential, liberty, and sacrifices it to his belly; nor does he buy pleasure for himself, but sells himself to pleasure.

15

"But what," asks our adversary, "is there to hinder virtue and pleasure being combined together, and a highest good being thus formed, so that honour and pleasure may be the same thing?" Because nothing except what is honourable can form a part of honour, and the highest good would lose its purity if it were to see within itself anything unlike its own better part. Even the joy which arises from virtue, although it be a good thing, yet is not a part of absolute good, any more than cheerfulness or peace of mind, which are indeed good things, but which merely follow the highest good, and do not contribute to its perfection, although they are generated by the noblest causes. Whoever on the other hand forms an alliance, and that, too, a one-sided one, between virtue and pleasure, clogs whatever strength the one may possess by the weakness of the other, and sends liberty under the yoke, for liberty can only remain unconquered as long as she knows nothing more valuable than herself: for he begins to need the help of Fortune, which is the most utter slavery: his life becomes anxious, full of suspicion, timorous, fearful of accidents, waiting in agony for critical moments of time. You do not afford virtue a solid immoveable base if you bid it stand on what is unsteady: and what can be so unsteady as dependence on mere chance, and the vicissitudes of the body and of those things which act on the body? How can such a man obey God and receive everything which comes to pass in a cheerful spirit, never complaining of fate, and putting a good construction upon everything that befalls him, if he be agitated by the petty pinpricks of pleasures and pains? A man cannot be a good protector of his country, a good avenger of her wrongs, or a good defender of his friends, if he be inclined to pleasures. Let the highest good, then, rise to that height from whence no force can dislodge it, whither neither pain can ascend, nor hope, nor fear, nor anything else that can impair the authority of the "highest good." Thither virtue alone can make her way: by her aid that hill must be climbed: she will bravely stand her ground and endure whatever may befall her not only resignedly, but even willingly: she will know that all hard times come in obedience to natural laws, and like a good soldier she will bear wounds, count scars, and when transfixed and dying will yet adore the general for whom she falls: she will bear in mind the old maxim, "Follow God." On the other hand, he who grumbles and complains and bemoans himself is nevertheless forcibly obliged to obey orders, and is dragged away, however much against his will, to carry them out: yet what madness is it to be dragged rather than to follow? as great, by Hercules, as it is folly and ignorance of one's true position to grieve because one has not got something or because something has caused us rough treatment, or to be surprised or indignant at those ills which befall good men as well as bad ones, I mean diseases, deaths, illnesses, and the other cross accidents of human life. Let us bear with magnanimity whatever the system of the universe makes it needful for us to bear: we are all bound by this oath: "To bear the ills of mortal life, and to submit with a good grace to what we cannot avoid." We have been born into a monarchy: our liberty is to obey God.

16

True happiness, therefore, consists in virtue: and what will this virtue bid you do? Not to think anything bad or good which is connected neither with virtue nor with wickedness: and in the next place, both to endure unmoved the assaults of evil, and, as far as is right, to form a god out of what is good. What reward does she promise you for this campaign? an enormous one, and one that raises you to the level of the gods: you shall be subject to no restraint and to no want; you shall be free, safe, unhurt; you shall fail in nothing that you attempt; you shall be debarred from nothing; everything shall turn out according to your wish; no misfortune shall befall you; nothing shall happen to you except what you expect and hope for. "What! does virtue alone suffice to make you happy?" why, of course, consummate and godlike virtue such as this not only suffices, but more than suffices: for when a man is placed beyond the reach of any desire, what can he possibly lack? if all that he needs is concentred in himself, how can he require anything from without? He, however, who is only on the road to virtue, although he may have made great progress along it, nevertheless needs some favour from Fortune while he is still struggling among mere human interests, while he is untying that knot, and all the bonds which bind him to mortality. What, then, is the difference between them? it is that some are tied more or less tightly by these bonds, and some have even tied themselves with them as well; whereas he who has made progress towards the upper regions and raised himself upwards drags a looser chain, and though not yet free, is yet as good as free.

17

If, therefore, any one of those dogs who yelp at philosophy were to say, as they are wont to do, "Why, then, do you talk so much more bravely than you live? why do you check your words in the presence of your superiors, and consider money to be a necessary implement: why are you disturbed when you sustain losses, and weep on hearing of the death of your wife or your friend? Why do you pay regard to common rumour, and feel annoyed by calumnious gossip? why is your estate more elaborately kept than its natural use requires? why do you not dine according to your own maxims? why is your furniture smarter than it need be? why do you drink wine that is older than yourself? why are your grounds laid out? Why do you plant trees which afford nothing except shade? why does your wife wear in her ears the price of a rich man's house? why are your children at school dressed in costly clothes? why is it a science to wait upon you at table? why is your silver plate not set down anyhow or at random, but skillfully disposed in regular order, with a superintendent to preside over the carving of the viands?" Add to this, if you like, the questions "Why do you own property beyond the seas? why do you own more than you know of? it is a shame to you not to know your slaves by sight: for you must be very neglectful of them if you only own a few, or very extravagant if you have too many for your memory to retain." I will add some reproaches afterwards, and will bring more accusations against myself than you think of: for the present I will make you the following answer. "I am not a wise man, and I will not be one in order to feed your spite: so do not require me to be on a level with the best of men, but merely to be better than the worst: I am satisfied, if every day I take away something from my vices and correct my faults. I have not arrived at perfect soundness of mind, indeed, I never shall arrive at it: I compound palliatives rather than remedies for my gout, and am satisfied if it comes at rarer interval—and does not shoot so painfully. Compared with your feet, which are lame, I am a racer." I make this speech, not on my own behalf, for I am steeped in vices of every kind, but on behalf of one who has made some progress in virtue.

18

"You talk one way," objects our adversary, "and live another." You most spiteful of creatures, you who always show the bitterest hatred to the best of men, this reproach was flung at Plato, at Epicurus, at Zeno: for all these declared how they ought to live, not how they did live. I speak of virtue, not of myself, and when I blame vices, I blame my own first of all: when I have the power, I shall live as I ought to do: spite, however deeply steeped in venom, shall not keep me back from what is best: that poison itself with which you bespatter others, with which you choke yourselves, shall not hinder me from continuing to praise that life which I do not, indeed, lead, but which I know I ought to lead, from loving virtue and from following after her, albeit a long way behind her and with halting gait. Am I to expect that evil speaking will respect anything, seeing that it respected neither Rutilius nor Cato? Will anyone care about being thought too rich by men for whom Diogenes the Cynic was not poor enough? That most energetic philosopher fought against all the desires of the body, and was poorer even than the other Cynics, in that besides having given up possessing anything he had also given up asking for anything: yet they reproached him for not being sufficiently in want: as though forsooth it were poverty, not virtue, of which he professed knowledge.

19

They say that Diodorus, the Epicurean philosopher, who within these last few days put an end to his life with his own hand, did not act according to the precepts of Epicurus, in cutting his throat: some choose to regard this act as the result of madness, others of recklessness; he, meanwhile, happy and filled with the consciousness of his own goodness, has borne testimony to himself by his manner of departing from life, has commended the repose of a life spent at anchor in a safe harbour, and has said what you do not like to hear, because you too ought to do it.

"I've lived, I've run the race which Fortune set me."

You argue about the life and death of another, and yelp at the name of men whom some peculiarly noble quality has rendered great, just as tiny curs do at the approach of strangers: for it is to your interest that no one should appear to be good, as if virtue in another were a reproach to all your crimes. You enviously compare the glories of others with your own dirty actions, and do not understand how greatly to your disadvantage it is to venture to do so: for if they who follow after virtue be greedy, lustful, and fond of power, what must you be, who hate the very name of virtue? You say that no one acts up to his professions, or lives according to the standard which he sets up in his discourses: what wonder, seeing that the words which they speak are brave, gigantic, and able to weather all the storms which wreck mankind, whereas they themselves are struggling to tear themselves away from crosses into which each one of you is driving his own nail. Yet men who are crucified hang from one single pole, but these who punish themselves are divided between as many crosses as they have lusts, but yet are given to evil speaking, and are so magnificent in their contempt of the vices of others that I should suppose that they had none of their own, were it not that some criminals when on the gibbet spit upon the spectators.

20

"Philosophers do not carry into effect all that they teach." No; but they effect much good by their teaching, by the noble thoughts which they conceive in their minds: would, indeed, that they could act up to their talk: what could be happier than they would be? but in the meanwhile you have no right to despise good sayings and hearts full of good thoughts. Men deserve praise for engaging in profitable studies, even though they stop short of producing any results. Why need we wonder if those who begin to climb a steep path do not succeed in ascending it very high? yet, if you be a man, look with respect on those who attempt great things, even though they fall. It is the act of a generous spirit to proportion its efforts not to its own strength but to that of human nature, to entertain lofty aims, and to conceive plans which are too vast to be carried into execution even by those who are endowed with gigantic intellects, who appoint for themselves the following rules: "I will look upon death or upon a comedy with the same expression of countenance: I will submit to labours, however great they may be, supporting the strength of my body by that of my mind: I will despise riches when I have them as much as when I have them not; if they be elsewhere I will not be more gloomy, if they sparkle around me I will not be more lively than I should otherwise be: whether Fortune comes or goes I will take no notice of her: I will view all lands as though they belong to me, and my own as though they belonged to all mankind: I will so live as to remember that I was born for others, and will thank Nature on this account: for in what fashion could she have done better for me? she has given me alone to all, and all to me alone. Whatever I may possess, I will neither hoard it greedily nor squander it recklessly. I will think that I have no possessions so real as those which I have given away to deserving people: I will not reckon benefits by their magnitude or number, or by anything except the value set upon them by the receiver: I never will consider a gift to be a large one if it be bestowed upon a worthy object. I will do nothing because of public opinion, but everything because of conscience: whenever I do anything alone by myself I will believe that the eyes of the Roman people are upon me while I do it. In eating and drinking my object shall be to quench the desires of Nature, not to fill and empty my belly. I will be agreeable with my friends, gentle and mild to my foes: I will grant pardon before I am asked for it, and will meet the wishes of honourable men half way: I will bear in mind that the world is my native city, that its governors are the gods, and that they stand above and around me, criticizing whatever I do or say. Whenever either Nature demands my breath again, or reason bids me dismiss it, I will quit this life, calling all to witness that I have loved a good conscience, and good pursuits; that no one's freedom, my own least of all, has been impaired through me." He who sets up these as the rules of his life will soar aloft and strive to make his way to the gods: of a truth, even though he fails, yet he

"Fails in a high emprise."[173]

But you, who hate both virtue and those who practise it, do nothing at which we need be surprised, for sickly lights cannot bear the sun, nocturnal creatures avoid the brightness of day, and at its first dawning become bewildered and all betake themselves to their dens together: creatures that fear the light hide themselves in crevices. So croak away, and exercise your miserable tongues in reproaching good men: open wide your jaws, bite hard: you will break many teeth before you make any impression.

21

"But how is it that this man studies philosophy and nevertheless lives the life of a rich man? Why does he say that wealth ought to be despised and yet possess it? that life should be despised, and yet live? that health should be despised, and yet guard it with the utmost care, and wish it to be as good as possible? Does he consider banishment to be an empty name, and say, 'What evil is there in changing one country for another?' and yet, if permitted, does he not grow old in his native land? does he declare that there is no difference between a longer and a shorter time, and yet, if he be not prevented, lengthen out his life and flourish in a green old age?" His answer is, that these things ought to be despised, not that he should not possess them, but that he should not possess them with fear and trembling: he does not drive them away from him, but when they leave him he follows after them unconcernedly. Where, indeed, can Fortune invest riches more securely than in a place from whence they can always be recovered without any squabble with their trustee? Marcus Cato, when he was praising Curius and Coruncanius and that century in which the possession of a few small silver coins were an offence which was punished by the Censor, himself owned four million sesterces; a less fortune, no doubt, than that of Crassus, but

---

[173] The quotation is from the epitaph on Phaeton. See Ovid, *Metamorphoses*, II, 327.

larger than of Cato the Censor. If the amounts be compared, he had outstripped his great-grandfather further than he himself was outdone by Crassus, and if still greater riches had fallen to his lot, he would not have spurned them: for the wise man does not think himself unworthy of any chance presents: he does not love riches, but he prefers to have them; he does not receive them into his spirit, but only into his house: nor does he cast away from him what he already possesses, but keeps them, and is willing that his virtue should receive a larger subject-matter for its exercise.

22

Who can doubt, however, that the wise man, if he is rich, has a wider field for the development of his powers than if he is poor, seeing that in the latter case the only virtue which he can display is that of neither being perverted nor crushed by his poverty, whereas if he has riches, he will have a wide field for the exhibition of temperance, generosity, laboriousness, methodical arrangement, and grandeur. The wise man will not despise himself, however short of stature he may be, but nevertheless he will wish to be tall: even though he be feeble and one-eyed he may be in good health, yet he would prefer to have bodily strength, and that too, while he knows all the while that he has something which is even more powerful: he will endure illness, and will hope for good health: for some things, though they may be trifles compared with the sum total, and though they may be taken away without destroying the chief good, yet add somewhat to that constant cheerfulness which arises from virtue. Riches encourage and brighten up such a man just as a sailor is delighted at a favourable wind that bears him on his way, or as people feel pleasure at a fine day or at a sunny spot in the cold weather. What wise man, I mean of our school, whose only good is virtue, can deny that even these matters which we call neither good nor bad have in themselves a certain value, and that some of them are preferable to others? to some of them we show a certain amount of respect, and to some a great deal. Do not, then, make any mistake: riches belong to the class of desirable things. "Why then," say you, "do you laugh at me, since you place them in the same position that I do?" Do you wish to know how different the position is in which we place them? If my riches leave me, they will carry away with them nothing except themselves: you will be bewildered and will seem to be left without yourself if they should pass away from you: with me riches occupy a certain place, but with you they occupy the highest place of all. In fine, my riches belong to me, you belong to your riches.

23

Cease, then, forbidding philosophers to possess money: no one has condemned wisdom to poverty. The philosopher may own ample wealth, but will not own wealth that which has been torn from another, or which is stained with another's blood: his must be obtained without wronging any man, and without its being won by base means; it must be alike honourably come by and honourably spent, and must be such as spite alone could shake its head at. Raise it to whatever figure you please, it will still be an honourable possession, if, while it includes much which every man would like to call his own, there be nothing which anyone can say is his own. Such a man will not forfeit his right to the favour of Fortune, and will neither boast of his inheritance nor blush for it if it was honourably acquired: yet he will have something to boast of, if he throw his house open, let all his countrymen come among his property, and say, "If anyone recognizes here anything belonging to him, let him take it." What a great man, how excellently rich will he be, if after this speech he possesses as much as he had before! I say, then, that if he can safely and confidently submit his accounts to the scrutiny of the people, and no one can find in them any item upon which he can lay hands, such a man may boldly and unconcealedly enjoy his riches. The wise man will not allow a single ill-won penny to cross his threshold: yet he will not refuse or close his door against great riches, if they are the gift of fortune and the product of virtue: what reason has he for grudging them good quarters: let them come and be his guests: he will neither brag of them nor hide them away: the one is the part of a silly, the other of a cowardly and paltry spirit, which, as it were, muffles up a good thing in its lap. Neither will he, as I said before, turn them out of his house: for what will he say? will he say, "You are useless," or, "I do not know how to use riches?" As he is capable of performing a journey upon his own feet, but yet would prefer to mount a carriage, just so he will be capable of being poor, yet will wish to be rich; he will own wealth, but will view it as an uncertain possession which will someday fly away from him. He will not allow it to be a burden either to himself or to anyone else: he will give it—why do you prick up your ears? why do you open your pockets?—he will give it either to good men or to those whom it may make into good men. He will give it after having taken the utmost pains to choose those who are fittest to receive it, as becomes one who bears in mind that he ought to give an account of what he spends as well as of what he receives. He will give for good and commendable reasons, for a gift ill bestowed counts as a shameful loss: he will have an easily opened pocket, but not one with a hole in it, so that much may be taken out of it, yet nothing may fall out of it.

24

He who believes giving to be an easy matter, is mistaken: it offers very great difficulties, if we bestow our bounty rationally, and do not scatter it impulsively and at random. I do this man a service, I requite a good turn done me by that one: I help this other, because I pity him: this man, again, I teach to be no fit object for poverty to hold down or degrade. I shall not give some men anything, although they are in want, because, even if I do give to them they will still be in want: I shall proffer my bounty to some, and shall forcibly thrust it upon others: I cannot be neglecting my own interests while I am doing this: at no time do I make more people in my debt than when I am giving things away. "What?" say you, "do you give that you may receive again?" At any rate I do not give that I may throw my bounty away: what I give should be so placed that although I cannot ask for its return, yet it may be given back to me. A benefit should be invested in the same manner as a treasure buried deep in the earth, which you would not dig up unless actually obliged. Why, what opportunities of conferring benefits the mere house of a rich man affords? for who considers generous behaviour due only to those who wear the toga? Nature bids me do good to mankind—what difference does it make whether they be slaves or freemen, freeborn or emancipated, whether their freedom be legally acquired or bestowed by arrangement among friends? Wherever there is a human being, there is an opportunity for a benefit: consequently, money may be distributed even within one's own threshold, and a field may be found there for the practice of freehandedness, which is not so called because it is our duty towards free men, but because it takes its rise in a freeborn mind. In the case of the wise man, this never falls upon base and unworthy recipients, and never becomes so exhausted as not, whenever it finds a worthy object, to flow as if its store was undiminished. You have, therefore, no grounds for misunderstanding the honourable, brave, and spirited language which you hear from those who are studying wisdom: and first of all observe this, that a student of wisdom is not the same thing as a man who has made himself perfect in wisdom. The former will say to you, "In my talk I express the most admirable sentiments, yet I am still weltering amid countless ills. You must not force me to act up to my rules: at the present time I am forming myself, moulding my character, and striving to rise myself to the height of a great example. If I should ever succeed in carrying out all that I have set myself to accomplish, you may then demand that my words and deeds should correspond." But he who has reached the summit of human perfection will deal otherwise with you, and will say, "In the first place, you have no business to allow yourself to sit in judgment upon your betters:" I have already obtained one proof of my righteousness in having become an object of dislike to bad men: however, to make you a rational answer, which I grudge to no man, listen to what I declare, and at what price I value all things. Riches, I say, are not a good thing; for if they were, they would make men good: now since that which is found even among bad men cannot be termed good, I do not allow them to be called so: nevertheless I admit that they are desirable and useful and contribute great comforts to our lives.

25

Learn, then, since we both agree that they are desirable, what my reason is amongst counting them among good things, and in what respects I should behave differently to you if I possessed them. Place me as master in the house of a very rich man: place me where gold and silver plate is used for the commonest purposes; I shall not think more of myself because of things which even though they are in my house are yet no part of me. Take me away to the wooden bridge[174] and put me down there among the beggars: I shall not despise myself because I am sitting among those who hold out their hands for alms: for what can the lack of a piece of bread matter to one who does not lack the power of dying? Well, then? I prefer the magnificent house to the beggar's bridge. Place me among magnificent furniture and all the appliances of luxury: I shall not think myself any happier because my cloak is soft, because my guests rest upon purple. Change the scene: I shall be no more miserable if my weary head rests upon a bundle of hay, if I lie upon a cushion from the circus, with all the stuffing on the point of coming out through its patches of threadbare cloth. Well, then? I prefer, as far as my feelings go, to show myself in public dressed in woollen and in robes of office, rather than with naked or half-covered shoulders: I should like every day's business to turn out just as I wish it to do, and new congratulations to be constantly following upon the former ones: yet I will not pride myself upon this: change all this good fortune for its opposite, let my spirit be distracted by losses, grief, various kinds of attacks: let no hour pass without some dispute: I shall not on this account, though beset by the greatest miseries, call myself the most miserable of beings, nor shall I curse any particular day, for I have taken care to have no unlucky days. What, then, is the upshot of all this? it is that I prefer to have to regulate joys than to stifle sorrows. The great Socrates would say the same thing to you. "Make me," he would say, "the conqueror of all nations: let

---

[174] The "Pons Sublicius," or "pile bridge," was built over the Tiber by Ancus Martius, one of the early kings of Rome, and was always kept in repair out of a superstitious feeling.

the voluptuous car of Bacchus bear me in triumph to Thebes from the rising of the sun: let the kings of the Persians receive laws from me: yet I shall feel myself to be a man at the very moment when all around salute me as a God. Straightaway connect this lofty height with a headlong fall into misfortune: let me be placed upon a foreign chariot that I may grace the triumph of a proud and savage conqueror: I will follow another's car with no more humility than I showed when I stood in my own. What then? In spite of all this, I had rather be a conqueror than a captive. I despise the whole dominion of Fortune, but still, if I were given my choice, I would choose its better parts. I shall make whatever befalls me become a good thing, but I prefer that what befalls me should be comfortable and pleasant and unlikely to cause me annoyance: for you need not suppose that any virtue exists without labour, but some virtues need spurs, while others need the curb. As we have to check our body on a downward path, and to urge it to climb a steep one; so also the path of some virtues leads downhill, that of others uphill. Can we doubt that patience, courage, constancy, and all the other virtues which have to meet strong opposition, and to trample fortune under their feet, are climbing, struggling, winning their way up a steep ascent? Why! is it not equally evident that generosity, moderation, and gentleness glide easily downhill? With the latter we must hold in our spirit, lest it run away with us: with the former we must urge and spur it on. We ought, therefore to apply these energetic, combative virtues to poverty, and to riches those other more thrifty ones which trip lightly along, and merely support their own weight. This being the distinction between them, I would rather have to deal with those which I could practise in comparative quiet, than those of which one can only make trial through blood and sweat. "Wherefore," says the sage, "I do not talk one way and live another: but you do not rightly understand what I say: the sound of my words alone reaches your ears, you do not try to find out their meaning."

26

"What difference, then, is there between me, who am a fool, and you, who are a wise man?" "All the difference in the world: for riches are slaves in the house of a wise man, but masters in that of a fool. You accustom yourself to them and cling to them as if somebody had promised that they should be yours forever, but a wise man never thinks so much about poverty as when he is surrounded by riches. No general ever trusts so implicitly in the maintenance of peace as not to make himself ready for a war, which, though it may not actually be waged, has nevertheless been declared; you are rendered overproud by a fine house, as though it could never be burned or fall down, and your heads are turned by riches as though they were beyond the reach of all dangers and were so great that Fortune has not sufficient strength to swallow them up. You sit idly playing with your wealth and do not foresee the perils in store for it, as savages generally do when besieged, for, not understanding the use of siege artillery, they look on idly at the labours of the besiegers and do not understand the object of the machines which they are putting together at a distance: and this is exactly what happens to you: you go to sleep over your property, and never reflect how many misfortunes loom menacingly around you on all sides, and soon will plunder you of costly spoils, but if one takes away riches from the wise man, one leaves him still in possession of all that is his: for he lives happy in the present, and without fear for the future. The great Socrates, or anyone else who had the same superiority to and power to withstand the things of this life, would say, 'I have no more fixed principle than that of not altering the course of my life to suit your prejudices: you may pour your accustomed talk upon me from all sides: I shall not think that you are abusing me, but that you are merely wailing like poor little babies.' " This is what the man will say who possesses wisdom, whose mind, being free from vices, bids him reproach others, not because he hates them, but in order to improve them: and to this he will add, "Your opinion of me affects me with pain, not for my own sake but for yours, because to hate perfection and to assail virtue is in itself a resignation of all hope of doing well. You do me no harm; neither do men harm the gods when they overthrow their altars: but it is clear that your intention is an evil one and that you will wish to do harm even where you are not able. I bear with your prating in the same spirit in which Jupiter, best and greatest, bears with the idle tales of the poets, one of whom represents him with wings, another with horns, another as an adulterer staying out all night, another is dealing harshly with the gods, another as unjust to men, another as the seducer of noble youths whom he carries off by force, and those, too, his own relatives, another as a parricide and the conqueror of another's kingdom, and that his father's. The only result of such tales is that men feel less shame at committing sin if they believe the gods to be guilty of such actions. But although this conduct of yours does not hurt me, yet, for your own sakes, I advise you, respect virtue: believe those who having long followed her cry aloud that what they follow is a thing of might, and daily appears mightier. Reverence her as you would the gods, and reverence her followers as you would the priests of the gods: and whenever any mention of sacred writings is made, *favete linguis*, favour us with silence: this word is not derived, as most people imagine, from *favour*, but commands silence, that divine service may be performed without being interrupted by any words of evil omen. It is much more necessary that you should be ordered to do this, in order that whenever utterance is made by that oracle, you may listen to it with attention and in silence. Whenever anyone beats a *sistrum*,[175] pretending to do so by divine command, any proficient in grazing his own skin covers his arms and shoulders with blood from light cuts, anyone crawls on his knees howling along the street, or any old man clad in linen comes forth in daylight with a lamp and laurel branch and cries out that one of the gods is angry, you crowd round him and listen to his words, and each increases the other's wonderment by declaring him to be divinely inspired.

27

Behold! from that prison of his, which by entering he cleansed from shame and rendered more honourable than any senate house, Socrates addresses you, saying: "What is this madness of yours? what is this disposition, at war alike with gods and men, which leads you to calumniate virtue and to outrage holiness with malicious accusations? Praise good men, if you are able: if not, pass them by in silence: if indeed you take pleasure in this offensive abusiveness, fall foul of one another: for when you rave against Heaven, I do not say that you commit sacrilege, but you waste your time. I once afforded Aristophanes with the subject of a jest: since then all the crew of comic poets have made me a mark for their envenomed wit: my virtue has been made to shine more brightly by the very blows which have been aimed at it, for it is to its advantage to be brought before the public and exposed to temptation, nor do any people understand its greatness more than those who by their assaults have made trial of its strength. The hardness of flint is known to none so well as to those who strike it. I offer myself to all attacks, like some lonely rock in a shallow sea, which the waves never cease to beat upon from whatever quarter they may come, but which they cannot thereby move from its place nor yet wear away, for however many years they may unceasingly dash against it. Bound upon me, rush upon me, I will overcome you by enduring your onset: whatever strikes against that which is firm and unconquerable merely injures itself by its own violence.

Wherefore, seek some soft and yielding object to pierce with your darts. But have you leisure to peer into other men's evil deeds and to sit in judgment upon anybody? to ask how it is that this philosopher has so roomy a house, or that one so good a dinner?

---

[175] A metallic rattle used by the Egyptians in celebrating the rites of Isis, etc.—Andrews.

Do you look at other people's pimples while you yourselves are covered with countless ulcers? This is as though one who was eaten up by the mange were to point with scorn at the moles and warts on the bodies of the handsomest men. Reproach Plato with having sought for money, reproach Aristotle with having obtained it,

Democritus with having disregarded it, Epicurus with having spent it: cast Phaedrus and Alcibiades in my own teeth, you who reach the height of enjoyment whenever you get an opportunity of imitating our vices! Why do you not rather cast your eyes around yourselves at the ills which tear you to pieces on every side, some attacking you from without, some burning in your own bosoms? However little you know your own place, mankind has not yet come to such a pass that you can have leisure to wag your tongues to the reproach of your betters.

28

This you do not understand, and you bear a countenance which does not befit your condition, like many men who sit in the circus or the theatre without having learned that their home is already in mourning: but I, looking forward from a lofty standpoint, can see what storms are either threatening you, and will burst in torrents upon you somewhat later, or are close upon you and on the point of sweeping away all that you possess. Why, though you are hardly aware of it, is there not a whirling hurricane at this moment spinning round and confusing your minds, making them seek and avoid the very same things, now raising them aloft and now dashing them below?

ON THE SHORTNESS OF LIFE

1

The greater part of mankind, my Paulinus, complains of the unkindness of Nature, because we are born only for a short space of time, and that this allotted period of life runs away so swiftly, nay so hurriedly, that with but few exceptions men's life comes to an end just as they are preparing to enjoy it: nor is it only the common herd and the ignorant vulgar who mourn over this universal misfortune, as they consider it to be: this reflection has wrung complaints even from great men. Hence comes that well-known saying of physicians, that art is long but life is short: hence arose that quarrel, so unbefitting a sage, which Aristotle picked with Nature, because she had indulged animals with such length of days that some of them lived for ten or fifteen centuries, while man, although born for many and such great exploits, had the term of his existence cut so much shorter. We do not have a very short time assigned to us, but we lose a great deal of it: life is long enough to carry out the most important projects: we have an ample portion, if we do but arrange the whole of it aright: but when it all runs to waste through luxury and carelessness, when it is not devoted to any good purpose, then at the last we are forced to feel that it is all over, although we never noticed how it glided away. Thus it is: we do not receive a short life, but we make it a short one, and we are not poor in days, but wasteful of them. When great and kinglike riches fall into the hands of a bad master, they are dispersed straightaway, but even a moderate fortune, when bestowed upon a wise guardian, increases by use: and in like manner our life has great opportunities for one who knows how to dispose of it to the best advantage.

2

Why do we complain of Nature? she has dealt kindly with us. Life is long enough, if you know how to use it. One man is possessed by an avarice which nothing can satisfy, another by a laborious diligence in doing what is totally useless: another is sodden by wine: another is benumbed by sloth: one man is exhausted by an ambition which makes him court the good will of others:[176] another, through his eagerness as a merchant, is led to visit every land and every sea by the hope of gain: some are plagued by the love of soldiering, and are always either endangering other men's lives or in trembling for their own: some wear away their lives in that voluntary slavery, the unrequited service of great men: many are occupied either in laying claim to other men's fortune or in complaining of their own: a great number have no settled purpose, and are tossed from one new scheme to another by a rambling, inconsistent, dissatisfied, fickle habit of mind: some care for no object sufficiently to try to attain it, but lie lazily yawning until their fate comes upon them: so that I cannot doubt the truth of that verse which the greatest of poets has dressed in the guise of an oracular response—

"We live a small part only of our lives."

But all duration is time, not life: vices press upon us and surround us on every side, and do not permit us to regain our feet, or to raise our eyes and gaze upon truth, but when we are down keep us prostrate and chained to low desires. Men who are in this condition are never allowed to come to themselves: if ever by chance they obtain any rest, they roll to and fro like the deep sea, which heaves and tosses after a gale, and they never have any respite from their lusts. Do you suppose that I speak of those whose ills are notorious? Nay, look at those whose prosperity all men run to see: they are choked by their own good things. To how many men do riches prove a heavy burden? how many men's eloquence and continual desire to display their own cleverness has cost them their lives?[177] how many are sallow with constant sensual indulgence? how many have no freedom left them by the tribe of clients that surges around them? Look through all these, from the lowest to the highest:—this man calls his friends to support him, this one is present in court, this one is the defendant, this one pleads for him, this one is on the jury: but no one lays claim to his own self, everyone wastes his time over someone else. Investigate those men, whose names are in everyone's mouth: you will find that they bear just the same marks: A is devoted to B, and B to C: no one belongs to himself. Moreover some men are full of most irrational anger: they complain of the insolence of their chiefs, because they have not granted them an audience when they wished for it; as if a man had any right to complain of being so haughtily shut out by another, when he never has leisure to

---

[176] "*L'un se consume en projets d'ambition, dont le succès dépend du suffrage de l'autrui.*" —La Grange.
[177] "*Combien d'orateurs qui s'épuisent de sang et de forces pour faire montrer de leur génie!*" —La Grange.

give his own conscience a hearing. This chief of yours, whoever he is, though he may look at you in an offensive manner, still will some day look at you, open his ears to your words, and give you a seat by his side: but you never design to look upon yourself, to listen to your own grievances. You ought not, then, to claim these services from another, especially since while you yourself were doing so, you did not wish for an interview with another man, but were not able to obtain one with yourself.[178]

3

Were all the brightest intellects of all time to employ themselves on this one subject, they never could sufficiently express their wonder at this blindness of men's minds: men will not allow anyone to establish himself upon their estates, and upon the most trifling dispute about the measuring of boundaries, they betake themselves to stones and cudgels; yet they allow others to encroach upon their lives, nay, they themselves actually lead others in to take possession of them. You cannot find anyone who wants to distribute his money; yet among how many people does everyone distribute his life? men covetously guard their property from waste, but when it comes to waste of time, they are most prodigal of that of which it would become them to be sparing. Let us take one of the elders, and say to him, "We perceive that you have arrived at the extreme limits of human life: you are in your hundredth year, or even older. Come now, reckon up your whole life in black and white: tell us how much of your time has been

---

[178] "*Pour vous, jamais vous ne daignâtes vous regarder seulement, ou vous entendre. Ne faites pas non plus valoir votre condescendance a écouter les autres. Lorsque vous vous y prêtez, ce n'est pas que vous aimiez a vous communiquer aux autres; c'est que vous craignez de vous trouver avec vous-même.*"—La Grange.

"It is a folly therefore beyond Sence,
When great men will not give us Audience
To count them proud; how dare we call it pride
When we the same have to ourselves deny'd.
Yet they how great, how proud so e're, have bin
Sometimes so courteous as to call thee in,
And hear thee speak; but thou could'st nere afford
Thyself the leisure of a look or word.
Thou should'st not then herein another blame,
Because when thou thyself do'st do the same,
Thou would'st not be with others, but we see
Plainly thou can'st not with thine own self be."

L. Annaeus Seneca, the Philosopher, his book of the Shortness of Life, translated into an English poem. Imprinted at London, by William Goldbird, for the Author.

spent upon your creditors, how much on your mistress, how much on your king, how much on your clients, how much in quarrelling with your wife, how much in keeping your slaves in order, how much in running up and down the city on business. Add to this the diseases which we bring upon us with our own hands, and the time which has laid idle without any use having been made of it; you will see that you have not lived as many years as you count. Look back in your memory and see how often you have been consistent in your projects, how many days passed as you intended them to do when you were at your own disposal, how often you did not change colour and your spirit did not quail, how much work you have done in so long a time, how many people have without your knowledge stolen parts of your life from you, how much you have lost, how large a part has been taken up by useless grief, foolish gladness, greedy desire, or polite conversation; how little of yourself is left to you: you will then perceive that you will die prematurely." What, then, is the reason of this? It is that people live as though they would live forever: you never remember your human frailty; you never notice how much of your time has already gone by: you spend it as though you had an abundant and overflowing store of it, though all the while that day which you devote to some man or to some thing is perhaps your last. You fear everything, like mortals as you are, and yet you desire everything as if you were immortals. You will hear many men say, "After my fiftieth year I will give myself up to leisure: my sixtieth shall be my last year of public office": and what guarantee have you that your life will last any longer? who will let all this go on just as you have arranged it? are you not ashamed to reserve only the leavings of your life for yourself, and appoint for the enjoyment of your own right mind only that time which you cannot devote to any business? How late it is to begin life just when we have to be leaving it! What a foolish forgetfulness of our mortality, to put off wholesome counsels until our fiftieth or sixtieth year, and to choose that our lives shall begin at a point which few of us ever reach.

4

You will find that the most powerful and highly-placed men let fall phrases in which they long for leisure, praise it, and prefer it to all the blessings which they enjoy. Sometimes they would fain descend from their lofty pedestal, if it could be safely done: for fortune collapses by its own weight, without any shock or interference from without. The late Emperor Augustus, upon whom the gods bestowed more blessings than on anyone else, never ceased to pray for rest and exemption from the troubles of empire: he used to enliven his labours with this sweet, though unreal consolation, that he would some day live for himself alone. In a letter which he addressed to the Senate, after promising that his rest shall not be devoid of dignity nor discreditable to his former glories, I find the following words:—"These things, however, it is more honourable to do than to promise: but my eagerness for that time, so earnestly longed for, has led me to derive a certain pleasure from speaking about it, though the reality is still far distant."[179] He thought leisure so important, that though he could not actually enjoy it, yet he did so by anticipation and by thinking about it. He, who saw everything depending upon himself alone, who swayed the fortunes of men and of nations, thought that his happiest day would be that on which he laid aside his greatness. He knew by experience how much labour was involved in that glory that shone through all lands, and how much secret anxiety was concealed within it: he had been forced to assert his rights by war, first with his countrymen, next with his colleagues, and lastly with his own relations, and had shed blood both by sea and by land: after marching his troops under arms through Macedonia, Sicily, Egypt, Syria, Asia Minor, and almost all the countries of the world, when they were weary with slaughtering Romans he had directed them against a foreign foe. While he was pacifying the Alpine regions, and subduing the enemies whom he found in the midst of the Roman empire, while he was extending its boundaries beyond the Rhine, the Euphrates, and the Danube, at Rome itself the swords of Murena, Caepio, Lepidus, Egnatius, and others were being sharpened to slay him. Scarcely had he escaped from their plot, when his already failing age was terrified by his daughter and all the noble youths who were pledged to her cause by adultery with her by way of oath of fidelity. Then there was Paulus and Antonius's mistress, a second time to be feared by Rome: and when he had cut out these ulcers from his very limbs, others grew in their place: the empire, like a body overloaded with blood, was always breaking out somewhere. For this reason he longed for leisure: all his labours were based upon hopes and thoughts of leisure: this was the wish of him who could accomplish the wishes of all other men.

---

[179] *"Dans une lettre qu'il envoya au Sénat apres avoir promis que son repos n'aura rièn indigne de la gloire de ses premières années, il ajoute: Mais l'execution y mettra un prix, que ne peuvent y mettre les promesses. J'obeis cependant à la vive passion que j'ai, de me voir a ce temps si désiré; et puisque l'heureuse situation d'affaires m'en tient encore éloigné, j'ai voulu du moins me satisfaire en partie, par la douceur que je trouve à vous en parler."*—La Grange.

"Such words I find. But these things rather ought
Be done, then said; yet so far hath the thought
Of that wish'd time prevail'd, that though the glad
Fruition of the thing be not yet had,
Yet I,"

5

While tossed hither and thither by Catiline and Clodius, Pompeius and Crassus, by some open enemies and some doubtful friends, while he struggled with the struggling republic and kept it from going to ruin, when at last he was banished, being neither able to keep silence in prosperity nor to endure adversity with patience, how often must Marcus Cicero have cursed that consulship of his which he never ceased to praise, and which nevertheless deserved it? What piteous expressions he uses in a letter to Atticus when Pompeius the father had been defeated, and his son was recruiting his shattered forces in Spain? "Do you ask," writes he, "what I am doing here? I am living in my Tusculan villa almost as a prisoner." He adds more afterwards, wherein he laments his former life, complains of the present, and despairs of the future. Cicero called himself "half a prisoner," but, by Hercules, the wise man never would have come under so lowly a title: he never would be half a prisoner, but would always enjoy complete and entire liberty, being free, in his own power, and greater than all others: for what can be greater than the man who is greater than Fortune?

6

When Livius Drusus, a vigorous and energetic man, brought forward bills for new laws and radical measures of the Gracchus pattern, being the centre of a vast mob of all the peoples of Italy, and seeing no way to solve the question, since he was not allowed to deal with it as he wished, and yet was not free to throw it up after having once taken part in it, complained bitterly of his life, which had been one of unrest from the very cradle, and said, we are told, that "he was the only person who had never had any holidays even when he was a boy." Indeed, while he was still under age and wearing the *praetexta*, he had the courage to plead the cause of accused persons in court, and to make use of his influence so powerfully that it is well known that in some causes his exertions gained a verdict. Where would such precocious ambition stop? You may be sure that one who showed such boldness as a child would end by becoming a great pest both in public and in private life: it was too late for him to complain that he had had no holidays, when from his boyhood he had been a firebrand and a nuisance in the courts. It is a stock question whether he committed suicide: for he fell by a sudden wound in the groin, and some doubted whether his death was caused by his own hand, though none disputed its having happened most seasonably. It would be superfluous to mention more who, while others thought them the happiest of men, have themselves borne true witness to their own feelings, and have loathed all that they have done for all the years of their lives: yet by these complaints they have effected no alteration either in others or in themselves: for after these words have escaped them their feelings revert to their accustomed frame. By Hercules, that life of you great men, even though it should last for more than a thousand years, is still a very short one: those vices of yours would swallow up any extent of time: no wonder if this our ordinary span, which, though Nature hurries on, can be enlarged by common sense, soon slips away from you: for you do not lay hold of it or hold it back, and try to delay the swiftest of all things, but you let it pass as though it were a useless thing and you could supply its place.

7

Among these I reckon in the first place those who devote their time to nothing but drinking and debauchery: for no men are busied more shamefully: the others, although the glory which they pursue is but a counterfeit, still deserve some credit for their pursuit of it—though you may tell me of misers, of passionate men, of men who hate and who even wage war without a cause—yet all such men sin like men: but the sin of those who are given up to gluttony and lust is a disgraceful one. Examine all the hours of their lives: consider how much time they spend in calculation, how much in plotting, how much in fear, how much in giving and receiving flattery, how much in entering into recognizances for themselves or for others, how much in banquets, which indeed become a serious business, you will see that they are not allowed any breathing time either by their pleasures or their pains. Finally, all are agreed that nothing, neither eloquence nor literature, can be done properly by one who is occupied with something else; for nothing can take deep root in a mind which is directed to some other subject, and which rejects whatever you try to stuff into it. No man knows less about living than a business man: there is nothing about which it is more difficult to gain knowledge. Other arts have many folk everywhere who profess to teach them: some of them can be so thoroughly learned by mere boys, that they are able to teach them to others: but one's whole life must be spent in learning how to live, and, which may perhaps surprise you more, one's whole life must be spent in learning how to die. Many excellent men have freed themselves from all hindrances, have given up riches, business, and pleasure, and have made it their duty to the very end of their lives to learn how to live: and yet the larger portion of them leave this life confessing that they do not yet know how to live, and still less know how to live as wise men. Believe me, it requires a great man and one who is superior to human frailties not to allow any of his time to be filched from him: and therefore it follows that his life is a very long one, because he devotes every possible part of it to himself: no portion lies idle or uncultivated, or in another man's power; for he finds nothing worthy of being exchanged for his time, which he husbands most grudgingly. He, therefore, had time enough: whereas those who gave up a great part of their lives to the people of necessity had not enough. Yet you need not suppose that the latter were not sometimes conscious of their loss: indeed, you will hear most of those who are troubled with great prosperity every now and then cry out amid their hosts of clients, their pleadings in court, and their other honourable troubles, "I am not allowed to live my own life." Why is he not allowed? because all those who call upon you to defend them, take you away from yourself. How many of your days have been spent by that defendant? by that candidate for office? by that old woman who is weary with burying her heirs? by that man who pretends to be ill, in order to excite the greed of those who hope to inherit his property? by that powerful friend of yours, who uses you to swell his train, not to be his friend? Balance your account, and run over all the days of your life; you will see that only a very few days, and only those which were useless for any other purpose, have been left to you. He who has obtained the fasces[180] for which he longed, is eager to get rid of them, and is constantly saying, "When will this year be over?" Another exhibits public games, and once would have given a great deal for the chance of doing so, but now "when," says he, "shall I escape from this?" Another is an advocate who is fought for in all the courts, and who draws immense audiences, who crowd all the forum to a far greater distance than they can hear him; "When," says he, "will vacation-time come?" Every man hurries through his life, and suffers from a yearning for the future, and a weariness of the present: but he who disposes of all his time for his own purposes, who arranges all his days as though he were arranging the plan of his life, neither wishes for nor fears the morrow: for what new pleasure can any hour now bestow upon him? he knows it all, and has indulged in it all even to satiety. Fortune may deal with the rest as she will, his life is already safe from her: such a man may gain something, but cannot lose anything: and, indeed, he can only gain anything in the same way as one who is already glutted and filled can get some extra food which he takes although he does not want it. You have no grounds, therefore, for supposing that anyone has lived long, because he has wrinkles or grey hairs: such a man has not lived long, but has only been long alive. Why! would you think that a man had voyaged much

---

[180] The rods carried by the lictors as symbols of office. See Smith's *Dictionary of Antiquities*, s.v.

if a fierce gale had caught him as soon as he left his port, and he had been driven round and round the same place continually by a succession of winds blowing from opposite quarters? such a man has not travelled much, he has only been much tossed about.

8

I am filled with wonder when I see some men asking others for their time, and those who are asked for it most willing to give it: both parties consider the object for which the time is given, but neither of them thinks of the time itself, as though in asking for this one asked for nothing, and in giving it one gave nothing: we play with what is the most precious of all things: yet it escapes men's notice, because it is an incorporeal thing, and because it does not come before our eyes; and therefore it is held very cheap, nay, hardly any value whatever is put upon it. Men set the greatest store upon presents or pensions, and hire out their work, their services, or their care in order to gain them: no one values time: they give it much more freely, as though it cost nothing. Yet you will see these same people clasping the knees of their physician as suppliants when they are sick and in present peril of death, and if threatened with a capital charge willing to give all that they possess in order that they may live: so inconsistent are they. Indeed, if the number of every man's future years could be laid before him, as we can lay that of his past years, how anxious those who found that they had but few years remaining would be to make the most of them? Yet it is easy to arrange the distribution of a quantity, however small, if we know how much there is: what you ought to husband most carefully is that which may run short you know not when. Yet you have no reason to suppose that they do not know how dear a thing time is: they are wont to say to those whom they especially love that they are ready to give them a part of their own years. They do give them, and know not that they are giving them; but they give them in such a manner that they themselves lose them without the others gaining them. They do not, however, know whence they obtain their supply, and therefore they are able to endure the waste of what is not seen: yet no one will give you back your years, no one will restore them to you again: your life will run its course when once it has begun, and will neither begin again or efface what it has done. It will make no disturbance, it will give you no warning of how fast it flies: it will move silently on: it will not prolong itself at the command of a king, or at the wish of a nation: as it started on its first day, so it will run: it will never turn aside, never delay. What follows, then? Why! you are busy, but life is hurrying on: death will be here some time or other, and you must attend to him, whether you will or no.

9

Can anything be mentioned which is more insane than the ideas of leisure of those people who boast of their worldly wisdom? They live laboriously, in order that they may live better; they fit themselves out for life at the expense of life itself, and cast their thoughts a long way forwards: yet postponement is the greatest waste of life: it wrings day after day from us, and takes away the present by promising something hereafter: there is no such obstacle to true living as waiting, which loses today while it is depending on the morrow. You dispose of that which is in the hand of Fortune, and you let go that which is in your own. Whither are you looking, whither are you stretching forward? everything future is uncertain: live now straightaway. See how the greatest of bards cries to you and sings in wholesome verse as though inspired with celestial fire:—

"The best of wretched mortals' days is that
Which is the first to fly."

Why do you hesitate, says he, why do you stand back? unless you seize it it will have fled: and even if you do seize it, it will still fly. Our swiftness in making use of our time ought therefore to vie with the swiftness of time itself, and we ought to drink of it as we should of a fast-running torrent which will not be always running. The poet, too, admirably satirizes our boundless thoughts, when he says, not "the first age," but "the first day." Why are you careless and slow while time is flying so fast, and why do you spread out before yourself a vision of long months and years, as many as your greediness requires? he talks with you about one day, and that a fast-fleeting one. There can, then, be no doubt that the best days are those which fly first for wretched, that is, for busy mortals, whose minds are still in their childhood when old age comes upon them, and they reach it unprepared and without arms to combat it. They have never looked forward: they have all of a sudden stumbled upon old age: they never noticed that it was stealing upon them day by day. As conversation, or reading, or deep thought deceives travellers, and they find themselves at their journey's end before they knew that it was drawing near, so in this fast and never-ceasing journey of life, which we make at the same pace whether we are asleep or awake, busy people never notice that they are moving till they are at the end of it.

10

If I chose to divide this proposition into separate steps, supported by evidence, many things occur to me by which I could prove that the lives of busy men are the shortest of all. Fabianus, who was none of your lecture-room philosophers, but one of the true antique pattern, used to say, "We ought to fight against the passions by main force, not by skirmishing, and upset their line of battle by a home charge, not by inflicting trifling wounds: I do not approve of dallying with sophisms; they must be crushed, not merely scratched." Yet, in order that sinners may be confronted with their errors, they must be taught, and not merely mourned for. Life is divided into three parts: that which has been, that which is, and that which is to come: of these three stages, that which we are passing through is brief, that which we are about to pass is uncertain, and that which we have passed is certain: this it is over which Fortune has lost her rights, and which can fall into no other man's power: and this is what busy men lose: for they have no leisure to look back upon the past, and even if they had, they take no pleasure in remembering what they regret: they are, therefore, unwilling to turn their minds to the contemplation of ill-spent time, and they shrink from reviewing a course of action whose faults become glaringly apparent when handled a second time, although they were snatched at when we were under the spell of immediate gratification. No one, unless all his acts have been submitted to the infallible censorship of his own conscience, willingly turns his thoughts back upon the past. He who has ambitiously desired, haughtily scorned, passionately vanquished, treacherously deceived, greedily snatched, or prodigally wasted much, must needs fear his own memory; yet this is a holy and consecrated part of our time, beyond the reach of all human accidents, removed from the dominion of Fortune, and which cannot be disquieted by want, fear, or attacks of sickness: this can neither be troubled nor taken away from one: we possess it forever undisturbed. Our present consists only of single days, and those, too, taken one hour at a time: but all the days of past times appear before us when bidden, and allow themselves to be examined and lingered over, albeit busy men cannot find time for so doing. It is the privilege of a tranquil and peaceful mind to review all the parts of its life: but the minds of busy men are like animals under the yoke, and cannot bend aside or look back. Consequently, their life passes away into vacancy, and as you do no good however much you may pour into a vessel which cannot keep or hold what you put there, so also it matters not how much time you give men if it can find no place to settle in, but leaks away through the chinks and holes of their minds. Present time is very short, so much so that to some it seems to be no time at all; for it is always in motion, and runs swiftly away: it ceases to exist before it comes, and can no more brook delay than can the universe or the host of heaven, whose unresting movement never lets them pause on their way. Busy men, therefore, possess present time alone, that being so short that they cannot grasp it, and when they are occupied with many things they lose even this.

11

In a word, do you want to know for how short a time they live? see how they desire to live long: broken-down old men beg in their prayers for the addition of a few more years: they pretend to be younger than they are: they delude themselves with their own lies, and are as willing to cheat themselves as if they could cheat Fate at the same time: when at last some weakness reminds them that they are mortal, they die as it were in terror: they may rather be said to be dragged out of this life than to depart from it. They loudly exclaim that they have been fools and have not lived their lives, and declare that if they only survive this sickness they will spend the rest of their lives at leisure: at such times they reflect how uselessly they have laboured to provide themselves with what they have never enjoyed, and how all their toil has gone for nothing: but those whose life is spent without any engrossing business may well find it ample: no part of it is made over to others, or scattered here and there; no part is entrusted to fortune, is lost by neglect, is spent in ostentatious giving, or is useless: all of it is, so to speak, invested at good interest. A very small amount of it, therefore, is abundantly sufficient, and so, when his last day arrives, the wise man will not hang back, but will walk with a steady step to meet death.

12

Perhaps you will ask me whom I mean by "busy men"? you need not think that I allude only to those who are hunted out of the courts of justice with dogs at the close of the proceedings, those whom you see either honourably jostled by a crowd of their own clients or contemptuously hustled in visits of ceremony by strangers, who call them away from home to hang about their patron's doors, or who make use of the praetor's sales by auction to acquire infamous gains which some day will prove their own ruin. Some men's leisure is busy: in their country house or on their couch, in complete solitude, even though they have retired from all men's society, they still continue to worry themselves: we ought not to say that such men's life is one of leisure, but their very business is sloth. Would you call a man idle who expends anxious finicking care in the arrangement of his Corinthian bronzes, valuable only through the mania of a few connoisseurs? and who passes the greater part of his days among plates of rusty metal? who sits in the palaestra (shame, that our very vices should be foreign) watching boys wrestling? who distributes his gangs of fettered slaves into pairs according to their age and colour? who keeps athletes of the latest fashion? Why do you call those men idle, who pass many hours at the barber's while the growth of the past night is being plucked out by the roots, holding councils over each several hair, while the scattered locks are arranged in order and those which fall back are forced forward on to the forehead? How angry they become if the shaver is a little careless, as though he were shearing a *man*! what a white heat they work themselves into if some of their mane is cut away, if some part of it is ill-arranged, if all their ringlets do not lie in regular order! who of them would not rather that the state were overthrown than that his hair should be ruffled? who does not care more for the appearance of his head than for his health? who would not prefer ornament to honour? Do you call these men idle, who make a business of the comb and looking-glass? what of those who devote their lives to composing, hearing, and learning songs who twist their voices, intended by Nature to sound best and simplest when used straightforwardly, through all the turns of futile melodies; whose fingers are always beating time to some music on which they are inwardly meditating; who, when invited to serious and even sad business may be heard humming an air to themselves?—such people are not at leisure, but are busy about trifles. As for their banquets, by Hercules, I cannot reckon them among their unoccupied times when I see with what anxious care they set out their plate, how laboriously they arrange the girdles of their waiters' tunics, how breathlessly they watch to see how the cook dishes up the wild boar, with what speed, when the signal is given, the slave-boys run to perform their duties, how skilfully birds are carved into pieces of the right size, how painstakingly wretched youths wipe up the spittings of drunken men. By these means men seek credit for taste and grandeur, and their vices follow them so far into their privacy that they can neither eat nor drink without a view to effect. Nor should I count those men idle who have themselves carried hither and thither in sedans and litters, and who look forward to their regular hour for taking this exercise as though they were not allowed to omit it: men who are reminded by someone else when to bathe, when to swim, when to dine: they actually reach such a pitch of languid effeminacy as not to be able to find out for themselves whether they are hungry. I have heard one of these luxurious folk—if indeed, we ought to give the name of luxury to unlearning the life and habits of a man—when he was carried in men's arms out of the bath and placed in his chair, say inquiringly, "Am I seated?" Do you suppose that such a man as this, who did not know when he was seated, could know whether he was alive, whether he could see, whether he was at leisure? I can hardly say whether I pity him more if he really did not know or if he pretended not to know this. Such people do really become unconscious of much, but they behave as though they were unconscious of much more: they delight in some failings because they consider them to be proofs of happiness: it seems the part of an utterly low and contemptible man to know what he is doing. After this, do you suppose that playwrights draw largely upon their imaginations in their burlesques upon luxury: by Hercules, they omit more than they invent; in this age, inventive in this alone, such a number of incredible vices have been produced, that already you are able to reproach the playwrights with omitting to notice them. To think that there should be anyone who had so far lost his senses through luxury as to take someone else's opinion as to whether he was sitting or not? This man certainly is not at leisure: you must bestow a different title on him: he is sick, or rather dead: he only is at leisure who feels that he is at leisure: but this creature is only half alive, if he wants someone to tell him what position his body is in. How can such a man be able to dispose of any time?

13

It would take long to describe the various individuals who have wasted their lives over playing at draughts, playing at ball, or toasting their bodies in the sun: men are not at leisure if their pleasures partake of the character of business, for no one will doubt that those persons are laborious triflers who devote themselves to the study of futile literary questions, of whom there is already a great number in Rome also. It used to be a peculiarly Greek disease of the mind to investigate how many rowers Ulysses had, whether the *Iliad* or the *Odyssey* was written first, and furthermore, whether they were written by the same author, with other matters of the same stamp, which neither please your inner consciousness if you keep them to yourself, nor make you seem more learned, but only more troublesome, if you publish them abroad. See, already this vain longing to learn what is useless has taken hold of the Romans: the other day I heard somebody telling who was the first Roman general who did this or that: Duillius was the first who won a sea-fight, Curius Dentatus was the first who drove elephants in his triumph: moreover, these stories, though they add nothing to real glory, do nevertheless deal with the great deeds of our countrymen: such knowledge is not profitable, yet it claims our attention as a fascinating kind of folly. I will even pardon those who want to know who first persuaded the Romans to go on board ship. It was Claudius, who for this reason was surnamed Caudex, because any piece of carpentry formed of many planks was called *caudex* by the ancient Romans, for which reason public records are called *codices*, and by old custom the ships which ply on the Tiber with provisions are called *codicariae*. Let us also allow that it is to the point to tell how Valerius Corvinus was the first to conquer Messana, and first of the family of the Valerii transferred the name of the captured city to his own, and was called Messana, and how the people gradually corrupted the pronunciation and called him Messalla: or would you let anyone find interest in Lucius Sulla having been the first to let lions loose in the circus, they having been previously exhibited in chains, and hurlers of darts having been sent by King Bocchus to kill them? This may be permitted to their curiosity: but can it serve any useful purpose to know that Pompeius was the first to exhibit eighteen elephants in the circus, who were matched in a mimic battle with some convicts? The leading man in the State, and one who, according to tradition, was noted among the ancient leaders of the State for his transcendent goodness of heart, thought it a notable kind of show to kill men in a manner hitherto unheard of. Do they fight to the death? that is not cruel enough: are they torn to pieces? that is not cruel enough: let them be crushed flat by animals of enormous bulk. It would be much better that such a thing should be forgotten, for fear that hereafter some potentate might hear of it and envy its refined barbarity. O, how doth excessive prosperity blind our intellects! at the moment at which he was casting so many troops of wretches to be trampled on by outlandish beasts, when he was proclaiming war between such different creatures, when he was shedding so much blood before the eyes of the Roman people, whose blood he himself was soon to shed even more freely, he thought himself the master of the whole world; yet he afterwards, deceived by the treachery of the Alexandrians, had to offer himself to the dagger of the vilest of slaves, and then at last discovered what an empty boast was his surname of "The Great." But to return to the point from which I have digressed, I will prove that even on this very subject some people expend useless pains. The same author tells us that Metellus, when he triumphed after having conquered the Carthaginians in Sicily, was the only Roman who ever had a hundred and twenty captured elephants led before his car: and that Sulla was the last Roman who extended the *pomoerium*[181] which it was not the custom of the ancients to extend on account of the conquest of provincial, but only of Italian territory. Is it more useful to know this, than to know that the Mount Aventine, according to him, is outside of the *pomoerium*, for one of two reasons, either because it was thither that the plebeians seceded, or because when Remus took his auspices on

---

[181] See Smith's *Dictionary of Antiquities*.

that place the birds which he saw were not propitious: and other stories without number of the like sort, which are either actual falsehoods or much the same as falsehoods? for even if you allow that these authors speak in all good faith, if they pledge themselves for the truth of what they write, still, whose mistakes will be made fewer by such stories? whose passions will be restrained? whom will they make more brave, more just, or more gentlemanly? My friend Fabianus used to say that he was not sure that it was not better not to apply oneself to any studies at all than to become interested in these.

14

The only persons who are really at leisure are those who devote themselves to philosophy: and they alone really live: for they do not merely enjoy their own lifetime, but they annex every century to their own: all the years which have passed before them belong to them. Unless we are the most ungrateful creatures in the world, we shall regard these noblest of men, the founders of divine schools of thought, as having been born for us, and having prepared life for us: we are led by the labour of others to behold most beautiful things which have been brought out of darkness into light: we are not shut out from any period, we can make our way into every subject, and, if only we can summon up sufficient strength of mind to overstep the narrow limit of human weakness, we have a vast extent of time wherein to disport ourselves: we may argue with Socrates, doubt with Carneades, repose with Epicurus, overcome human nature with the Stoics, exceed it with the Cynics. Since Nature allows us to commune with every age, why do we not abstract ourselves from our own petty fleeting span of time, and give ourselves up with our whole mind to what is vast, what is eternal, what we share with better men than ourselves? Those who gad about in a round of calls, who worry themselves and others, after they have indulged their madness to the full, and crossed every patron's threshold daily, leaving no open door unentered, after they have hawked about their interested greetings in houses of the most various character—after all, how few people are they able to see out of so vast a city, divided among so many different ruling passions: how many will be moved by sloth, self-indulgence, or rudeness to deny them admittance: how many, after they have long plagued them, will run past them with feigned hurry? how many will avoid coming out through their entrance-hall with its crowds of clients, and will escape by some concealed backdoor? as though it were not ruder to deceive their visitor than to deny him admittance!—how many, half asleep and stupid with yesterday's debauch, can hardly be brought to return the greeting of the wretched man who has broken his own rest in order to wait on that of another, even after his name has been whispered to them for the thousandth time, save by a most offensive yawn of his half-opened lips. We may truly say that those men are pursuing the true path of duty, who wish every day to consort on the most familiar terms with Zeno, Pythagoras, Democritus, and the rest of those high priests of virtue, with Aristotle and with Theophrastus. None of these men will be "engaged," none of these will fail to send you away after visiting him in a happier frame of mind and on better terms with yourself, none of them will let you leave him empty-handed: yet their society may be enjoyed by all men, and by night as well as by day.

15

None of these men will force you to die, but all of them will teach you how to die: none of these will waste your time, but will add his own to it. The talk of these men is not dangerous, their friendship will not lead you to the scaffold, their society will not ruin you in expenses: you may take from them whatsoever you will; they will not prevent your taking the deepest draughts of their wisdom that you please. What blessedness, what a fair old age awaits the man who takes these for his patrons! he will have friends with whom he may discuss all matters, great and small, whose advice he may ask daily about himself, from whom he will hear truth without insult, praise without flattery, and according to whose likeness he may model his own character. We are wont to say that we are not able to choose who our parents should be, but that they were assigned to us by chance; yet we may be born just as we please: there are several families of the noblest intellects: choose which you would like to belong to: by your adoption you will not receive their name only, but also their property, which is not intended to be guarded in a mean and miserly spirit: the more persons you divide it among the larger it becomes. These will open to you the path which leads to eternity, and will raise you to a height from whence none shall cast you down. By this means alone can you prolong your mortal life, nay, even turn it into an immortal one. High office, monuments, all that ambition records in decrees or piles up in stone, soon passes away: lapse of time casts down and ruins everything; but those things on which Philosophy has set its seal are beyond the reach of injury: no age will discard them or lessen their force, each succeeding century will add somewhat to the respect in which they are held: for we look upon what is near us with jealous eyes, but we admire what is further off with less prejudice. The wise man's life, therefore, includes much: he is not hedged in by the same limits which confine others: he alone is exempt from the laws by which mankind is governed: all ages serve him like a god. If any time be past, he recalls it by his memory; if it be present, he uses it; if it be future, he anticipates it: his life is a long one because he concentrates all times into it.

16

Those men lead the shortest and unhappiest lives who forget the past, neglect the present, and dread the future: when they reach the end of it the poor wretches learn too late that they were busied all the while that they were doing nothing. You need not think, because sometimes they call for death, that their lives are long: their folly torments them with vague passions which lead them into the very things of which they are afraid: they often, therefore, wish for death because they live in fear. Neither is it, as you might think, a proof of the length of their lives that they often find the days long, that they often complain how slowly the hours pass until the appointed time arrives for dinner: for whenever they are left without their usual business, they fret helplessly in their idleness, and know not how to arrange or to spin it out. They betake themselves, therefore, to some business, and all the intervening time is irksome to them; they would wish, by Hercules, to skip over it, just as they wish to skip over the intervening days before a gladiatorial contest or some other time appointed for a public spectacle or private indulgence: all postponement of what they wish for is grievous to them. Yet the very time which they enjoy is brief and soon past, and is made much briefer by their own fault: for they run from one pleasure to another, and are not able to devote themselves consistently to one passion: their days are not long, but odious to them: on the other hand, how short they find the nights which they spend with courtesans or over wine? Hence arises that folly of the poets who encourage the errors of mankind by their myths, and declare that Jupiter to gratify his voluptuous desires doubled the length of the night. Is it not adding fuel to our vices to name the gods as their authors, and to offer our distempers free scope by giving them deity for an example? How can the nights for which men pay so dear fail to appear of the shortest? they lose the day in looking forward to the night, and lose the night through fear of the dawn.

17

Such men's very pleasures are restless and disturbed by various alarms, and at the most joyous moment of all there rises the anxious thought: "How long will this last?" This frame of mind has led kings to weep over their power, and they have not been so much delighted at the grandeur of their position, as they have been terrified by the end to which it must some day come. That most arrogant Persian king,[182] when his army stretched over vast plains and could not be counted but only measured, burst into tears at the thought that in less than a hundred years none of all those warriors would be alive: yet their death was brought upon them by the very man who wept over it, who was about to destroy some of them by sea, some on land, some in battle, and some in flight, and who would in a very short space of time put an end to those about whose hundredth year he showed such solicitude. Why need we wonder at their very joys being mixed with fear? they do not rest upon any solid grounds, but are disturbed by the same emptiness from which they spring. What must we suppose to be the misery of such times as even they acknowledge to be wretched, when even the joys by which they elevate themselves and raise themselves above their fellows are of a mixed character. All the greatest blessings are enjoyed with fear, and nothing is so untrustworthy as extreme prosperity: we require fresh strokes of good fortune to enable us to keep that which we are enjoying, and even those of our prayers which are answered require fresh prayers. Everything for which we are dependent on chance is uncertain: the higher it rises, the more opportunities it has of falling. Moreover, no one takes any pleasure in what is about to fall into ruin: very wretched, therefore, as well as very short must be the lives of those who work very hard to gain what they must work even harder to keep: they obtain what they wish with infinite labour, and they hold what they have obtained with fear and trembling. Meanwhile they take no account of time, of which they will never have a fresh and larger supply: they substitute new occupations for old ones, one hope leads to another, one ambition to another: they do not seek for an end to their wretchedness, but they change its subject. Do our own preferments trouble us? nay, those of other men occupy more of our time. Have we ceased from our labours in canvassing? then we begin others in voting. Have we got rid of the trouble of accusation? then we begin that of judging. Has a man ceased to be a judge? then he becomes an examiner. Has he grown old in the salaried management of other people's property? then he becomes occupied with his own. Marius is discharged from military service; he becomes consul many times: Quintius is eager to reach the end of his dictatorship; he will be called a second time from the plough: Scipio marched against the Carthaginians before he was of years sufficient for so great an undertaking; after he has conquered Hannibal, conquered Antiochus, been the glory of his own consulship and the surety

---

[182] Xerxes.

for that of his brother, he might, had he wished it, have been set on the same pedestal with Jupiter; but civil factions will vex the saviour of the State, and he who when a young man disdained to receive divine honours, will take pride as an old man in obstinately remaining in exile. We shall never lack causes of anxiety, either pleasurable or painful: our life will be pushed along from one business to another: leisure will always be wished for, and never enjoyed.

18

Wherefore, my dearest Paulinus, tear yourself away from the common herd, and since you have seen more rough weather than one would think from your age, betake yourself at length to a more peaceful haven: reflect what waves you have sailed through, what storms you have endured in private life, and brought upon yourself in public. Your courage has been sufficiently displayed by many toilsome and wearisome proofs; try how it will deal with leisure: the greater, certainly the better part of your life, has been given to your country; take now some part of your time for yourself as well. I do not urge you to practise a dull or lazy sloth, or to drown all your fiery spirit in the pleasures which are dear to the herd: that is not rest: you can find greater works than all those which you have hitherto so manfully carried out, upon which you may employ yourself in retirement and security. You manage the revenues of the entire world, as unselfishly as though they belonged to another, as laboriously as if they were your own, as scrupulously as though they belonged to the public: you win love in an office in which it is hard to avoid incurring hatred; yet, believe me, it is better to understand your own mind than to understand the corn-market. Take away that keen intellect of yours, so well capable of grappling with the greatest subjects, from a post which may be dignified, but which is hardly fitted to render life happy, and reflect that you did not study from childhood all the branches of a liberal education merely in order that many thousand tons of corn might safely be entrusted to your charge: you have given us promise of something greater and nobler than this. There will never be any want of strict economists or of laborious workers: slow-going beasts of burden are better suited for carrying loads than well-bred horses, whose generous swiftness no one would encumber with a heavy pack. Think, moreover, how full of risk is the great task which you have undertaken: you have to deal with the human stomach: a hungry people will not endure reason, will not be appeased by justice, and will not hearken to any prayers. Only just a few days ago, when G. Caesar perished, grieving for nothing so much (if those in the other world can feel grief) as that the Roman people did not die with him, there was said to be only enough corn for seven or eight days' consumption: while he was making bridges with ships[183] and playing with the resources of the empire, want of provisions, the worst evil that can befall even a besieged city, was at hand: his imitation of a crazy outlandish and misproud king very nearly ended in ruin, famine, and the general revolution which follows famine. What must then have been the feelings of those who had the charge of supplying the city with corn, who were in danger of stoning, of fire and sword, of Gaius himself? With consummate art they concealed the vast internal evil by which the State was menaced, and were quite right in so doing; for some diseases must be cured without the patient's knowledge: many have died through discovering what was the matter with them.

19

Betake yourself to these quieter, safer, larger fields of action; do you think that there can be any comparison between seeing that corn is deposited in the public granary without being stolen by the fraud or spoilt by the carelessness of the importer, that it does not suffer from damp or overheating, and that it measures and weighs as much as it ought, and beginning the study of sacred and divine knowledge, which will teach you of what elements the gods are formed, what are their pleasures, their position, their form? to what changes your soul has to look forward? where Nature will place us when we are dismissed from our bodies? what that principle is which holds all the heaviest particles of our universe in the middle, suspends the lighter ones above, puts fire highest of all, and causes the stars to rise in their courses, with many other matters, full of marvels? Will you not[184] cease to grovel on Earth and turn your mind's eye on these themes? nay, while your blood still flows swiftly, before your knees grow feeble, you ought to take the better path. In this course of life there await you many good things, such as love and practice of the virtues, forgetfulness of passions, knowledge of how to live and die, deep repose. The position of all busy men is unhappy, but most unhappy of all is that of those who do not even labour at their own affairs, but have to regulate their rest by another man's sleep, their walk by another man's pace, and whose very love and hate, the freest things in the world, are at another's bidding. If such men wish to know how short their lives are, let them think how small a fraction of them is their own.

---

[183] "*Sénéque parle ici du pont que Caligula fit construire sur le golphe de Baies, l'an de Rome 791, 40 de J. C. ... Il rassembla et fit entrer dans la construction de son pont tous les vaisseaux qui se trouverent dans les ports d'Italie et des contrées voisines. Il n'excepta pas même ceux qui etoient destinés a y apporter des grains étrangers,*" etc.—La Grange.

[184] For *vis tu* see Juvenal V, *vis tu consuetis*, etc. Mayor's note.

20

When, therefore, you see a man often wear the purple robes of office, and hear his name often repeated in the forum, do not envy him: he gains these things by losing so much of his life. Men throw away all their years in order to have one year named after them as consul: some lose their lives during the early part of the struggle, and never reach the height to which they aspired: some after having submitted to a thousand indignities in order to reach the crowning dignity, have the miserable reflection that the only result of their labours will be the inscription on their tombstone. Some, while telling off extreme old age, like youth, for new aspirations, have found it fail from sheer weakness amid great and presumptuous enterprises. It is a shameful ending, when a man's breath deserts him in a court of justice, while, although well stricken in years, he is still striving to gain the sympathies of an ignorant audience for some obscure litigant: it is base to perish in the midst of one's business, wearied with living sooner than with working; shameful, too, to die in the act of receiving payments, amid the laughter of one's long-expectant heir. I cannot pass over an instance which occurs to me: Turannius was an old man of the most painstaking exactitude, who after entering upon his ninetieth year, when he had by Gr. Caesar's own act been relieved of his duties as collector of the revenue, ordered himself to be laid out on his bed and mourned for as though he were dead. The whole house mourned for the leisure of its old master, and did not lay aside its mourning until his work was restored to him. Can men find such pleasure in dying in harness? Yet many are of the same mind: they retain their wish for labour longer than their capacity for it, and fight against their bodily weakness; they think old age an evil for no other reason than because it lays them on the shelf. The law does not enroll a soldier after his fiftieth year, or require a senator's attendance after his sixtieth: but men have more difficulty in obtaining their own consent than that of the law to a life of leisure. Meanwhile, while they are plundering and being plundered, while one is disturbing another's repose, and all are being made wretched alike, life remains without profit, without pleasure, without any intellectual progress: no one keeps death well before his eyes, no one refrains from far-reaching hopes. Some even arrange things which lie beyond their own lives, such as huge sepulchral buildings, the dedication of public works, and exhibitions to be given at their funeral-pyre, and ostentatious processions: but, by Hercules, the funerals of such men ought to be conducted by the light of torches and wax tapers,[185] as though they had lived but a few days.

---

[185] As those of children were.

ON PEACE OF MIND

1

(Serenus)

When I examine myself, Seneca, some vices appear on the surface, and so that I can lay my hands upon them, while others are less distinct and harder to reach, and some are not always present, but recur at intervals: and these I should call the most troublesome, being like a roving enemy that assails one when he sees his opportunity, and who will neither let one stand on one's guard as in war, nor yet take one's rest without fear as in peace. The position in which I find myself more especially (for why should I not tell you the truth as I would to a physician), is that of neither being thoroughly set free from the vices which I fear and hate, nor yet quite in bondage to them: my state of mind, though not the worst possible, is a particularly discontented and sulky one: I am neither ill nor well. It is of no use for you to tell me that all virtues are weakly at the outset, and that they acquire strength and solidity by time, for I am well aware that even those which do but help our outward show, such as grandeur, a reputation for eloquence, and everything that appeals to others, gain power by time. Both those which afford us real strength and those which do but trick us out in a more attractive form, require long years before they gradually are adapted to us by time. But I fear that custom, which confirms most things, implants this vice more and more deeply in me. Long acquaintance with both good and bad people leads one to esteem them all alike. What this state of weakness really is, when the mind halts between two opinions without any strong inclination towards either good or evil, I shall be better able to show you piecemeal than all at once. I will tell you what befalls me, you must find out the name of the disease. I have to confess the greatest possible love of thrift: I do not care for a bed with gorgeous hangings, nor for clothes brought out of a chest, or pressed under weights and made glossy by frequent manglings, but for common and cheap ones, that require no care either to keep them or to put them on. For food I do not want what needs whole troops of servants to prepare it and admire it, nor what is ordered many days before and served up by many hands, but something handy and easily come at, with nothing farfetched or costly about it, to be had in every part of the world, burdensome neither to one's fortune nor one's body, not likely to go out of the body by the same path by which it came in. I like[186] a rough and unpolished homebred servant, I like my servant born in my house: I like my country-bred father's heavy silver plate stamped with no maker's name: I do not want a table that is beauteous with dappled spots, or known to all the town by the number of fashionable people to whom it has successively belonged, but one which stands merely for use, and which causes no guest's eye to dwell upon it with pleasure or to kindle at it with envy. While I am well satisfied with this, I am reminded of the clothes of a certain schoolboy, dressed with no ordinary care and splendour, of slaves bedecked with gold and a whole regiment of glittering attendants. I think of houses too, where one treads on precious stones, and where valuables lie about in every corner, where the very roof is brilliantly painted, and a whole nation attends and accompanies an inheritance on the road to ruin. What shall I say of waters, transparent to the very bottom, which flow round the guests, and banquets worthy of the theatre in which they take place? Coming as I do from a long course of dull thrift, I find myself surrounded by the most brilliant luxury, which echoes around me on every side: my sight becomes a little dazzled by it: I can lift up my heart against it more easily than my eyes. When I return from seeing it I am a sadder, though not a worse man, I cannot walk amid my own paltry possessions with so lofty a step as before, and silently there steals over me a feeling of vexation, and a doubt whether that way of life may not be better than mine. None of these things alter my principles, yet all of them disturb me. At one time I would obey the maxims of our school and plunge into public life, I would obtain office and become consul, not because the purple robe and lictor's axes attract me, but in order that I may be able to be of use to my friends, my relatives, to all my countrymen, and indeed to all mankind. Ready and determined, I follow the advice of Zeno, Cleanthes, and Chrysippus, all of whom bid one take part in public affairs, though none of them ever did so himself: and then, as soon as something disturbs my mind, which is not used to receiving shocks, as soon as something occurs which is either disgraceful, such as often occurs in all men's lives, or which does not proceed quite easily, or when subjects of very little importance require me to devote a great deal of time to them, I go back to my life of leisure, and, just as even tired cattle go faster when they are going home, I wish to retire and pass my life within the walls of my

---

[186] Cf. Juvenal II, 150.

house. "No one," I say, "that will give me no compensation worth such a loss shall ever rob me of a day. Let my mind be contained within itself and improve itself: let it take no part with other men's affairs, and do nothing which depends on the approval of others: let me enjoy a tranquility undisturbed by either public or private troubles." But whenever my spirit is roused by reading some brave words, or some noble example spurs me into action, I want to rush into the law courts, to place my voice at one man's disposal, my services at another's, and to try to help him even though I may not succeed, or to quell the pride of some lawyer who is puffed up by ill-deserved success: but I think, by Hercules, that in philosophical speculation it is better to view things as they are, and to speak of them on their own account, and as for words, to trust to things for them, and to let one's speech, simply follow whither they lead. "Why do you want to construct a fabric that will endure for ages? Do you not wish to do this in order that posterity may talk of you: yet you were born to die, and a silent death is the least wretched. Write something therefore in a simple style, merely to pass the time, for your own use, and not for publication. Less labour is needed when one does not look beyond the present." Then again, when the mind is elevated by the greatness of its thoughts, it becomes ostentatious in its use of words, the loftier its aspirations, the more loftily it desires to express them, and its speech rises to the dignity of its subject. At such times I forget my mild and moderate determination and soar higher than is my wont, using a language that is not my own. Not to multiply examples, I am in all things attended by this weakness of a well-meaning mind, to whose level I fear that I shall be gradually brought down, or what is even more worrying, that I may always hang as though about to fall, and that there may be more the matter with me than I myself perceive: for we take a friendly view of our own private affairs, and partiality always obscures our judgment. I fancy that many men would have arrived at wisdom had they not believed themselves to have arrived there already, had they not purposely deceived themselves as to some parts of their character, and passed by others with their eyes shut: for you have no grounds for supposing that other people's flattery is more ruinous to us than our own. Who dares to tell himself the truth? Who is there, by however large a troop of caressing courtiers he may be surrounded, who in spite of them is not his own greatest flatterer? I beg you, therefore, if you have any remedy by which you could stop this vacillation of mine, to deem me worthy to owe my peace of mind to you. I am well aware that these oscillations of mind are not perilous and that they threaten me with no serious disorder: to express what I complain of by an exact simile, I am not suffering from a storm, but from seasickness. Take from me, then, this evil, whatever it may be, and help one who is in distress within sight of land.

2

(Seneca)

I have long been silently asking myself, my friend Serenus, to what I should liken such a condition of mind, and I find that nothing more closely resembles it than the conduct of those who, after having recovered from a long and serious illness, occasionally experience slight touches and twinges, and, although they have passed through the final stages of the disease, yet have suspicions that it has not left them, and though in perfect health yet hold out their pulse to be felt by the physician, and whenever they feel warm suspect that the fever is returning. Such men, Serenus, are not unhealthy, but they are not accustomed to being healthy; just as even a quiet sea or lake nevertheless displays a certain amount of ripple when its waters are subsiding after a storm. What you need, therefore, is, not any of those harsher remedies to which allusion has been made, not that you should in some cases check yourself, in others be angry with yourself, in others sternly reproach yourself, but that you should adopt that which comes last in the list, have confidence in yourself, and believe that you are proceeding on the right path, without being led aside by the numerous divergent tracks of wanderers which cross it in every direction, some of them circling about the right path itself. What you desire, to be undisturbed, is a great thing, nay, the greatest thing of all, and one which raises a man almost to the level of a god. The Greeks call this calm steadiness of mind *euthymia*, and Democritus's treatise upon it is excellently written: I call it peace of mind: for there is no necessity for translating so exactly as to copy the words of the Greek idiom: the essential point is to mark the matter under discussion by a name which ought to have the same meaning as its Greek name, though perhaps not the same form. What we are seeking, then, is how the mind may always pursue a steady, unruffled course, may be pleased with itself, and look with pleasure upon its surroundings, and experience no interruption of this joy, but abide in a peaceful condition without being ever either elated or depressed: this will be "peace of mind." Let us now consider in a general way how it may be attained: then you may apply as much as you choose of the universal remedy to your own case. Meanwhile we must drag to light the entire disease, and then each one will recognize his own part of it: at the same time you will understand how much less you suffer by your self-depreciation than those who are bound by some showy declaration which they have made, and are oppressed by some grand title of honour, so that shame rather than their own free will forces them to keep up the pretence. The same thing applies both to those who suffer from fickleness and continual changes of purpose, who always are fondest of what they have given up, and those who merely yawn and dawdle: add to these those who, like bad sleepers, turn from side to side, and settle themselves first in one manner and then in another, until at last they find rest through sheer weariness: in forming the habits of their lives they often end by adopting some to which they are not kept by any dislike of change, but in the practice of which old age, which is slow to alter, has caught them living: add also those who are by no means fickle, yet who must thank their dullness, not their consistency for being so, and who go on living not in the way they wish, but in the way they have begun to live. There are other special forms of this disease without number, but it has but one effect, that of making people dissatisfied with themselves. This arises from a distemperature of mind and from desires which one is afraid to express or unable to fulfill, when men either dare not attempt as much as they wish to do, or fail in their efforts and depend entirely upon hope: such people are always fickle and changeable, which is a necessary consequence of living in a state of suspense: they take any way to arrive at their ends, and teach and force themselves to use both dishonourable and difficult means to do so, so that when their toil has been in vain they are made wretched by the disgrace of failure, and do not regret having longed for what was wrong, but having longed for it in vain. They then begin to feel sorry for what they have done, and afraid to begin again, and their mind falls by degrees into a state of endless vacillation, because they can neither command nor obey their passions, of hesitation, because their life cannot properly develop itself, and of decay, as the mind becomes stupefied by disappointments. All these symptoms become aggravated when their dislike of a laborious misery has driven them to idleness and to secret studies, which are unendurable to a mind eager to take part in public affairs, desirous of action and naturally restless, because, of course, it finds too few resources within itself: when therefore it loses the amusement which business itself affords to busy men, it cannot endure home, loneliness, or the walls of a room, and regards itself with dislike when left to itself. Hence arises that weariness and dissatisfaction with oneself, that tossing to and fro of a mind which can nowhere find rest, that unhappy and unwilling endurance of enforced leisure. In all cases where one feels ashamed to confess the real cause of one's suffering, and where modesty leads one to drive one's sufferings inward, the desires pent up in a little space without any vent choke one another. Hence comes melancholy and drooping of spirit, and a thousand waverings of the unsteadfast mind, which is held in suspense by unfulfilled hopes, and saddened by disappointed ones: hence comes the state of mind of those who loathe their idleness, complain that they have nothing to do, and view the progress of others with the bitterest jealousy: for an unhappy sloth favours the growth of envy, and men who cannot succeed themselves wish everyone else to be ruined. This dislike of other men's progress and despair of one's own produces a mind angered against fortune, addicted to complaining of the age in which it lives to retiring into corners and brooding over its misery, until it becomes sick and weary of itself: for the human mind is naturally nimble and apt at movement: it delights in every opportunity of excitement and forgetfulness of itself, and the worse a man's disposition the more he delights in this, because he likes to wear himself out with busy action, just as some sores long for the hands that injure them and delight in being touched, and the foul itch enjoys anything that scratches it. Similarly I assure you that these minds over which desires have spread like evil ulcers, take pleasure in toils and troubles, for there are some things which please our body while at the same time they give it a certain amount of pain, such as turning oneself over and changing one's side before it is wearied, or cooling oneself in one position after another. It is like Homer's Achilles lying first upon its face, then upon its back, placing itself in various attitudes, and, as sick people are wont, enduring none of them for long, and using changes as though they were remedies. Hence men undertake aimless wanderings, travel along distant shores, and at one time at sea, at another by land, try to soothe that fickleness of disposition which always is dissatisfied with the present. "Now let us make for Campania: now I am sick of rich cultivation: let us see wild regions, let us thread the passes of Bruttii and Lucania: yet amid this wilderness one wants some thing of beauty to relieve our pampered eyes after so long dwelling on savage wastes: let us seek Tarentum with its famous harbour, its mild winter climate, and its district, rich enough to support even the great hordes of ancient times. Let us now return to town: our ears have too long missed its shouts and noise: it would be pleasant also to enjoy the sight of human bloodshed." Thus one journey succeeds another, and one sight is changed for another. As Lucretius says:—

"Thus every mortal from himself doth flee;"

but what does he gain by so doing if he does not escape from himself? he follows himself and weighs himself down by his own most burdensome companionship. We must understand, therefore, that what we suffer from is not the fault of the places but of ourselves: we are weak when there is anything to be endured, and cannot support either labour or pleasure, either one's own business or anyone else's for long. This has driven some men to death, because by frequently altering their purpose they were always brought back to the same point, and had left themselves no room for anything new. They had become sick of life and of the world itself, and as all indulgences palled upon them they began to ask themselves the question, "How long are we to go on doing the same thing?"

3

You ask me what I think we had better make use of to help us to support this ennui. "The best thing," as Athenodorus says, "is to occupy oneself with business, with the management of affairs of state and the duties of a citizen: for as some pass the day in exercising themselves in the sun and in taking care of their bodily health, and athletes find it most useful to spend the greater part of their time in feeding up the muscles and strength to whose cultivation they have devoted their lives; so too for you who are training your mind to take part in the struggles of political life, it is far more honourable to be thus at work than to be idle. He whose object is to be of service to his countrymen and to all mortals, exercises himself and does good at the same time when he is engrossed in business and is working to the best of his ability both in the interests of the public and of private men. But," continues he, "because innocence is hardly safe among such furious ambitions and so many men who turn one aside from the right path, and it is always sure to meet with more hindrance than help, we ought to withdraw ourselves from the forum and from public life, and a great mind even in a private station can find room wherein to expand freely. Confinement in dens restrains the springs of lions and wild creatures, but this does not apply to human beings, who often effect the most important works in retirement. Let a man, however, withdraw himself only in such a fashion that wherever he spends his leisure his wish may still be to benefit individual men and mankind alike, both with his intellect, his voice, and his advice. The man that does good service to the State is not only he who brings forward candidates for public office, defends accused persons, and gives his vote on questions of peace and war, but he who encourages young men in well-doing, who supplies the present dearth of good teachers by instilling into their minds the principles of virtue, who seizes and holds back those who are rushing wildly in pursuit of riches and luxury, and, if he does nothing else, at least checks their course—such a man does service to the public though in a private station. Which does the most good, he who decides between foreigners and citizens (as *praetor peregrinus*), or, as *praetor urbanus*, pronounces sentence to the suitors in his court at his assistant's dictation, or he who shows them what is meant by justice, filial feeling, endurance, courage, contempt of death and knowledge of the gods, and how much a man is helped by a good conscience? If then you transfer to philosophy the time which you take away from the public service, you will not be a deserter or have refused to perform your proper task. A soldier is not merely one who stands in the ranks and defends the right or the left wing of the army, but he also who guards the gates—a service which, though less dangerous, is no sinecure—who keeps watch, and takes charge of the arsenal: though all these are bloodless duties, yet they count as military service. As soon as you have devoted yourself to philosophy, you will have overcome all disgust at life: you will not wish for darkness because you are weary of the light, nor will you be a trouble to yourself and useless to others: you will acquire many friends, and all the best men will be attracted towards you: for virtue, in however obscure a position, cannot be hidden, but gives signs of its presence: anyone who is worthy will trace it out by its footsteps: but if we give up all society, turn our backs upon the whole human race, and live communing with ourselves alone, this solitude without any interesting occupation will lead to a want of something to do: we shall begin to build up and to pull down, to dam out the sea, to cause waters to flow through natural obstacles, and generally to make a bad disposal of the time which Nature has given us to spend: some of us use it grudgingly, others wastefully; some of us spend it so that we can show a profit and loss account, others so that they have no assets remaining: than which nothing can be more shameful. Often a man who is very old in years has nothing beyond his age by which he can prove that he has lived a long time."

4

To me, my dearest Serenus, Athenodorus seems to have yielded too completely to the times, to have fled too soon: I will not deny that sometimes one must retire, but one ought to retire slowly, at a foot's pace, without losing one's ensigns or one's honour as a soldier: those who make terms with arms in their hands are more respected by their enemies and more safe in their hands. This is what I think ought to be done by virtue and by one who practises virtue: if Fortune get the upper hand and deprive him of the power of action, let him not straightaway turn his back to the enemy, throw away his arms, and run away seeking for a hiding-place, as if there were any place whither Fortune could not pursue him, but let him be more sparing in his acceptance of public office, and after due deliberation discover some means by which he can be of use to the State. He is not able to serve in the army: then let him become a candidate for civic honours: must he live in a private station? then let him be an advocate: is he condemned to keep silence? then let him help his countrymen with silent counsel. Is it dangerous for him even to enter the forum? then let him prove himself a good comrade, a faithful friend, a sober guest in people's houses, at public shows, and at wine-parties. Suppose that he has lost the status of a citizen; then let him exercise that of a man: our reason for magnanimously refusing to confine ourselves within the walls of one city, for having gone forth to enjoy intercourse with all lands and for professing ourselves to be citizens of the world is that we may thus obtain a wider theatre on which to display our virtue. Is the bench of judges closed to you, are you forbidden to address the people from the hustings, or to be a candidate at elections? then turn your eyes away from Rome, and see what a wide extent of territory, what a number of nations present themselves before you. Thus, it is never possible for so many outlets to be closed against your ambition that more will not remain open to it: but see whether the whole prohibition does not arise from your own fault. You do not choose to direct the affairs of the State except as consul or prytanis[187] or meddix[188] or sufes:[189] what should we say if you refused to serve in the army save as general or military tribune? Even though others may form the first line, and your lot may have placed you among the veterans of the third, do your duty there with your voice, encouragement, example, and spirit: even though a man's hands be cut off, he may find means to help his side in a battle, if he stands his ground and cheers on his comrades. Do something of that sort yourself: if Fortune removes you from the front rank, stand your ground nevertheless and cheer on your comrades, and if somebody stops your mouth, stand nevertheless and help your side in silence. The services of a good citizen are never thrown away: he does good by being heard and seen, by his expression, his gestures, his silent determination, and his very walk. As some remedies benefit us by their smell as well as by their their taste and touch, so virtue even when concealed and at a distance sheds usefulness around. Whether she moves at her ease and enjoys her just rights, or can only appear abroad on sufferance and is forced to shorten sail to the tempest, whether it be unemployed, silent, and pent up in a narrow lodging, or openly displayed, in whatever guise she may appear, she always does good. What? do you think that the example of one who can rest nobly has no value? It is by far the best plan, therefore, to mingle leisure with business, whenever chance impediments or the state of public affairs forbid one's leading an active life: for one is never so cut off from all pursuits as to find no room left for honourable action.

5

Could you anywhere find a miserable city than that of Athens when it was being torn to pieces by the thirty tyrants? they slew thirteen hundred citizens, all the best men, and did not leave off because they had done so, but their cruelty became stimulated by exercise. In the city which possessed that most reverend tribunal, the Court of the Areopagus, which possessed a Senate, and a popular

---

[187] The chief magistrate of the Greeks.
[188] The chief magistrate of the Uscans.
[189] The chief magistrate of the Carthaginians.

assembly which was like a Senate, there met daily a wretched crew of butchers, and the unhappy Senate House was crowded with tyrants. A state, in which there were so many tyrants that they would have been enough to form a bodyguard for one, might surely have rested from the struggle; it seemed impossible for men's minds even to conceive hopes of recovering their liberty, nor could they see any room for a remedy for such a mass of evil: for whence could the unhappy state obtain all the Harmodiuses it would need to slay so many tyrants? Yet Socrates was in the midst of the city, and consoled its mourning Fathers, encouraged those who despaired of the republic, by his reproaches brought rich men, who feared that their wealth would be their ruin, to a tardy repentance of their avarice, and moved about as a great example to those who wished to imitate him, because he walked a free man in the midst of thirty masters. However, Athens herself put him to death in prison, and Freedom herself could not endure the freedom of one who had treated a whole band of tyrants with scorn: you may know, therefore, that even in an oppressed state a wise man can find an opportunity for bringing himself to the front, and that in a prosperous and flourishing one wanton insolence, jealousy, and a thousand other cowardly vices bear sway. We ought therefore, to expand or contract ourselves according as the State presents itself to us, or as Fortune offers us opportunities: but in any case we ought to move and not to become frozen still by fear: nay, he is the best man who, though peril menaces him on every side and arms and chains beset his path, nevertheless neither impairs nor conceals his virtue: for to keep oneself safe does not mean to bury oneself. I think that Curius Dentatus spoke truly when he said that he would rather be dead than alive: the worst evil of all is to leave the ranks of the living before one dies; yet it is your duty, if you happen to live in an age when it is not easy to serve the State, to devote more time to leisure and to literature. Thus, just as though you were making a perilous voyage, you may from time to time put into harbour, and set yourself free from public business without waiting for it to do so.

6

We ought, however, first to examine our own selves, next the business which we propose to transact, next those for whose sake or in whose company we transact it.

It is above all things necessary to form a true estimate of oneself, because as a rule we think that we can do more than we are able: one man is led too far through confidence in his eloquence, another demands more from his estate than it can produce, another burdens a weakly body with some toilsome duty.

Some men are too shamefaced for the conduct of public affairs, which require an unblushing front: some men's obstinate pride renders them unfit for courts: some cannot control their anger, and break into unguarded language on the slightest provocation: some cannot rein in their wit or resist making risky jokes: for all these men leisure is better than employment: a bold, haughty and impatient nature ought to avoid anything that may lead it to use a freedom of speech which will bring it to ruin. Next we must form an estimate of the matter which we mean to deal with, and compare our strength with the deed we are about to attempt: for the bearer ought always to be more powerful than his load: indeed, loads which are too heavy for their bearer must of necessity crush him: some affairs also are not so important in themselves as they are prolific and lead to much more business, which employments, as they involve us in new and various forms of work, ought to be refused. Neither should you engage in anything from which you are not free to retreat: apply yourself to something which you can finish, or at any rate can hope to finish: you had better not meddle with those operations which grow in importance, while they are being transacted, and which will not stop where you intended them to stop.

7

In all cases one should be careful in one's choice of men, and see whether they be worthy of our bestowing a part of our life upon them, or whether we shall waste our own time and theirs also: for some even consider us to be in their debt because of our services to them. Athenodorus said that "he would not so much as dine with a man who would not be grateful to him for doing so": meaning, I imagine, that much less would he go to dinner with those who recompense the services of their friends by their table, and regard courses of dishes as donatives, as if they overate themselves to do honour to others. Take away from these men their witnesses and spectators: they will take no pleasure in solitary gluttony. You must decide whether your disposition is better suited for vigorous action or for tranquil speculation and contemplation, and you must adopt whichever the bent of your genius inclines you for. Socrates laid hands upon Ephorus and led him away from the forum, thinking that he would be more usefully employed in compiling chronicles; for no good is done by forcing one's mind to engage in uncongenial work: it is vain to struggle against Nature. Yet nothing delights the mind so much as faithful and pleasant friendship: what a blessing it is when there is one whose breast is ready to receive all your secrets with safety, whose knowledge of your actions you fear less than your own conscience, whose conversation removes your anxieties, whose advice assists your plans, whose cheerfulness dispels your gloom, whose very sight delights you! We should choose for our friends men who are, as far as possible, free from strong desires: for vices are contagious, and pass from a man to his neighbour, and injure those who touch them. As, therefore, in times of pestilence we have to be careful not to sit near people who are infected and in whom the disease is raging, because by so doing, we shall run into danger and catch the plague from their very breath; so, too, in choosing our friends' dispositions, we must take care to select those who are as far as may be unspotted by the world; for the way to breed disease is to mix what is sound with what is rotten. Yet I do not advise you to follow after or draw to yourself no one except a wise man: for where will you find him whom for so many centuries we have sought in vain? in the place of the best possible man take him who is least bad. You would hardly find any time that would have enabled you to make a happier choice than if you could have sought for a good man from among the Platos and Xenophons and the rest of the produce of the brood of Socrates, or if you had been permitted to choose one from the age of Cato: an age which bore many men worthy to be born in Cato's time (just as it also bore many men worse than were ever known before, planners of the blackest crimes: for it needed both classes in order to make Cato understood: it wanted both good men, that he might win their approbation, and bad men, against whom he could prove his strength): but at the present day, when there is such a dearth of good men, you must be less squeamish in your choice. Above all, however, avoid dismal men who grumble at whatever happens, and find something to complain of in everything. Though he may continue loyal and friendly towards you, still one's peace of mind is destroyed by a comrade whose mind is soured and who meets every incident with a groan.

8

Let us now pass on to the consideration of property, that most fertile source of human sorrows: for if you compare all the other ills from which we suffer—deaths, sicknesses, fears, regrets, endurance of pains and labours–with those miseries which our money inflicts upon us, the latter will far outweigh all the others. Reflect, then, how much less a grief it is never to have had any money than to have lost it: we shall thus understand that the less poverty has to lose, the less torment it has with which to afflict us: for you are mistaken if you suppose that the rich bear their losses with greater spirit than the poor: a wound causes the same amount of pain to the greatest and the smallest body. It was a neat saying of Bion's, "that it hurts bald men as much as hairy men to have their hairs pulled out": you may be assured that the same thing is true of rich and poor people, that their suffering is equal: for their money clings to both classes, and cannot be torn away without their feeling it: yet it is more endurable, as I have said, and easier not to gain property than to lose it, and therefore you will find that those upon whom Fortune has never smiled are more cheerful than those whom she has deserted. Diogenes, a man of infinite spirit, perceived this, and made it impossible that anything should be taken from him. Call this security from loss poverty, want, necessity, or any contemptuous name you please: I shall consider such a man to be happy, unless you find me another who can lose nothing. If I am not mistaken, it is a royal attribute among so many misers, sharpers, and robbers, to be the one man who cannot be injured. If anyone doubts the happiness of Diogenes, he would doubt whether the position of the immortal gods was one of sufficient happiness, because they have no farms or gardens, no valuable estates let to strange tenants, and no large loans in the money market. Are you not ashamed of yourself, you who gaze upon riches with astonished admiration? Look upon the universe: you will see the gods quite bare of property, and possessing nothing though they give everything. Do you think that this man who has stripped himself of all fortuitous accessories is a pauper, or one like to the immortal gods? Do you call Demetrius, Pompeius's freedman, a happier man, he who was not ashamed to be richer than Pompeius, who was daily furnished with a list of the number of his slaves, as a general is with that of his army, though he had long deserved that all his riches should consist of a pair of underlings, and a roomier cell than the other slaves? But Diogenes's only slave ran away from him, and when he was pointed out to Diogenes, he did not think him worth fetching back. "It is a shame," he said, "that Manes should be able to live without Diogenes, and that Diogenes should not be able to live without Manes." He seems to me to have said, "Fortune, mind your own business: Diogenes has nothing left that belongs to you. Did my slave run away? nay, he went away from me as a free man." A household of slaves requires food and clothing: the bellies of so many hungry creatures have to be filled: we must buy raiment for them, we must watch their most thievish hands, and we must make use of the services of people who weep and execrate us. How far happier is he who is indebted to no man for anything except for what he can deprive himself of with the greatest ease! Since we, however, have not such strength of mind as this, we ought at any rate to diminish the extent of our property, in order to be less exposed to the assaults of fortune: those men whose bodies can be within the shelter of their armour, are more fitted for war than those whose huge size everywhere extends beyond it, and exposes them to wounds:

the best amount of property to have is that which is enough to keep us from poverty, and which yet is not far removed from it.

9

We shall be pleased with this measure of wealth if we have previously taken pleasure in thrift, without which no riches are sufficient, and with which none are insufficient, especially as the remedy is always at hand, and poverty itself by calling in the aid of thrift can convert itself into riches. Let us accustom ourselves to set aside mere outward show, and to measure things by their uses, not by their ornamental trappings: let our hunger be tamed by food, our thirst quenched by drinking, our lust confined within needful bounds; let us learn to use our limbs, and to arrange our dress and way of life according to what was approved of by our ancestors, not in imitation of newfangled models: let us learn to increase our continence, to repress luxury, to set bounds to our pride, to assuage our anger, to look upon poverty without prejudice, to practise thrift, albeit many are ashamed to do so, to apply cheap remedies to the wants of nature, to keep all undisciplined hopes and aspirations as it were under lock and key, and to make it our business to get our riches from ourselves and not from Fortune. We never can so thoroughly defeat the vast diversity and malignity of misfortune with which we are threatened as not to feel the weight of many gusts if we offer a large spread of canvas to the wind: we must draw our affairs into a small compass, to make the darts of Fortune of no avail. For this reason, sometimes slight mishaps have turned into remedies, and more serious disorders have been healed by slighter ones. When the mind pays no attention to good advice, and cannot be brought to its senses by milder measures, why should we not think that its interests are being served by poverty, disgrace, or financial ruin being applied to it? one evil is balanced by another. Let us then teach ourselves to be able to dine without all Rome to look on, to be the slaves of fewer slaves, to get clothes which fulfill their original purpose, and to live in a smaller house. The inner curve is the one to take, not only in running races and in the contests of the circus, but also in the race of life; even literary pursuits, the most becoming thing for a gentleman to spend money upon, are only justifiable as long as they are kept within bounds. What is the use of possessing numberless books and libraries, whose titles their owner can hardly read through in a lifetime? A student is overwhelmed by such a mass, not instructed, and it is much better to devote yourself to a few writers than to skim through many. Forty thousand books were burned at Alexandria: some would have praised this library as a most noble memorial of royal wealth, like Titus Livius, who says that it was "a splendid result of the taste and attentive care of the kings."[190] It had nothing to do with taste or care, but was a piece of learned luxury, nay, not even learned, since they amassed it, not for the sake of learning, but to make a show, like many men who know less about letters than a slave is expected to know, and who uses his books not to help him in his studies but to ornament his dining-room. Let a man, then, obtain as many books as he wants, but none for show. "It is more respectable," say you, "to spend one's money on such books than on vases of Corinthian brass and paintings." Not so: everything that is carried to excess is wrong. What excuses can you find for a man who is eager to buy bookcases of ivory and citrus wood, to collect the works of unknown or discredited authors, and who sits yawning amid so many thousands of books, whose backs and titles please him more than any other part of them? Thus in the houses of the laziest of men you will see the works of all the orators and historians stacked upon bookshelves reaching right up to the ceiling. At the present day a library has become as necessary an appendage to a house as a hot and cold bath. I would excuse them straightaway if they really were carried away by an excessive zeal for literature; but as it is, these costly works of sacred genius, with all the illustrations that adorn them, are merely bought for display and to serve as wall-furniture.

10

Suppose, however, that your life has become full of trouble, and that without knowing what you were doing you have fallen into some snare which either public or private fortune has set for you, and that you can neither untie it nor break it: then remember that fettered men suffer much at first from the burdens and clogs upon their legs: afterwards, when they have made up their minds not to fret themselves about them, but to endure them, necessity teaches them to bear them bravely, and habit to bear them easily. In every station of life you will find amusements, relaxations, and enjoyments; that is, provided you be willing to make light of evils rather than to hate them. Knowing to what sorrows we were born, there is nothing for which Nature more deserves our thanks than for having invented habit as an alleviation of misfortune, which soon accustoms us to the severest evils. No one could hold out against misfortune if

---

[190] "Livy himself styled the Alexandrian library *elegantiae regum curaeque egregium opus*: a liberal encomium, for which he is pertly criticised by the narrow stoicism of Seneca ('On Peace of Mind,' Chapter II), whose wisdom, on this occasion, deviates into nonsense."
—Gibbon, Decline and Fall, Chapter LI, note.

it permanently exercised the same force as at its first onset. We are all chained to fortune: some men's chain is loose and made of gold, that of others is tight and of meaner metal: but what difference does this make? we are all included in the same captivity, and even those who have bound us are bound themselves, unless you think that a chain on the left side is lighter to bear: one man may be bound by public office, another by wealth: some have to bear the weight of illustrious, some of humble birth: some are subject to the commands of others, some only to their own: some are kept in one place by being banished thither, others by being elected to the priesthood. All life is slavery: let each man therefore reconcile himself to his lot, complain of it as little as possible, and lay hold of whatever good lies within his reach. No condition can be so wretched that an impartial mind can find no compensations in it. Small sites, if ingeniously divided, may be made use of for many different purposes, and arrangement will render ever so narrow a room habitable. Call good sense to your aid against difficulties: it is possible to soften what is harsh, to widen what is too narrow, and to make heavy burdens press less severely upon one who bears them skillfully. Moreover, we ought not to allow our desires to wander far afield, but we must make them confine themselves to our immediate neighbourhood, since they will not endure to be altogether locked up. We must leave alone things which either cannot come to pass or can only be effected with difficulty, and follow after such things as are near at hand and within reach of our hopes, always remembering that all things are equally unimportant, and that though they have a different outward appearance, they are all alike empty within. Neither let us envy those who are in high places: the heights which look lofty to us are steep and rugged. Again, those whom unkind fate has placed in critical situations will be safer if they show as little pride in their proud position as may be, and do all they are able to bring down their fortunes to the level of other men's. There are many who must needs cling to their high pinnacle of power, because they cannot descend from it save by falling headlong: yet they assure us that their greatest burden is being obliged to be burdensome to others, and that they are nailed to their lofty post rather than raised to it: let them then, by dispensing justice, clemency, and kindness with an open and liberal hand, provide themselves with assistance to break their fall, and looking forward to this maintain their position more hopefully. Yet nothing sets as free from these alternations of hope and fear so well as always fixing some limit to our successes, and not allowing fortune to choose when to stop our career, but to halt of our own accord long before we apparently need do so. By acting thus certain desires will rouse up our spirits, and yet being confined within bounds, will not lead us to embark on vast and vague enterprises.

11

These remarks of mine apply only to imperfect, commonplace, and unsound natures, not to the wise man, who needs not to walk with timid and cautious gait: for he has such confidence in himself that he does not hesitate to go directly in the teeth of Fortune, and never will give way to her. Nor indeed has he any reason for fearing her, for he counts not only chattels, property, and high office, but even his body, his eyes, his hands, and everything whose use makes life dearer to us, nay, even his very self, to be things whose possession is uncertain; he lives as though he had borrowed them, and is ready to return them cheerfully whenever they are claimed. Yet he does not hold himself cheap, because he knows that he is not his own, but performs all his duties as carefully and prudently as a pious and scrupulous man would take care of property left in his charge as trustee. When he is bidden to give them up, he will not complain of Fortune, but will say, "I thank you for what I have had possession of: I have managed your property so as largely to increase it, but since you order me, I give it back to you and return it willingly and thankfully. If you still wish me to own anything of yours, I will keep it for you: if you have other views, I restore into your hands and make restitution of all my wrought and coined silver, my house and my household. Should Nature recall what she previously entrusted us with, let us say to her also: 'Take back my spirit, which is better than when you gave it me: I do not shuffle or hang back. Of my own free will I am ready to return what you gave me before I could think: take me away.'" What hardship can there be in returning to the place from whence one came? a man cannot live well if he knows not how to die well. We must, therefore, take away from this commodity its original value, and count the breath of life as a cheap matter. "We dislike gladiators," says Cicero, "if they are eager to save their lives by any means whatever: but we look favourably upon them if they are openly reckless of them." You may be sure that the same thing occurs with us: we often die because we are afraid of death. Fortune, which regards our lives as a show in the arena for her own enjoyment, says, "Why should I spare you, base and cowardly creature that you are? you will be pierced and hacked with all the more wounds because you know not how to offer your throat to the knife: whereas you, who receive the stroke without drawing away your neck or putting up your hands to stop it, shall both live longer and die more quickly." He who fears death will never act as becomes a living man: but he who knows that this fate was laid upon him as soon as he was conceived will live according to it, and by this strength of mind will gain this further advantage, that nothing can befall him unexpectedly: for by looking forward to everything which can happen as though it would happen to him, he takes the sting out of all evils, which can make no difference to those who expect it and are prepared to meet it: evil only comes hard upon those who have lived without giving it a thought and whose attention has been exclusively directed to happiness. Disease, captivity, disaster, conflagration, are none of them unexpected: I always knew with what disorderly company Nature had associated me. The dead have often been wailed for in my neighbourhood: the torch and taper have often been borne past my door before the bier of one who has died before his time: the crash of falling buildings has often resounded by my side: night has snatched away many of those with whom I have become intimate in the forum, the Senate-house, and in society, and has sundered the hands which were joined in friendship: ought I to be surprised if the dangers which have always been circling around me at last assail me? How large a part of mankind never think of storms when about to set sail? I shall never be ashamed to quote a good saying because it comes from a bad author. Publilius, who was a more powerful writer than any of our other playwrights, whether comic or tragic, whenever he chose to rise above farcical absurdities and speeches addressed to the gallery, among many other verses too noble even for tragedy, let alone for comedy, has this one:—

"What one hath suffered may befall us all."

If a man takes this into his inmost heart and looks upon all the misfortunes of other men, of which there is always a great plenty, in this spirit, remembering that there is nothing to prevent their coming upon him also, he will arm himself against them long before they attack him. It is too late to school the mind to endurance of peril after peril has come. "I did not think this would happen," and "Would you ever have believed that this would have happened?" say you. But why should it not? Where are the riches after which want, hunger, and beggary do not follow? what office is there whose purple robe, augur's staff, and patrician reins have not as their accompaniment rags and banishment, the brand of infamy, a thousand disgraces, and utter reprobation? what kingdom is there for which ruin, trampling under foot, a tyrant and a butcher are not ready at hand? nor are these matters divided by long periods of time, but there is but the space of an hour between sitting on the throne ourselves and clasping the knees of someone else as suppliants. Know then that every station of life is transitory, and that what has ever happened to anybody may happen to you also. You are wealthy: are you wealthier than Pompeius?[191] Yet when Gaius,[192] his old relative

---

[191] Haase reads "Ptolemaeus."
[192] Caligula.

and new host, opened Caesar's house to him in order that he might close his own, he lacked both bread and water: though he owned so many rivers which both rose and discharged themselves within his dominions, yet he had to beg for drops of water: he perished of hunger and thirst in the palace of his relative, while his heir was contracting for a public funeral for one who was in want of food. You have filled public offices: were they either as important, as unlooked for, or as all-embracing as those of Sejanus? Yet on the day on which the Senate disgraced him, the people tore him to pieces: the executioner[193] could find no part left large enough to drag to the Tiber, of one upon whom gods and men had showered all that could be given to man. You are a king: I will not bid you go to Croesus for an example, he who while yet alive saw his funeral pile both lighted and extinguished, being made to outlive not only his kingdom but even his own death, nor to Jugurtha, whom the people of Rome beheld as a captive within the year in which they had feared him. We have seen Ptolemaeus King of Africa, and Mithridates King of Armenia, under the charge of Gaius's[194] guards: the former was sent into exile, the latter chose it in order to make his exile more honourable. Among such continual topsy-turvy changes, unless you expect that whatever can happen will happen to you, you give adversity power against you, a power which can be destroyed by anyone who looks at it beforehand.

12

The next point to these will be to take care that we do not labour for what is vain, or labour in vain: that is to say, neither to desire what we are not able to obtain, nor yet, having obtained our desire too late, and after much toil to discover the folly of our wishes: in other words, that our labour may not be without result, and that the result may not be unworthy of our labour: for as a rule sadness arises from one of these two things, either from want of success or from being ashamed of having succeeded. We must limit the running to and fro which most men practise, rambling about houses, theatres, and marketplaces. They mind other men's business, and always seem as though they themselves had something to do. If you ask one of them as he comes out of his own door, "Whither are you going?" he will answer, "By Hercules, I do not know: but I shall see some people and do something." They wander purposelessly seeking for something to do, and do, not what they have made up their minds to do, but what has casually fallen in their way. They move uselessly and without any plan, just like ants

---

[193] It was the duty of the executioner to fasten a hook to the neck of condemned criminals, by which they were dragged to the Tiber.
[194] Caligula.

crawling over bushes, which creep up to the top and then down to the bottom again without gaining anything. Many men spend their lives in exactly the same fashion, which one may call a state of restless indolence. You would pity some of them when you see them running as if their house was on fire: they actually jostle all whom they meet, and hurry along themselves and others with them, though all the while they are going to salute someone who will not return their greeting, or to attend the funeral of someone whom they did not know: they are going to hear the verdict on one who often goes to law, or to see the wedding of one who often gets married: they will follow a man's litter, and in some places will even carry it: afterwards returning home weary with idleness, they swear that they themselves do not know why they went out, or where they have been, and on the following day they will wander through the same round again. Let all your work, therefore, have some purpose, and keep some object in view: these restless people are not made restless by labour, but are driven out of their minds by mistaken ideas: for even they do not put themselves in motion without any hope: they are excited by the outward appearance of something, and their crazy mind cannot see its futility. In the same way every one of those who walk out to swell the crowd in the streets, is led round the city by worthless and empty reasons; the dawn drives him forth, although he has nothing to do, and after he has pushed his way into many men's doors, and saluted their nomenclators one after the other, and been turned away from many others, he finds that the most difficult person of all to find at home is himself. From this evil habit comes that worst of all vices, talebearing and prying into public and private secrets, and the knowledge of many things which it is neither safe to tell nor safe to listen to.

13

It was, I imagine, following out this principle that Democritus taught that "he who would live at peace must not do much business either public or private," referring of course to unnecessary business: for if there be any necessity for it we ought to transact not only much but endless business, both public and private; in cases, however, where no solemn duty invites us to act, we had better keep ourselves quiet: for he who does many things often puts himself in Fortune's power, and it is safest not to tempt her often, but always to remember her existence, and never to promise oneself anything on her security. I will set sail unless anything happens to prevent me, I shall be praetor, if nothing hinders me, my financial operations will succeed, unless anything goes wrong with them. This is why we say that nothing befalls the wise man which he did not expect—we do not make him exempt from the chances of human life, but from its mistakes, nor does everything happen to him as he wished it would, but as he thought it would: now his first thought was that his purpose might meet with some resistance, and the pain of disappointed wishes must affect a man's mind less severely if he has not been at all events confident of success.

14

Moreover, we ought to cultivate an easy temper, and not become over fond of the lot which fate has assigned to us, but transfer ourselves to whatever other condition chance may lead us to, and fear no alteration, either in our purposes or our position in life, provided that we do not become subject to caprice, which of all vices is the most hostile to repose: for obstinacy, from which Fortune often wrings some concession, must needs be anxious and unhappy, but caprice, which can never restrain itself, must be more so. Both of these qualities, both that of altering nothing, and that of being dissatisfied with everything, are enemies to repose. The mind ought in all cases to be called away from the contemplation of external things to that of itself: let it confide in itself, rejoice in itself, admire its own works; avoid as far as may be those of others, and devote itself to itself; let it not feel losses, and put a good construction even upon misfortunes. Zeno, the chief of our school, when he heard the news of a shipwreck, in which all his property had been lost, remarked, "Fortune bids me follow philosophy in lighter marching order." A tyrant threatened Theodorus with death, and even with want of burial. "You are able to please yourself," he answered, "my half pint of blood is in your power: for, as for burial, what a fool you must be if you suppose that I care whether I rot above ground or under it." Julius Kanus, a man of peculiar greatness, whom even the fact of his having been born in this century does not prevent our admiring, had a long dispute with Gaius, and when as he was going away that Phalaris of a man said to him, "That you may not delude yourself with any foolish hopes, I have ordered you to be executed," he answered, "I thank you, most excellent prince." I am not sure what he meant: for many ways of explaining his conduct occur to me. Did he wish to be reproachful, and to show him how great his cruelty must be if death became a kindness? or did he upbraid him with his accustomed insanity? for even those whose children were put to death, and whose goods were confiscated, used to thank him: or was it that he willingly received death, regarding it as freedom? Whatever he meant, it was a magnanimous answer. Someone may say, "After this Gaius might have let him live." Kanus had no fear of this: the good faith with which Gaius carried out such orders as these was well known. Will you believe that he passed the ten intervening days before his execution without the slightest despondency? it is marvellous how that man spoke and acted, and how peaceful he was. He was playing at draughts when the centurion in charge of a number of those who were going to be executed bade him join them: on the summons he counted his men and said to his companion, "Mind you do not tell a lie after my death, and say that you won;" then, turning to the centurion, he said, "You will bear me witness that I am one man ahead of him." Do you think that Kanus played upon that draught-board? nay, he played with it. His friends were sad at being about to lose so great a man: "Why," asked he, "are you sorrowful? you are enquiring whether our souls are immortal, but I shall presently know." Nor did he up to the very end cease his search after truth, and raised arguments upon the subject of his own death. His own teacher of philosophy accompanied him, and they were not far from the hill on which the daily sacrifice to Caesar our god was offered, when he said, "What are you thinking of now, Kanus? or what are your ideas?" "I have decided," answered Kanus, "at that most swiftly-passing moment of all to watch whether the spirit will be conscious of the act of leaving the body." He promised, too, that if he made any discoveries, he would come round to his friends and tell them what the condition of the souls of the departed might be. Here was peace in the very midst of the storm: here was a soul worthy of eternal life, which used its own fate as a proof of truth, which when at the last step of life experimented upon his fleeting breath, and did not merely continue to learn until he died, but learned something even from death itself. No man has carried the life of a philosopher further. I will not hastily leave the subject of a great man, and one who deserves to be spoken of with respect: I will hand thee down to all posterity, thou most noble heart, chief among the many victims of Gaius.

15

Yet we gain nothing by getting rid of all personal causes of sadness, for sometimes we are possessed by hatred of the human race. When you reflect how rare simplicity is, how unknown innocence, how seldom faith is kept, unless it be to our advantage, when you remember such numbers of successful crimes, so many equally hateful losses and gains of lust, and ambition so impatient even of its own natural limits that it is willing to purchase distinction by baseness, the mind seems as it were cast into darkness, and shadows rise before it as though the virtues were all overthrown and we were no longer allowed to hope to possess them or benefited by their possession. We ought therefore to bring ourselves into such a state of mind that all the vices of the vulgar may not appear hateful to us, but merely ridiculous, and we should imitate Democritus rather than Heraclitus. The latter of these, whenever he appeared in public, used to weep, the former to laugh: the one thought all human doings to be follies, the other thought them to be miseries. We must take a higher view of all things, and bear with them more easily: it better becomes a man to scoff at life than to lament over it. Add to this that he who laughs at the human race deserves better of it than he who mourns for it, for the former leaves it some good hopes of improvement, while the latter stupidly weeps over what he has given up all hopes of mending. He who after surveying the universe cannot control his laughter shows, too, a greater mind than he who cannot restrain his tears, because his mind is only affected in the slightest possible degree, and he does not think that any part of all this apparatus is either important, or serious, or unhappy. As for the several causes which render us happy or sorrowful, let everyone describe them for himself, and learn the truth of Bion's saying, "That all the doings of men were very like what he began with, and that there is nothing in their lives which is more holy or decent than their conception." Yet it is better to accept public morals and human vices calmly without bursting into either laughter or tears; for to be hurt by the sufferings of others is to be forever miserable, while to enjoy the sufferings of others is an inhuman pleasure, just as it is a useless piece of humanity to weep and pull a long face because someone is burying his son. In one's own misfortunes, also, one ought so to conduct oneself as to bestow upon them just as much sorrow as reason, not as much as custom requires: for many shed tears in order to show them, and whenever no one is looking at them their eyes are dry, but they think it disgraceful not to weep when everyone does so. So deeply has this evil of being guided by the opinion of others taken root in us, that even grief, the simplest of all emotions, begins to be counterfeited.

16

There comes now a part of our subject which is wont with good cause to make one sad and anxious: I mean when good men come to bad ends; when Socrates is forced to die in prison, Rutilius to live in exile, Pompeius and Cicero to offer their necks to the swords of their own followers, when the great Cato, that living image of virtue, falls upon his sword and rips up both himself and the republic, one cannot help being grieved that Fortune should bestow her gifts so unjustly: what, too, can a good man hope to obtain when he sees the best of men meeting with the worst fates. Well, but see how each of them endured his fate, and if they endured it bravely, long in your heart for courage as great as theirs; if they died in a womanish and cowardly manner, nothing was lost: either they deserved that you should admire their courage, or else they did not deserve that you should wish to imitate their cowardice: for what can be more shameful than that the greatest men should die so bravely as to make people cowards. Let us praise one who deserves such constant praises, and say, "The braver you are the happier you are! You have escaped from all accidents, jealousies, diseases: you have escaped from prison: the gods have not thought you worthy of ill fortune, but have thought that fortune no longer deserved to have any power over you": but when anyone shrinks back in the hour of death and looks longingly at life, we must lay hands upon him. I will never weep for a man who dies cheerfully, nor for one who dies weeping: the former wipes away my tears, the latter by his tears makes himself unworthy that any should be shed for him. Shall I weep for Hercules because he was burned alive, or for Regulus because he was pierced by so many nails, or for Cato because he tore open his wounds a second time? All these men discovered how at the cost of a small portion of time they might obtain immortality, and by their deaths gained eternal life.

17

It also proves a fertile source of troubles if you take pains to conceal your feelings and never show yourself to anyone undisguised, but, as many men do, live an artificial life, in order to impose upon others: for the constant watching of himself becomes a torment to a man, and he dreads being caught doing something at variance with his usual habits, and, indeed, we never can be at our ease if we imagine that everyone who looks at us is weighing our real value: for many things occur which strip people of their disguise, however reluctantly they may part with it, and even if all this trouble about oneself is successful, still life is neither happy nor safe when one always has to wear a mask. But what pleasure there is in that honest straightforwardness which is its own ornament, and which conceals no part of its character? Yet even this life, which hides nothing from anyone runs some risk of being despised; for there are people who disdain whatever they come close to: but there is no danger of virtue's becoming contemptible when she is brought near our eyes, and it is better to be scorned for one's simplicity than to bear the burden of unceasing hypocrisy. Still, we must observe moderation in this matter, for there is a great difference between living simply and living slovenly. Moreover, we ought to retire a great deal into ourselves: for association with persons unlike ourselves upsets all that we had arranged, rouses the passions which were at rest, and rubs into a sore any weak or imperfectly healed place in our minds. Nevertheless we ought to mix up these two things, and to pass our lives alternately in solitude and among throngs of people; for the former will make us long for the society of mankind, the latter for that of ourselves, and the one will counteract the other: solitude will cure us when we are sick of crowds, and crowds will cure us when we are sick of solitude. Neither ought we always to keep the mind strained to the same pitch, but it ought sometimes to be relaxed by amusement. Socrates did not blush to play with little boys, Cato used to refresh his mind with wine after he had wearied it with application to affairs of state, and Scipio would move his triumphal and soldierly limbs to the sound of music, not with a feeble and halting gait, as is the fashion nowadays, when we sway in our very walk with more than womanly weakness, but dancing as men were wont in the days of old on sportive and festal occasions, with manly bounds, thinking it no harm to be seen so doing even by their enemies. Men's minds ought to have relaxation: they rise up better and more vigorous after rest. We must not force crops from rich fields, for an unbroken course of heavy crops will soon exhaust their fertility, and so also the liveliness of our minds will be detroyed by unceasing labour, but they will recover their strength after a short period of rest and relief: for continuous toil produces a sort of numbness and sluggishness. Men would not be so eager for this, if play and amusement did not possess natural attractions for them, although constant indulgence in them takes away all gravity and all strength from the mind: for sleep, also, is necessary for our refreshment, yet if you prolong it for days and nights together it will become death. There is a great difference between slackening your hold of a thing and letting it go. The founders of our laws appointed festivals, in order that men might be publicly encouraged to be cheerful, and they thought it necessary to vary our labours with amusements, and, as I said before, some great men have been wont to give themselves a certain number of holidays in every month, and some divided every day into playtime and work-time. Thus, I remember that great orator Asinius Pollio would not attend to any business after the tenth hour: he would not even read letters after that time for fear some new trouble should arise, but in those two hours[195] used to get rid of the weariness which he had contracted during the whole day. Some rest in the middle of the day, and reserve some light occupation for the afternoon. Our ancestors, too, forbade any new motion to be made in the Senate after the tenth hour. Soldiers divide their watches, and those who have just returned from active service are allowed to sleep the whole night undisturbed. We must humour our minds and grant them rest from time to time, which acts upon them like food, and restores their strength. It does good also to take walks out of doors, that our spirits may be raised and refreshed by the open air and fresh breeze: sometimes we gain strength by driving in a

---

[195] The Romans reckoned twelve hours from sunrise to sunset. These "two hours" were therefore the two last of the day.

carriage, by travel, by change of air, or by social meals and a more generous allowance of wine: at times we ought to drink even to intoxication, not so as to drown, but merely to dip ourselves in wine: for wine washes away troubles and dislodges them from the depths of the mind, and acts as a remedy to sorrow as it does to some diseases. The inventor of wine is called Liber, not from the licence which he gives to our tongues, but because he liberates the mind from the bondage of cares, and emancipates it, animates it, and renders it more daring in all that it attempts. Yet moderation is wholesome both in freedom and in wine. It is believed that Solon and Arcesilaus used to drink deep. Cato is reproached with drunkenness: but whoever casts this in his teeth will find it easier to turn his reproach into a commendation than to prove that Cato did anything wrong: however, we ought not to do it often, for fear the mind should contract evil habits, though it ought sometimes to be forced into frolic and frankness, and to cast off dull sobriety for a while. If we believe the Greek poet, "it is sometimes pleasant to be mad"; again, Plato always knocked in vain at the door of poetry when he was sober; or, if we trust Aristotle, no great genius has ever been without a touch of insanity. The mind cannot use lofty language, above that of the common herd, unless it be excited. When it has spurned aside the commonplace environments of custom, and rises sublime, instinct with sacred fire, then alone can it chant a song too grand for mortal lips: as long as it continues to dwell within itself it cannot rise to any pitch of splendour: it must break away from the beaten track, and lash itself to frenzy, till it gnaws the curb and rushes away bearing up its rider to heights whither it would fear to climb when alone.

I have now, my beloved Serenus, given you an account of what things can preserve peace of mind, what things can restore it to us, what can arrest the vices which secretly undermine it: yet be assured, that none of these is strong enough to enable us to retain so fleeting a blessing, unless we watch over our vacillating mind with intense and unremitting care.

ON PROVIDENCE

1

You have asked me, Lucilius, why, if the world be ruled by providence, so many evils befall good men? The answer to this would be more conveniently given in the course of this work, after we have proved that providence governs the universe, and that God is amongst us: but, since you wish me to deal with one point apart from the whole, and to answer one replication before the main action has been decided, I will do what is not difficult, and plead the cause of the gods. At the present time it is superfluous to point out that it is not without some guardian that so great a work maintains its position, that the assemblage and movements of the stars do not depend upon accidental impulses, or that objects whose motion is regulated by chance often fall into confusion and soon stumble, whereas this swift and safe movement goes on, governed by eternal law, bearing with it so many things both on sea and land, so many most brilliant lights shining in order in the skies; that this regularity does not belong to matter moving at random, and that particles brought together by chance could not arrange themselves with such art as to make the heaviest weight, that of the Earth, remain unmoved, and behold the flight of the heavens as they hasten round it, to make the seas pour into the valleys and so temper the climate of the land, without any sensible increase from the rivers which flow into them, or to cause huge growths to proceed from minute seeds. Even those phenomena which appear to be confused and irregular, I mean showers of rain and clouds, the rush of lightning from the heavens, fire that pours from the riven peaks of mountains, quakings of the trembling Earth, and everything else which is produced on Earth by the unquiet element in the universe, do not come to pass without reason, though they do so suddenly: but they also have their causes, as also have those things which excite our wonder by the strangeness of their position, such as warm springs amidst the waves of the sea, and new islands that spring up in the wide ocean. Moreover, anyone who has watched how the shore is laid bare by the retreat of the sea into itself, and how within a short time it is again covered, will believe that it is in obedience to some hidden law of change that the waves are at one time contracted and driven inwards, at another burst forth and regain their bed with a strong current, since all the while they wax in regular proportion, and come up at their appointed day and hour greater or less, according as the moon, at whose pleasure the ocean flows, draws them. Let these matters be set aside for discussion at their own proper season, but I, since you do not doubt the existence of providence but complain of it, will on that account more readily reconcile you to gods who are most excellent to excellent men: for indeed the nature of things does not ever permit good to be injured by good. Between good men and the gods there is a friendship which is brought about by virtue—friendship do I say? nay, rather relationship and likeness, since the good man differs from a god in time alone, being his pupil and rival and true offspring, whom his glorious parent trains more severely than other men, insisting sternly on virtuous conduct, just as strict fathers do. When therefore you see men who are good and acceptable to the gods toiling, sweating, painfully struggling upwards, while bad men run riot and are steeped in pleasures, reflect that modesty pleases us in our sons, and forwardness in our house-born slave-boys; that the former are held in check by a somewhat stern rule, whereas the boldness of the latter is encouraged. Be thou sure that God acts in like manner: He does not pet the good man: He tries him, hardens him, and fits him for Himself.

2

Why do many things turn out badly for good men? Why, no evil can befall a good man; contraries cannot combine. Just as so many rivers, so many showers of rain from the clouds, such a number of medicinal springs, do not alter the taste of the sea, indeed, do not so much as soften it, so the pressure of adversity does not affect the mind of a brave man; for the mind of a brave man maintains its balance and throws its own complexion over all that takes place, because it is more powerful than any external circumstances. I do not say that he does not feel them, but he conquers them, and on occasion calmly and tranquilly rises superior to their attacks, holding all misfortunes to be trials of his own firmness. Yet who is there who, provided he be a man and have honourable ambition, does not long for due employment, and is not eager to do his duty in spite of danger? Is there any hardworking man to whom idleness is not a punishment? We see athletes, who study only their bodily strength, engage in contests with the strongest of men, and insist that those who train them for the arena should put out their whole strength when practising with them: they endure blows and maltreatment, and, if they cannot find any single person who is their match, they engage with several at once: their strength and courage droop without an antagonist: they can only prove how great and how mighty it is by proving how much they can endure. You should know that good men ought to act in like manner, so as not to fear troubles and difficulties, nor to lament their hard fate, to take in good part whatever befalls them, and force it to become a blessing to them. It does not matter what you bear, but how you bear it. Do you not see how differently fathers and mothers indulge their children? How the former urge them to begin their tasks betimes, will not suffer them to be idle even on holidays, and exercise them till they perspire, and sometimes till they shed tears—while their mothers want to cuddle them in their laps, and keep them out of the sun, and never wish them to be vexed, or to cry, or to work. God bears a fatherly mind towards good men, and loves them in a manly spirit. "Let them," says He, "be exercised by labours, sufferings, and losses, that so they may gather true strength." Those who are surfeited with ease break down not only with labour, but with mere motion and by their own weight. Unbroken prosperity cannot bear a single blow; but he who has waged an unceasing strife with his misfortunes has gained a thicker skin by his sufferings, yields to no disaster, and even though he fall yet fights on his knee. Do you wonder that God, who so loves the good, who would have them attain the highest goodness and preeminence, should appoint Fortune to be their adversary? I should not be surprised if the gods sometimes experience a wish to behold great men struggling with some misfortune. We sometimes are delighted when a youth of steady courage receives on his spear the wild beast that attacks him; or when he meets the charge of a lion without flinching; and the more eminent the man is who acts thus,[196] the more attractive is the sight: yet these are not matters which can attract the attention of the gods, but are mere pastime and diversions of human frivolity. Behold a sight worthy to be viewed by a god interested in his own work, behold a pair[197] worthy of a god, a brave man matched with evil fortune, especially if he himself has given the challenge. I say, I do not know what nobler spectacle Jupiter could find on Earth, should he turn his eyes thither, than that of Cato, after his party had more than once been defeated, still standing upright amid the ruins of the commonwealth. Quoth he, "What though all be fallen into one man's power, though the land be guarded by his legions, the sea by his fleets, though Caesar's soldiers beset the city gate? Cato has a way out of it: with one hand he will open a

---

[196] *Honestior* is opposed to the gladiator—the loftier the station of the combatant. The Gracchus of Juvenal, *Satires* II and VIII, illustrates the passage.

[197] *Par*, a technical term in the language of sport (worthy of such a spectator).

wide path to freedom; his sword, which he has borne unstained by disgrace and innocent of crime even in a civil war, will still perform good and noble deeds; it will give to Cato that freedom which it could not give to his country. Begin, my soul, the work which thou so long hast contemplated, snatch thyself away from the world of man. Already Petreius and Juba have met and fallen, each slain by the other's hand—a brave and noble compact with fate, yet not one befitting my greatness: it is as disgraceful for Cato to beg his death of anyone as it would be for him to beg his life."

It is clear to me that the gods must have looked on with great joy, while that man, his own most ruthless avenger, took thought for the safety of others and arranged the escape of those who departed, while even on his last night he pursued his studies, while he drove the sword into his sacred breast, while he tore forth his vitals and laid his hand upon that most holy life which was unworthy to be defiled by steel. This, I am inclined to think, was the reason that his wound was not well-aimed and mortal: the gods were not satisfied with seeing Cato die once: his courage was kept in action and recalled to the stage, that it might display itself in a more difficult part: for it needs a greater mind to return a second time to death. How could they fail to view their pupil with interest when leaving his life by such a noble and memorable departure? Men are raised to the level of the gods by a death which is admired even by those who fear them.

3

However, as my argument proceeds, I shall prove that what appear to be evils are not so; for the present I say this, that what you call hard measure, misfortunes, and things against which we ought to pray, are really to the advantage, firstly, of those to whom they happen, and secondly, of all mankind, for whom the gods care more than for individuals; and next, that these evils befall them with their own good will, and that men deserve to endure misfortunes, if they are unwilling to receive them. To this I shall add, that misfortunes proceed thus by destiny, and that they befall good men by the same law which makes them good. After this, I shall prevail upon you never to pity any good man; for though he may be called unhappy, he cannot be so.

Of all these propositions that which I have stated first appears the most difficult to prove, I mean, that the things which we dread and shudder at are to the advantage of those to whom they happen. "Is it," say you, "to their advantage to be driven into exile, to be brought to want, to carry out to burial their children and wife, to be publicly disgraced, to lose their health?" Yes! if you are surprised at these being to any man's advantage, you will also be surprised at any man being benefited by the knife and cautery, or by hunger and thirst as well. Yet if you consider that some men, in order to be cured, have their bones scraped, and pieces of them extracted, that their veins are pulled out, and that some have limbs cut off, which could not remain in their place without ruin to the whole body, you will allow me to prove to you this also, that some misfortunes are for the good of those to whom they happen, just as much, by Hercules, as some things which are praised and sought after are harmful to those who enjoy them, like indigestions and drunkenness and other matters which kill us through pleasure. Among many grand sayings of our Demetrius is this, which I have but just heard, and which still rings and thrills in my ears: "No one," said he, "seems to me more unhappy than the man whom no misfortune has ever befallen." He never has had an opportunity of testing himself; though everything has happened to him according to his wish, nay, even before he has formed a wish, yet the gods have judged him unfavourably; he has never been deemed worthy to conquer ill fortune, which avoids the greatest cowards, as though it said, "Why should I take that man for my antagonist? He will straightaway lay down his arms: I shall not need all my strength against him: he will be put to flight by a mere menace: he dares not even face me; let me look around for some other with whom I may fight hand to hand: I blush to join battle with one who is prepared to be beaten." A gladiator deems it a disgrace to be matched with an inferior, and knows that to win without danger is to win without glory. Just so doth Fortune; she seeks out the bravest to match herself with, passes over some with disdain, and makes for the most unyielding and upright of men, to exert her strength against them. She tried Mucius by fire, Fabricius by poverty, Rutilius by exile, Regulus by torture, Socrates by poison, Cato by death: it is ill fortune alone that discovers these glorious examples. Was Mucius unhappy, because he grasped the enemy's fire with his right hand, and of his own accord paid the penalty of his mistake? because he overcame the King with his hand when it was burned, though he could not when it held a sword? Would he have been happier, if he had warmed his hand in his mistress's bosom; Was Fabricius unhappy, because when the State could spare him, he dug his own land? because he waged war against riches as keenly as against Pyrrhus? because he supped beside his hearth off the very roots and herbs which he himself, though an old man, and one who had enjoyed a triumph, had grubbed up while clearing his field of weeds? What then? would he have been happier if he had gorged himself with fishes from distant shores, and birds caught in foreign lands? if he had roused the torpor of his queasy stomach with shellfish from the upper and the lower sea? if he had piled a great heap of fruits round game of the first head, which many huntsmen had been killed in capturing? Was Rutilius unhappy, because those who condemned him will have to plead their cause for all ages? because he endured the loss of his country more composedly than that of his banishment? because he was the only man who refused anything to Sulla the dictator, and when recalled from exile all but went further away and banished himself still more. "Let those," said he, "whom thy fortunate reign catches at Rome, see to the forum drenched with blood,[198] and the heads of Senators above the Pool of Servilius—the place where the victims of Sulla's proscriptions were stripped—the bands of assassins roaming at large through the city, and many thousands of Roman citizens slaughtered in one place, after, nay, by means of a promise of quarter. Let those who are unable to go into exile behold these things." Well! is Lucius Sulla happy, because when he comes down into the forum room is made for him with sword-strokes, because he allows the heads of consulars to be shown to him, and counts out the price of blood through the quaestor and the state exchequer? And this, this was the man who passed the Lex Cornelia! Let us now come to Regulus: what injury did Fortune do him when she made him an example of good faith, an example of endurance? They pierce his skin with nails: wherever he leans his weary body, it rests on a wound; his eyes are fixed forever open; the greater his sufferings, the greater is his glory. Would you know how far he is from regretting that he valued his honour at such a price? Heal his wounds and send him again into the senate-house; he will give the same advice. So, then, you think Maecenas a happier man, who when troubled by love, and weeping at the daily repulses of his ill-natured wife, sought for sleep by listening to distant strains of music? Though he drug himself with wine, divert himself with the sound of falling waters, and distract his troubled thoughts with a thousand pleasures, yet Maecenas will no more sleep on his down cushions than Regulus on the rack. Yet it consoles the latter that he suffers for the sake of honour, and he looks away from his torments to their cause: whilst the other, jaded with pleasures and sick with over-enjoyment, is more hurt by the cause of his sufferings than by the sufferings themselves. Vice has not so utterly taken possession of the human race that, if men were allowed to choose their destiny, there can be any doubt but that more would choose to be Reguluses than to be Maecenases: or if there were anyone who dared to say that he would prefer to be born Maecenas than Regulus, that man, whether he says so or not, would rather have been Terentia (than Cicero).

---

[198] *Vidirint*—Let them see to it: it is no matter of mine.

Do you consider Socrates to have been badly used, because he took that draught which the State assigned to him as though it were a charm to make him immortal, and argued about death until death itself? Was he ill treated, because his blood froze and the current of his veins gradually stopped as the chill of death crept over them? How much more is this man to be envied than he who is served on precious stones, whose drink a creature trained to every vice, a eunuch or much the same, cools with snow in a golden cup? Such men as these bring up again all that they drink, in misery and disgust at the taste of their own bile, while Socrates cheerfully and willingly drains his poison. As for Cato, enough has been said, and all men must agree that the highest happiness was reached by one who was chosen by Nature herself as worthy to contend with all her terrors: "The enmity," says she, "of the powerful is grievous, therefore let him be opposed at once by Pompeius, Caesar, and Crassus: it is grievous, when a candidate for public offices, to be defeated by one's inferiors; therefore let him be defeated by Vatinius: it is grievous to take part in civil wars, therefore let him fight in every part of the world for the good cause with equal obstinacy and ill-luck: it is grievous to lay hands upon oneself, therefore let him do so. What shall I gain by this? That all men may know that these things, which I have deemed Cato worthy to undergo, are not real evils."

4

"Prosperity comes to the mob, and to low-minded men as well as to great ones; but it is the privilege of great men alone to send under the yoke[199] the disasters and terrors of mortal life: whereas to be always prosperous, and to pass through life without a twinge of mental distress, is to remain ignorant of one half of nature. You are a great man; but how am I to know it, if fortune gives you no opportunity of showing your virtue? You have entered the arena of the Olympic games, but no one else has done so: you have the crown, but not the victory: I do not congratulate you as I would a brave man, but as one who has obtained a consulship or praetorship. You have gained dignity. I may

---

[199] That is, to triumph over.

"Two spears were set upright ... and a third was fastened across them at the top; and through this gateway the vanquished army marched out, as a token that they had been conquered in war, and owed their lives to the enemy's mercy. It was no peculiar insult devised for this occasion, but a common usage, so far as appears, in similar cases; like the modern ceremony of piling arms when a garrison or army surrender themselves as prisoners of war."

—Arnold's *History of Rome*, Chapter XXXI.

say the same of a good man, if troublesome circumstances have never given him a single opportunity of displaying the strength of his mind. I think you unhappy because you never have been unhappy: you have passed through your life without meeting an antagonist: no one will know your powers, not even you yourself." For a man cannot know himself without a trial; no one ever learnt what he could do without putting himself to the test; for which reason many have of their own free will exposed themselves to misfortunes which no longer came in their way, and have sought for an opportunity of making their virtue, which otherwise would have been lost in darkness, shine before the world. Great men, I say, often rejoice at crosses of fortune just as brave soldiers do at wars. I remember to have heard Triumphus, who was a gladiator[200] in the reign of Tiberius Caesar, complaining about the scarcity of prizes. "What a glorious time," said he, "is past." Valour is greedy of danger, and thinks only of whither it strives to go, not of what it will suffer, since even what it will suffer is part of its glory. Soldiers pride themselves on their wounds, they joyously display their blood flowing over their breastplate.[201] Though those who return unwounded from battle may have done as bravely, yet he who returns wounded is more admired. God, I say, favours those whom He wishes to enjoy the greatest honours, whenever He affords them the means of performing some exploit with spirit and courage, something which is not easily to be accomplished: you can judge of a pilot in a storm, of a soldier in a battle. How can I know with how great a spirit you could endure poverty, if you overflow with riches? How can I tell with how great firmness you could bear up against disgrace, dishonour, and public hatred, if you grow old to the sound of applause, if popular favour cannot be alienated from you, and seems to flow to you by the natural bent of men's minds? How can I know how calmly you would endure to be childless, if you see all your children around you? I have heard what you said when you were consoling others: then I should have seen whether you could have consoled yourself, whether you could have forbidden yourself to grieve. Do not, I beg you, dread those things which the immortal gods apply to our minds like spurs: misfortune is virtue's opportunity. Those men may justly be called unhappy who are stupified with excess of enjoyment, whom sluggish contentment keeps as it were becalmed in a quiet sea: whatever befalls them will come strange to them. Misfortunes press hardest on those who are unacquainted with them: the yoke feels heavy to the tender neck. The recruit turns pale at the thought of a wound: the veteran,

---

[200] He was a *mirmillo*, a kind of gladiator who was armed with a Gaulish helmet.
[201] *E lorica*.

who knows that he has often won the victory after losing blood, looks boldly at his own flowing gore. In like manner God hardens, reviews, and exercises those whom He tests and loves: those whom He seems to indulge and spare, He is keeping out of condition to meet their coming misfortunes: for you are mistaken if you suppose that anyone is exempt from misfortune: he who has long prospered will have his share some day; those who seem to have been spared them have only had them put off. Why does God afflict the best of men with ill-health, or sorrow, or other troubles? Because in the army the most hazardous services are assigned to the bravest soldiers: a general sends his choicest troops to attack the enemy in a midnight ambuscade, to reconnoitre his line of march, or to drive the hostile garrisons from their strong places. No one of these men says as he begins his march, "The general has dealt hardly with me," but "He has judged well of me." Let those who are bidden to suffer what makes the weak and cowardly weep, say likewise, "God has thought us worthy subjects on whom to try how much suffering human nature can endure." Avoid luxury, avoid effeminate enjoyment, by which men's minds are softened, and in which, unless something occurs to remind them of the common lot of humanity, they lie unconscious, as though plunged in continual drunkenness. He whom glazed windows have always guarded from the wind, whose feet are warmed by constantly renewed fomentations, whose dining-room is heated by hot air beneath the floor and spread through the walls, cannot meet the gentlest breeze without danger. While all excesses are hurtful, excess of comfort is the most hurtful of all; it affects the brain; it leads men's minds into vain imaginings; it spreads a thick cloud over the boundaries of truth and falsehood. Is it not better, with virtue by one's side, to endure continual misfortune, than to burst with an endless surfeit of good things? It is the overloaded stomach that is rent asunder: death treats starvation more gently. The gods deal with good men according to the same rule as schoolmasters with their pupils, who exact most labour from those of whom they have the surest hopes. Do you imagine that the Lacedaemonians, who test the mettle of their children by public flogging, do not love them? Their own fathers call upon them to endure the strokes of the rod bravely, and when they are torn and half dead, ask them to offer their wounded skin to receive fresh wounds. Why then should we wonder if God tries noble spirits severely? There can be no easy proof of virtue. Fortune lashes and mangles us: well, let us endure it: it is not cruelty, it is a struggle, in which the oftener we engage the braver we shall become. The strongest part of the body is that which is exercised by the most frequent use: we must entrust ourselves to Fortune to be hardened by her against herself: by degrees she will make us a match for herself. Familiarity with danger leads us to despise it. Thus the bodies of sailors are hardened by endurance of the sea, and the hands of farmers by work; the arms of soldiers are powerful to hurl darts, the legs of runners are active: that part of each man which he exercises is the strongest: so by endurance the mind becomes able to despise the power of misfortunes. You may see what endurance might effect in us if you observe what labour does among tribes that are naked and rendered stronger by want. Look at all the nations that dwell beyond the Roman Empire: I mean the Germans and all the nomad tribes that war against us along the Danube. They suffer from eternal winter, and a dismal climate, the barren soil grudges them sustenance, they keep off the rain with leaves or thatch, they bound across frozen marshes, and hunt wild beasts for food. Do you think them unhappy? There is no unhappiness in what use has made part of one's nature: by degrees men find pleasure in doing what they were first driven to do by necessity. They have no homes and no resting-places save those which weariness appoints them for the day; their food, though coarse, yet must be sought with their own hands; the harshness of the climate is terrible, and their bodies are unclothed. This, which you think a hardship, is the mode of life of all these races: how then can you wonder at good men being shaken, in order that they may be strengthened? No tree which the wind does not often blow against is firm and strong; for it is stiffened by the very act of being shaken, and plants its roots more securely: those which grow in a sheltered valley are brittle: and so it is to the advantage of good men, and causes them to be undismayed, that they should live much amidst alarms, and learn to bear with patience what is not evil save to him who endures it ill.

5

Add to this that it is to the advantage of everyone that the best men should, so to speak, be on active service and perform labours: God has the same purpose as the wise man, that is, to prove that the things which the herd covets and dreads are neither good nor bad in themselves. If, however, He only bestows them upon good men, it will be evident that they are good things, and bad, if He only inflicts them upon bad men. Blindness would be execrable if no one lost his eyes except those who deserve to have them pulled out; therefore let Appius and Metellus be doomed to darkness. Riches are not a good thing: therefore let Elius the pander possess them, that men who have consecrated money in the temple, may see the same in the brothel: for by no means can God discredit objects of desire so effectually as by bestowing them upon the worst of men, and removing them from the best. "But," you say, "it is unjust that a good man should be enfeebled, or transfixed, or chained, while bad men swagger at large with a whole skin." What! is it not unjust that brave men should bear arms, pass the night in camps, and stand on guard along the rampart with their wounds still bandaged, while within the city eunuchs and professional profligates live at their ease? what? is it not unjust that maidens of the highest birth should be roused at night to perform Divine service, while fallen women enjoy the soundest sleep? Labour calls for the best men: the senate often passes the whole day in debate, while at the same time every scoundrel either amuses his leisure in the Campus Martius, or lurks in a tavern, or passes his time in some pleasant society. The same thing happens in this great commonwealth (of the world): good men labour, spend and are spent, and that too of their own free will; they are not dragged along by Fortune, but follow her and take equal steps with her; if they knew how, they would outstrip her. I remember, also, to have heard this spirited saying of that stoutest-hearted of men, Demetrius. "Ye immortal Gods," said he, "the only complaint which I have to make of you is that you did not make your will known to me earlier; for then I would sooner have gone into that state of life to which I now have been called. Do you wish to take my children? it was for you that I brought them up. Do you wish to take some part of my body? take it: it is no great thing that I am offering you, I shall soon have done with the whole of it. Do you wish for my life? why should I hesitate to return to you what you gave me? whatever you ask you shall receive with my good will: nay, I would rather give it than be forced to hand it over to you: what need had you to take away what you did? you might have received it from me: yet even as it is you cannot take anything from me, because you cannot rob a man unless he resists."

I am constrained to nothing, I suffer nothing against my will, nor am I God's slave, but his willing follower, and so much the more because I know that everything is ordained and proceeds according to a law that endures forever. The fates guide us, and the length of every man's days is decided at the first hour of his birth: every cause depends upon some earlier cause: one long chain of destiny decides all things, public or private. Wherefore, everything must be patiently endured, because events do not fall in our way, as we imagine, but come by a regular law. It has long ago been settled at what you should rejoice and at what you should weep, and although the lives of individual men appear to differ from one another in a great variety of particulars, yet the sum total comes to one and the same thing: we soon perish, and the gifts which we receive soon perish. Why, then, should we be angry? why should we lament? we are prepared for our fate: let nature deal as she will with her own bodies; let us be cheerful whatever befalls, and stoutly reflect that it is not anything of our own that perishes. What is the duty of a good man? To submit himself to fate: it is a great consolation to be swept away together with the entire universe: whatever law is laid upon us that thus we must live and thus we must die, is laid upon the gods also: one unchangeable stream bears along men and gods alike: the creator and ruler of the universe himself, though he has given laws to the fates, yet is guided by them: he always obeys, he only once commanded. "But why was God so unjust in His distribution of fate, as to assign poverty, wounds, and untimely deaths to good men?" The workman cannot alter his materials: this is their nature. Some qualities cannot be separated from some others: they cling together; are indivisible. Dull minds, tending to sleep or to a waking state exactly like sleep, are composed of sluggish elements: it requires stronger stuff to form a man meriting careful description. His course will not be straightforward; he must go upwards and downwards, be tossed about, and guide his vessel through troubled waters: he must make his way in spite of fortune: he will meet with much that is hard which he must soften, much that is rough that he must make smooth. Fire tries gold, misfortune tries brave men. See how high virtue has to climb: you may be sure that it has no safe path to tread.

> "Steep is the path at first: the steeds, though strong,
> Fresh from their rest, can hardly crawl along;
> The middle part lies through the topmost sky,
> Whence oft, as I the earth and sea descry,
> I shudder, terrors through my bosom thrill.
> The ending of the path is sheer down hill,
> And needs the careful guidance of the rein,
> Forever when I sink beneath the main,
> Old Tethys trembles in her depths below
> Lest headlong down upon her I should go."[202]

When the spirited youth heard this, he said, "I have no fault to find with the road: I will mount it, it is worthwhile to go through these places, even though one fall." His father did not cease from trying to scare his brave spirit with terrors:—

---

[202] The lines occur in Ovid's *Metamorphoses*, II, 63. Phoebus is telling Phaethon how to drive the chariot of the Sun.

"Then, too, that thou may'st hold thy course aright,
And neither turn aside to left nor right,
Straight through the Bull's fell horns thy path must go,
Through the fierce Lion, and the Archer's bow."

After this Phaethon says:—

"Harness the chariot which you yield to me,

I am encouraged by these things with which you think to scare me: I long to stand where the Sun himself trembles to stand." It is the part of grovellers and cowards to follow the safe track; courage loves a lofty path.

6

"Yet, why does God permit evil to happen to good men?" He does not permit it: he takes away from them all evils, such as crimes and scandalous wickedness, daring thoughts, grasping schemes, blind lusts, and avarice coveting its neighbour's goods. He protects and saves them. Does anyone besides this demand that God should look after the baggage of good men also? Why, they themselves leave the care of this to God: they scorn external accessories. Democritus forswore riches, holding them to be a burden to a virtuous mind: what wonder then, if God permits that to happen to a good man, which a good man sometimes chooses should happen to himself? Good men, you say, lose their children: why should they not, since sometimes they even put them to death? They are banished: why should they not be, since sometimes they leave their country of their own free will, never to return? They are slain: why not, since sometimes they choose to lay violent hands on themselves? Why do they suffer certain miseries? it is that they may teach others how to do so. They are born as patterns. Conceive, therefore, that God says:—"You, who have chosen righteousness, what complaint can you make of me? I have encompassed other men with unreal good things, and have deceived their inane minds as it were by a long and misleading dream: I have bedecked them with gold, silver, and ivory, but within them there is no good thing. Those men whom you regard as fortunate, if you could see, not their outward show, but their hidden life, are really unhappy, mean, and base, ornamented on the outside like the walls of their houses: that good fortune of theirs is not sound and genuine: it is only a veneer, and that a thin one. As long, therefore, as they can stand upright and display themselves as they choose, they shine and impose upon one; when something occurs to shake and unmask them, we see how deep and real a rottenness was hidden by that factitious magnificence. To you I have given sure and lasting good things, which become greater and better the more one turns them over and views them on every side: I have granted to you to scorn danger, to disdain passion. You do not shine outwardly, all your good qualities are turned inwards; even so does the world neglect what lies without it, and rejoices in the contemplation of itself. I have placed every good thing within your own breasts: it is your good fortune not to need any good fortune. 'Yet many things befall you which are sad, dreadful, hard to be borne.' Well, as I have not been able to remove these from your path, I have given your minds strength to combat all: bear them bravely. In this you can surpass God himself; He is beyond suffering evil; you are above it. Despise poverty; no man lives as poor as he was born: despise pain; either it will cease or you will cease: despise death; it either ends you or takes you elsewhere: despise fortune; I have given her no weapon that can reach the mind. Above all, I have taken care that no one should hold you captive against your will: the way of escape lies open before you: if you do not choose to fight, you may fly. For this reason, of all those matters which I have deemed essential for you, I have made nothing easier for you than to die. I have set man's life as it were on a mountain side: it soon slips down.[203] Do but watch, and you will see how short and how ready a path leads to freedom. I have not imposed such long delays upon those who quit the world as upon those who enter it: were it not so, fortune would hold a wide dominion over you, if a man died as slowly as he is born. Let all time, let every place teach you, how simple it is to renounce nature, and to fling back her gifts to her: before the altar itself and during the solemn rites of sacrifice, while life is being prayed for, learn how to die. Fat oxen fall dead with a tiny wound; a blow from a man's hand fells animals of great strength: the sutures of the neck are severed by a thin blade, and when the joint which connects the head and neck is cut, all that great mass falls. The breath of life is not deep seated, nor only to be let forth by steel—the vitals

---

[203] Compare Walter Scott:

"All ... must have felt that but for the dictates of religion, or the natural recoil of the mind from the idea of dissolution, there have been times when they would have been willing to throw away life as a child does a broken toy. I am sure I know one who has often felt so. O God! what are we?—Lords of nature?—Why, a tile drops from a housetop, which an elephant would not feel more than a sheet of pasteboard, and there lies his lordship. Or something of inconceivably minute origin, the pressure of a bone, or the inflammation of a particle of the brain takes place, and the emblem of the Deity destroys himself or someone else. We hold our health and our reason on terms slighter than anyone would desire, were it in their choice, to hold an Irish cabin."

—Lockhart's *Life of Sir Walter Scott*, Volume VII, p. 11.

need not be searched throughout by plunging a sword among them to the hilt: death lies near the surface. I have not appointed any particular spot for these blows—the body may be pierced wherever you please. That very act which is called dying, by which the breath of life leaves the body, is too short for you to be able to estimate its quickness: whether a knot crushes the windpipe, or water stops your breathing: whether you fall headlong from a height and perish upon the hard ground below, or a mouthful of fire checks the drawing of your breath—whatever it is, it acts swiftly. Do you not blush to spend so long a time in dreading what takes so short a time to do?"

www.ingramcontent.com/pod-product-compliance
Lightning Source LLC
LaVergne TN
LVHW091533070526
838199LV00001B/50